ENGLISH AS A LINGUA FRANCA IN ASEAN

Asian Englishes Today

Series Editor: Kingsley Bolton
　　　　　　　　Chair Professor of English, City University of Hong Kong

---

The volumes in this series set out to provide a contemporary record of the spread and development of the English language in South, Southeast, and East Asia from both linguistic and literary perspectives. They reflect themes related to English that cut across national and linguistic boundaries, including the study of language policies; globalization and linguistic imperialism; English in the media; English in law, government and education; 'hybrid' Englishes; and the bilingual creativity manifested by the vibrant creative writing found in many societies in Asia.

The editorial advisory board comprises a number of leading scholars in the field of world Englishes, including Maria Lourdes S. Bautista (De La Salle University-Manila, the Philippines), Susan Butler (Macquarie Dictionary, Australia), Braj B. Kachru (University of Illinois, Urbana-Champaign), Yamuna Kachru (University of Illinois, Urbana-Champaign), Shirley Geok-lin Lim (University of California, Santa Barbara), Tom McArthur (founding editor of *English Today*), Anne Pakir (National University of Singapore), Larry E. Smith (co-founding editor of *World Englishes*), and Yasukata Yano (Waseda University, Japan).

Also in the series:

Hong Kong English: Autonomy and Creativity
Edited by Kingsley Bolton

Japanese English: Language and Culture Contact
James Stanlaw

China's English: A History of English in Chinese Education
Bob Adamson

Asian Englishes: Beyond the Canon
Braj B. Kachru

World Englishes in Asian Contexts
Yamuna Kachru and Cecil L. Nelson

Philippine English: Linguistic and Literary Perspectives
Edited by Ma. Lourdes S. Bautista and Kingsley Bolton

English in Singapore: Modernity and Management
Edited by Lisa Lim, Anne Pakir and Lionel Wee

ENGLISH AS A LINGUA FRANCA IN ASEAN
A MULTILINGUAL MODEL

ANDY KIRKPATRICK

香港大學出版社
HONG KONG UNIVERSITY PRESS

Hong Kong University Press
14/F Hing Wai Centre
7 Tin Wan Praya Road
Aberdeen
Hong Kong

© Hong Kong University Press 2010

Hardback   ISBN 978-988-8028-78-8
Paperback   ISBN 978-988-8028-79-5

All rights reserved. No portion of this publication may be reproduced or transmitted in any form or by any means, electronic or mechanical, including photocopy, recording, or any information storage or retrieval system, without permission in writing from the publisher.

Secure On-line Ordering
http://www.hkupress.org

British Library Cataloguing-in-Publication Data
A catalogue record for this book is available from the British Library.

Printed and bound by Liang Yu Printing Factory Co. Ltd., Hong Kong, China

To all my ASEAN students, colleagues and friends
who have given me so much over so many years

Contents

Series editor's preface	ix
Preface	xi
Part I: ASEAN and English	1
1 The origins of ASEAN and the role of English	3
2 Malaysia, Singapore, Brunei and the Philippines: Linguistic context and the role of English	19
3 Burma, Cambodia, Indonesia, Laos, Thailand and Vietnam: Linguistic context and the role of English	43
Part II: Linguistic Features of English as a Lingua Franca in Asia	65
Introduction to Part II	67
4 Pronunciation, intelligibility and lexis	73
5 Grammar, discourse and pragmatics	95
6 The communicative strategies of ASEAN ELF users	123
Part III: Implications for Policy and Pedagogy	143
Introduction to Part III	145
7 Implications for language education policy	147

8	Pedagogical implications: The multilingual model and the lingua franca approach	169
Appendices		191
Notes		193
References		195
Index		213

Series editor's preface

From the mid-1990s onwards, the topic of English as a lingua franca has attracted a great deal of attention among various groups of linguists. Initially, this largely arose in the context of a Europe dealing with increasing multilingualism due not only to immigration and the growth of immigrant communities, but also as a result of the wide diversity of students attending European universities. Over the last ten years, linguistic research on English as a Lingua Franca (ELF) has emerged as an energetic and productive strand of research in the European context. Hitherto, however, there have been very few studies adopting an ELF approach within the Asian region.

What is both noteworthy and outstanding about this present volume from Professor Andy Kirkpatrick is that, while there have been a large number of books and theses dealing with the issue of ELF in the European context, this present volume, to my knowledge, is a first of its kind: a detailed book-length study of English as a lingua franca in the Asian context. In addition, the strength of the present volume rests not merely on theorization, but also on original empirical investigation and data collection, as well as the detailed personal knowledge of a leading educator whose experience of language education in Asia is measured in decades.

In this volume, Professor Kirkpatrick's discussion of English in ASEAN ranges from the historical to the sociolinguistic and to the pedagogic. The early sections of the book provide an overview of the foundation and development of ASEAN from the 1960s to the present, a description of the status and functions of English in the member ASEAN societies, and the spread of English as a dominant foreign language in the largely postcolonial context of national development. The middle sections focus on the linguistic features of English as a lingua franca in ASEAN, at the levels of phonology, vocabulary, discourse and pragmatics, and the communicative strategies of ASEAN ELF users. The final sections of the volume are devoted to a discussion of language policies and pedagogical implications relating to the teaching of English. In these sections, Professor Kirkpatrick makes a strong case for the adoption of a multilingual approach to English language in education. This requires a re-thinking of language policies in many ASEAN societies, in order, not least, to avoid the worst consequences of imposing English as a medium of instruction in primary schools in the region.

Professor Kirkpatrick's challenge to the orthodoxies of current language policies is supported by careful argumentation and detailed exemplification from particular case studies. This volume presents a fresh and welcome challenge to any complacency that one might have concerning the wholesale spread of English in Asian education systems, reminding us throughout that the place of English in these contexts must be viewed against the linguistic ecologies of such societies. This is an issue that is at the heart of the volume, and, one appreciates, at the heart of the author, who communicates a deep and genuine concern for the multilingual cultures and diversity of the Asian region.

Kingsley Bolton
August 2010

Preface

The major role that English plays in today's world is as a lingua franca.[1] That is to say, the majority of speakers are multilinguals who have learned English as a second or later language. They use English as a common language with fellow multilinguals. This lingua franca use of English is prevalent throughout the ten nations which make up the Association of Southeast Asian Nations (ASEAN). Indeed, this regional role of English has now been enshrined by the ASEAN Charter, as English has been formally adopted as the Association's sole working and official language.

This lingua franca role of English, coupled with its formal status as the official language of ASEAN, has important implications for language policy and language education. These include the relationship between English, the respective national languages of ASEAN and the literally thousands of the region's local languages. How, for example, can the demand for English be balanced against the need for people of the region to acquire their respective national language and mother tongue? Ideally, people need to be able to develop their identity and cultural roots from their mother tongue. In many cases, they will also need a *regional* lingua franca along with the national language. Thus, for example, a Filipino or an Indonesian will learn their mother tongue, may need to know a regional lingua franca such as Cebuano in the Philippines or Javanese in Indonesia, and then need to learn the national language, Filipino or Bahasa Indonesia respectively. On top of this, English is considered to be so essential that it is taught as the first foreign language in each of the countries of ASEAN. It is introduced as a compulsory subject in primary school in each country except Indonesia, where it is an optional subject in primary school and a compulsory subject in secondary school. In many countries, however, it is introduced as a compulsory subject from Primary 1, and in three countries, Brunei, Malaysia and the Philippines, English is also a medium of instruction. In Singapore, it is *the* medium of instruction.

But might not this early introduction of English into the school curriculum threaten local languages on the one hand, and children's ability to learn on the other? Is there not a danger that this early introduction of English into the school curriculum will mean that no place for local languages can be found? Is there not a danger that too early an introduction to English as a medium of instruction will place too heavy a cognitive load on children with the result that they fail or drop out of school? Or can English be introduced and taught in such a way that it can complement local languages rather than replace them?

The aim of this book is to explore questions such as these and then make recommendations on language policy and language education. The book should be important for regional policymakers and language education professionals. It should also benefit language teachers, especially, but by no means exclusively, English language teachers. The book should also be of interest to all who are interested in the development of English as an international language and the possible implications of this upon local languages and cultures.

The book is arranged in three parts. Part I comprises Chapters 1–3 and describes the history behind the formation of ASEAN and the development of English and the respective national language in each of the ten member states of ASEAN.

Chapter 1 recalls the reasons behind the original formation of ASEAN and the Bangkok Declaration of 1967, signed by the five founding nations, Indonesia, Malaysia, the Philippines, Singapore, and Thailand. The chapter then describes how ASEAN developed and was enlarged to ten member states with the joining of Burma,[2] Brunei, Cambodia, Laos and Vietnam, culminating in the signing of the ASEAN Charter in February 2009.

Chapter 2 describes the linguistic context and the development and role of English in Brunei, Malaysia, the Philippines and Singapore. Each of these countries were colonies of English-speaking imperial powers and the place and role of English has been affected by this colonial history, although, as will be illustrated, in significantly different ways. While Burma was also a colony, its recent history as a closed military dictatorship means that English has no institutional role there and so Burma will be considered in Chapter 3.

Chapter 3 describes the linguistic context and records how English has gradually become the dominant foreign language in Burma and also in the remaining five countries, namely Cambodia, Indonesia, Laos, Thailand and Vietnam. Cambodia, Laos and Vietnam all share a history of French colonial rule which was followed by a period of Soviet influence. Indonesia was a Dutch colony. Thailand is the only ASEAN member state without a colonial past.

The focus of Part II shifts to an analysis of the linguistic features of English when used as a lingua franca in ASEAN.

Chapters 4 and 5 will illustrate selected linguistic features of the phonology, lexis and grammar of this lingua franca use of English.

Chapter 6 identifies and illustrates the communicative strategies adopted by people when using English as a lingua franca. It will be argued that these linguistic features and communicative strategies have important implications for language policy and pedagogy.

Part III comprises two chapters.

Chapter 7 considers the policy implications arising from the discussions covered in Part I, and from the linguistic features and communicative strategies illustrated in Part II. In particular, the need to see the goal of English language learning in ASEAN as the ability to use English successfully in lingua franca communication is stressed. Tenets commonly associated with successful language learning, such as the need to start early and to use it as a medium of instruction, are challenged and alternatives proposed. This chapter closes with a specific proposal for a language education policy for Hong Kong. While Hong Kong is not a member of ASEAN, the Hong Kong government's goal of making its citizens trilingual in Cantonese, Putonghua (Mandarin) and English, and biliterate in Chinese and English means that it faces many of the issues which confront the member states of ASEAN.

Chapter 8, the final chapter, considers a number of pedagogical implications of the history and current role of English in ASEAN and the chapter concludes with a number of recommendations which represent a radical departure from current pedagogical policy and practice. These proposals include the need to invest in multilinguals as language teachers and the importance of deriving linguistic targets for learners from multilinguals rather than from monolingual native speakers. It is also suggested that the teaching of English should be delayed until later in the school curriculum than at present. The early years should be devoted to local languages. It is argued that the adoption of the recommendations made in Chapter 8 would lead to, among other things, a more equitable balance between local languages and English; to better retention rates in primary schools across the region; and to multilingual secondary school graduates, whose linguistic repertoires would include literacy and fluency in their home and national languages, and functional proficiency in English.

I conclude this preface on a personal note. I grew up in Malaysia and Singapore and have spent many years of my teaching and academic life working and living in ASEAN countries. The great benefit of living and working in such countries has been to experience the extraordinary and rich array of cultural and linguistic diversity which each provides. To sacrifice this linguistic and cultural diversity on the altar of English would not only be tragic, but also unnecessary. By valuing multilingualism and local languages on the one hand, and with a clearer understanding of the real roles and needs for English on the other, I believe we can produce school graduates who are not only multilingual in local languages but who also have functional proficiency in English. ASEAN can remain a site of cultural and linguistic diversity, *and* be able to produce sufficient quantities of people with high levels of proficiency in English, but only if it moves swiftly in the ways proposed above.

Part I
ASEAN and English

1

The origins of ASEAN and the role of English

This chapter will give a brief summary of the context in which the Association of Southeast Asian Nations (ASEAN) was established with the signing of the Bangkok Declaration in August 1967 by the five founding member countries. The circumstances surrounding the joining of the remaining five countries will also be reviewed. The main principles of the original 1967 Bangkok Declaration will be compared with those of the recently signed ASEAN Charter. An introduction to the role that English plays within the Association and the place and role of other languages underpins the chapter.

Background

The Bangkok Declaration of 8 August 1967 heralded the formation of the Association of Southeast Asian Nations (ASEAN). While today all ten nations of Southeast Asia are members, the number of founder member states was only five: Indonesia, Malaysia, the Philippines, Singapore, and Thailand. Brunei joined in 1984, Vietnam in 1995, Laos and Burma (Myanmar) in 1997 and finally, Cambodia, in 1999.

ASEAN was born at a time of political uncertainty and 'in the most unpromising circumstances' (Severino 2008: 3). Previous regional alliances or groupings had been tried but failed for various political reasons (Curley and Thomas 2007). These included the Association of South Asia (ASA) of 1961, the 1963 grouping of Malaysia, Indonesia and the Philippines (MAPHILINDO) and the Asia and Pacific Council (ASPAC). In 1967, the regional political situation was one of conflict. The Vietnam war was raging and the Chinese Cultural Revolution was in full swing, both of which threatened to spill over into Southeast Asia and threaten the stability of the region (Severino 2008). Rajaratnam, the foreign minister of Singapore at the time and one of the signatories to the Bangkok Declaration, has recently recalled that ASEAN was born out of a common fear. 'Regional countries were faced with managing the effects of de-colonisation, confrontation with the forces of communism, and separatism. These newly independent countries were also pre-occupied with building their economies and national identities'(Kesavapany 2005: vii). It was this combination of common interests expressed primarily through an anti-communist position and fear of regional instability that was the major motivating force for the foundation of ASEAN (Hagiwara 1992).

The countries of ASEAN are characterized by 'political, cultural and historical diversity' (Severino 2005: 15). All the world's great religions have significant numbers of adherents in countries throughout the region; there is extraordinary ethnic diversity, with more than 300 ethnic groups in Indonesia alone, and the region is home to more than 1,000 languages including Sinitic, Tai, Malayo-Polynesian, Mon-Khmer, Viet-Muong and Papuan, not to mention the languages of the earlier colonizers, of which English is now the most important, and whose role in ASEAN is the major topic of this book.

Given the political uncertainty of the times and the range of diversity within and between the five founding countries of ASEAN, one might have expected the Bangkok Declaration to be a highly detailed and juridical document. In fact, the opposite was true, as the Bangkok Declaration contains only five Articles and covers only two pages of text (http://www.aseansec.org/1212.htm). The seven aims and purposes of ASEAN, as expressed in the original declaration, were:

1. To accelerate the economic growth, social progress and cultural development in the region through joint endeavours in the spirit of equality and partnership in order to strengthen the foundation for a prosperous and peaceful community of South-East Asian Nations;
2. To promote regional peace and stability through abiding respect for justice and the rule of law in the relationship among countries of the region and adherence to the principles of the United Nations Charter;
3. To promote active collaboration and mutual assistance on matters of common interest in the economic, social, cultural, technical, scientific and administrative fields;
4. To provide assistance to each other in the form of training and research facilities in the educational, professional, technical and administrative spheres;
5. To collaborate more effectively for the greater utilization of their agriculture and industries, the expansion of their trade, including the study of the problems of international commodity trade, the improvement of their transportation and communications facilities and the raising of the living standards of their peoples;
6. To promote South-East Asian studies;

7. To maintain close and beneficial co-operation with existing international and regional organizations with similar aims and purposes, and explore all avenues for even closer co-operation among themselves.

There is no mention here of a working language or languages for the Association; nor is there any mention of the languages of the region as a whole, points which will be further considered later.

As Severino has noted (2005: 4), and as signalled by the tone of the original Declaration, the Bangkok Declaration heralded an 'ASEAN' way of doing things, which relied not on juridical documents but on consensus building in a loose and informal way. The ASEAN way is based on two Malay concepts, namely *musyawarah* (dialogue) and *muafakat* (consensus) (Curley and Thomas 2007: 9). In its original formulation, therefore, ASEAN had no central authority, no juridical personality or legal standing under international law (Severino 2005: 6).

After more than forty years of this loose structure and consensual approach to decision making, however, politicians from the region recognized the need for a more formal and legal organization and structure. This resulted in the ASEAN Charter, a document of fifty-five articles and some thirty-five pages of text, (http://www.aseansec.org/21069.pdf) and which is, in effect, the group's constitution. The Charter was adopted at the 13th ASEAN summit in November 2007, but in order to become legally binding, all ten member countries needed to ratify it. The charter attempts to define 'a more cohesive structure with specific rules of engagement for member countries', including 'enforceable obligations' (Kumar and Siddique 2008: 75), while, at the same time, maintaining the sanctity of the sovereign state through the principle of non-supra-nationality, a balancing act which is likely to prove difficult. As Kumar and Siddique point out, the 'one word that is anathema to ASEAN ... is integration' (2008: 86). It is not clear how such a diverse and disparate group of nations can work together in any significant way. The principles listed under Article 2 of the new Charter specify the policy of unity in diversity. How nations so intent on guarding their own sovereign rights will work together to implement a policy of unity in diversity also remains unclear.

The Charter was finally signed into law in February 2009 at the ASEAN summit held in Hua Hin, Thailand, after an unscheduled delay of some two months. Rather embarrassingly, given the circumstances, the delay was caused by the closure of Thailand's international airport by anti-government supporters of the ousted Thai prime minister, Thaksin Sinawatra, an issue about which ASEAN members kept characteristically silent.

Article 1 of the new Charter lists fifteen purposes of ASEAN, up from the seven of the original Declaration. They are:

1. To maintain and enhance peace, security and stability and to further strengthen peace-oriented values in the region;
2. To enhance regional resilience by promoting greater political, security, economic and socio-cultural co-operation;
3. To preserve Southeast Asia as a Nuclear Weapon-Free Zone and free of all other weapons of mass destruction;
4. To ensure that the peoples and Member States of ASEAN live in peace with the world at large in a just, democratic and harmonious environment;
5. To create a single market and production base which is stable, prosperous, highly competitive and economically integrated with effective facilitation for trade and investment in which there is free flow of goods, services and investment; facilitated movement of business persons, professionals, talents and labour; and freer flow of capital;
6. To alleviate poverty and narrow the development gap within ASEAN through mutual assistance and co-operation;
7. To strengthen democracy, enhance good governance and the rule of law, and to promote and protect human rights and fundamental freedoms, with due regard to the rights and responsibilities of the Member States of ASEAN;
8. To respond effectively, in accordance with the principle of comprehensive security, to all forms of threats, transnational crimes and transboundary challenges;
9. To promote sustainable development so as to ensure the protection of the region's environment, the sustainability of its natural resources, the preservation of its cultural heritage and the high quality of life of its peoples;
10. To develop human resources through closer co-operation in education and life-long learning, and in science and technology, for the empowerment of the peoples of ASEAN and for the strengthening of the ASEAN Community;
11. To enhance the well-being and livelihood of the peoples of ASEAN by providing them with equitable access to opportunities for human development, social welfare and justice;
12. To strengthen co-operation in building a safe, secure and drug-free environment for the peoples of ASEAN;
13. To promote a people-oriented ASEAN in which all sectors of society are encouraged to participate in, and benefit from, the process of ASEAN integration and community building;
14. To promote an ASEAN identity through the fostering of greater awareness of the diverse culture and heritage of the region; and
15. To maintain the centrality and proactive role of ASEAN as the primary driving force in its relations and co-operation with its external partners in a regional architecture that is open, transparent and inclusive.

There are a number of interesting points of difference between the fifteen purposes listed in the Charter when compared with the original seven of the Declaration. The Charter is more specific — it mentions the creation of a single market (#5) and the determination to make Southeast Asia a Nuclear Weapon-free zone (#3), for example. The Charter is also politically bolder and makes direct reference to democracy (#4 and #7) and to Human Rights (#7). One area where the original Declaration was specific concerned the promotion of Southeast Asian studies as one of its seven purposes. The new Charter makes no reference to this, but rather seeks to promote an ASEAN identity 'through the fostering of greater awareness of the diverse culture and heritage of the region' (#14).

Article 2 of the Charter lists fourteen 'principles' which member states are expected to follow and promote. As noted earlier, these include 'respect for the different cultures, languages and religions of the peoples of ASEAN while emphasizing their common values in the spirit of unity in diversity'. It is interesting to note that 'unity in diversity' is also the slogan of Indonesia (*bhinneka tunggal ita*), where Bahasa Indonesia, the national lingua franca, provides the 'glue' to bind the diversity together. 'Unity in diversity' slogans may actually be signalling unity at some cost to diversity.

Although Article 2 lists 'respect for the different languages of the peoples of ASEAN' as one of the principles, this does not translate into any official commitment into the study, teaching or learning of these languages by member states, a position which, as will be shown below, stands in stark contrast to that taken by member states of the European Union (EU). Unlike the original Declaration, however, language is mentioned in the Charter, albeit only once. Article 34, the 'Working Language of ASEAN', states that 'the working language of ASEAN shall be English'. There are, however, no other references to language or languages in the Charter.

The adoption of English

The lack of mention of languages and the decision to adopt English as the sole working language of ASEAN will no doubt strike many readers as remarkable, given, for example, the language policies of the other successful regional organization, the European Union and the intense debate which surround these (cf. Wright 2007a, Phillipson 2003, Tosi 2003). In striking contrast to ASEAN, the European Union has twenty-three official and working languages.[1] Important documents are translated into every official language. The European Parliament provides translation into all languages for documents for its plenary sessions. However, these are usually first translated into the so-called major languages. As a result, many who do not read these major languages are disadvantaged as 'the translation of essential documents and amendments may take longer to appear in the "small" languages than the "big", and may sometimes arrive too late to be studied properly before the meeting' (Wright 2007b: 157). Interpreting also follows a similar 'relay' pattern by which a speech of, for example, an Estonian delegate, is first interpreted from Estonian into English or French before then being translated from English or French into the other languages.

The Council of Europe has established the European Centre for Modern Languages whose task is to promote the teaching and learning of European languages. To quote from its website, 'Europe needs citizens who can all communicate in some of the many languages spoken within its borders'. It promotes policies which aim to maintain linguistic diversity and plurilingualism, by which is meant the ability of Europeans to achieve functional levels of proficiency in European languages according to their needs (Beacco and Byram 2003). These aims are further strengthened by the European Cultural Convention, which commits the states party to the Convention to promote the reciprocal teaching and learning of their languages. Each Contracting Party shall, insofar as may be possible:

> a. encourage the study by its own nationals of the languages, history and civilisation of the other Contracting Parties and grant facilities to those Parties to promote such studies in its territory,
> b. endeavour to promote the study of its languages, history and civilisation in the territory of the other Contracting Parties and grant facilities to the nationals of those Parties to pursue such studies in its territory.
> (http://conventions.coe.int/Treaty/Commun/QueVoulezVous.asp?NT=018&CM=2&DF=13/12/2005&CL=ENG)

The Council of Europe and the European Commission both promote the importance of Europeans learning languages other than their first language. The European Commission's Action Plan for Language Learning hopes to see people learning their mother tongue and two other European languages, and the European Charter for Regional or Minority Languages has the protection of these languages as its goal (Baetens Beardsmore 2009). While it is true that English is becoming the increasingly dominant language, there are policies in place to encourage the learning of other European languages.

While no one would argue that the language policy of the EU was perfect, especially with regard to the increasing dominance of English, the contrast between the official EU and ASEAN policies is remarkable. Indeed, as has been noted above, language was not mentioned in the original Bangkok Declaration of 1967. There was no mention even of which language(s) was (were) to be used as working languages. In the event, English immediately became the one and only de facto working language.

In her study of the process behind this de facto adoption of English as the only working and official language for the original members of ASEAN, Okudaira interviewed a number of key ASEAN figures. The three answers listed below are representative of their replies:

> 'the idea of English as the common language came out automatically',
>
> 'there has been no regulation for the use of English but it has been used in all the actual situations', and
>
> 'we took it for granted' (1999: 95–96)

Further evidence that the use of English as the sole working language was quietly accepted by the founding member states comes from an article on ASEAN negotiating styles. Although the author describes in detail the negotiating styles of speakers from different countries, no reference is made to the language in which the negotiations are conducted (Thambipillai 1992). It is automatically assumed that this is English. This lack of a mention of the language is particularly interesting as the author makes reference to national negotiating styles, and says that the Singaporeans seem 'to be the most articulate with well substantiated arguments and facts to support claims' (1992: 74). The fact that the negotiations were being conducted through English and that this might have given the Singaporeans an advantage is not considered, even though the negotiations were 'direct and forthright' (75), which would suggest a strong influence from an 'Anglo' negotiating style. In contrast, Philippine negotiators are classified as 'less specific' and 'not too clear of their wants', while the Malaysians are 'less open and more rigid' (75). Differences in national negotiating styles are also discussed by Ahmad (1992), but again there is no mention of the language used in decision making.

These articles come from *The ASEAN Reader* (Sandhu 1992). There is a companion volume, *The Second ASEAN Reader* (Siddique 2003), which provides a fount of information about ASEAN on a whole host of topics but does not discuss language at all. That there is not one chapter out of the total of the almost two hundred chapters in these volumes which discusses language issues in any form is surprising. It also underlines, however, how uncontroversial the notion of using English as the sole working language of ASEAN has been and how unconcerned regional politicians appear to be about local languages. The attitude has been well captured by Okudaira (1999: 96), 'There was a shared mutual understanding among the member countries regarding the use of English'. And in a volume in which those involved in the writing of the ASEAN Charter give their thoughts on the process, only one person mentions any issues connected with the use of English during the process. Ong Keng Yong, an ambassador-at-large in the Singaporean Ministry of Foreign Affairs recalls:

> The use of the English language as the working language of ASEAN produced an unintended outcome! There is a multiplicity of grammatical and spelling preferences originating from the peculiar usage of English in each member state. At the Charter drafting sessions, such differences delayed a quick consensus on wording and many formulations had to be put in square brackets (to be revisited later) (Ong 2009: 111).

It is therefore worth recalling ASEAN's founding membership to see if this provides any possible explanation for the lack of concern about which languages might be working languages. The five founding member states were Indonesia, Malaysia, the Philippines, Singapore, and Thailand. The roles and status of English were quite different in these countries and a detailed account of the development and roles of English in the ASEAN countries will be provided in Chapters 2 and 3. Here, therefore, only a brief review of the situation in selected countries will be provided.

Following Kachru (1992c), countries can be classified into one of three circles depending on the history, role and status of English within them. Countries where English has been traditionally spoken as the major language are classified as 'inner circle countries'. These include countries such as Britain, the United States and Australia. Countries which were British or American colonies and where English plays an institutional role are classified as 'outer circle' countries. ASEAN member states which fall into this category include Brunei, Malaysia, the Philippines and Singapore, where, because of their colonial past, English continues to play major institutional roles, and where it is possible to talk about local varieties of English, such as Singaporean and Filipino English. While Burma seems to fit this category in the sense that it was once a British colony and where English played a major role, the inward-looking xenophobic policies initiated by U Ne Win and the Burmese Socialist Programme Party (BSPP) from 1962 led to the marginalization of English. There has been some attempt to reverse such marginalization in recent years, but with little success. Kachru's third group of countries are classified as expanding circle countries. In such countries, English traditionally played no internal role and was taught only as a foreign language. Indonesia presents such an example. Not only was it a colony of a non-English-speaking colonizer, the Dutch, but it is also a land with a hugely diverse range of languages and cultures. After freedom from, first the Dutch, and then the Japanese, Indonesia has sought to promote a local language, a variety of Malay, to become the national lingua franca. In this, it has been remarkably successful, so that the great majority of Indonesians are now able to communicate through what is called Bahasa Indonesia. English is the second language of the educated urban elite and is also the first foreign language taught in schools, but often with only limited success (Dardjowidjojo 2000). Thailand, another expanding circle country, is the only country within ASEAN that has never been colonized. As in

Indonesia, English is now the first second language but, as in Indonesia, it is not being taught or learned very successfully.

Finally, there are the expanding circle countries which are made up of the former French colony of Indo-China, namely Cambodia, Laos and Vietnam. While these countries have seen a dramatic increase in the number of English learners, largely at the expense of French, levels of English even among the elite — particularly in Laos and Cambodia — remain comparatively low, and this disadvantages them in ASEAN seminars and meetings.

To return to the original five founding member states, English operated as an institutional language in the outer circle countries of Malaysia, the Philippines and Singapore to the extent that specific local varieties of English had developed. This could not be said of Indonesia, where English really only existed as a school language and where the real language planning focus was on the adoption of Bahasa Indonesia as the national lingua franca. In Thailand, English also only occupied the position of a school language. Thai language policy centred on the national adoption of Standard Thai.

Despite the comparable history of English as a colonial language in Malaysia, the Philippines and Singapore, however, the role of and attitudes to English were quite different in these three countries. For example, in the very year of the Bangkok Declaration, Malaysia introduced the National Language Act which decreed that the medium of instruction in education, from primary through to tertiary, would gradually switch from English to Malay, a process that was given some twenty years to complete. This was the start of the period of Malaysianization, brought to its culmination with the policies of Dr Mahathir, who became prime minister in 1981, a position he held until 2003. It is only relatively recently, from 2002, that Malaysia has seen a change in policy, with, for example, the revival of English as the medium of instruction for science and maths subjects in primary and secondary schools. Recent developments, however, have led to the abandonment of this policy and a reversal to Malay as the medium of instruction for maths and science in primary schools. This will be reviewed in more detail in Chapter 2.

Malaysia's policies of Malaysianization were at least partly responsible for the split between Singapore and Malaysia in 1965. Language policies played a significant part. Malaysia was keen to promote the status of Malays and used language policy to help in this. In contrast, the prime minister of the newly independent Singapore, Lee Kuan Yew, was adamant that English would play a major role in the education of Singaporeans. This campaign has been so successful that Singapore can now be classified as a country where English is spoken as the first language by a significant and increasing proportion of its citizens. The recent census showed that 60% of children in Primary 1 reported using English as their first home language. Whether the campaign has been as successful in developing bilingualism among Singaporeans is another question, and one which will be revisited later.

While English may have held important institutional roles in three of the five founder member states, the same and more could be said about Malay. Malay is the national language of both Malaysia and Singapore. And Bahasa Indonesia, which is a variety of Malay, is the national lingua franca of Indonesia. In addition, many people in the Southern Philippines and some in Southern Thailand speak varieties of Malay, or languages related to Malay. And, as we have seen, Malaysia was embarking on a policy to promote the use of Malay. Despite all this, there was no call at this stage for Malay to be at least one of the working languages of ASEAN.

Possible explanations for the 'natural' adoption of English as the working language include the view that it represented the language of modernization and advancement on the one hand (Rappa and Wee 2006), and the language of democratically supported power on the other, a particularly important motivation, given the Vietnam war and the anti-communist stance of the ASEAN states.

There have, however, been periodic, if infrequent, calls for other languages to be adopted as working languages in ASEAN and these will be considered below.

Calls for other languages

As new states joined ASEAN, one might have expected some debate over the use of English only, and indeed there was some. Brunei was the next country to join, in 1984, the year it achieved independence from Britain. Hardly surprisingly, however, given its small size on the one hand and the institutional role of English on the other, its membership occasioned no radical re-thinking of the language policy. It was not until Vietnam's membership in 1995 that the role of English only was questioned. It is not difficult to see why Vietnam did so, given its history of being a French colony and then under Russian influence during the communist period. Ironically, however, in the discussions leading to their membership, Vietnam asked for consideration to be given to adopting a second 'colonial' language, French, as ASEAN's second official language, but this request was rebuffed with the curt, 'No, English only' (Okudaira 1999: 101).

As outlined above, it was surprising, given the passing of the National Language Act in Malaysia in 1967 and the relatively widespread role of Malay within the founder member countries of ASEAN that there was no call for the adoption of Malay in the early years of ASEAN's existence. An official request for Malay to be adopted had to wait until 1997 to be tabled.

At a meeting of the ASEAN Committee on Culture and Information, the Malaysian minister of information suggested the adoption of Malay as ASEAN's second official language. Even though, as we have seen, there was some justification for this — Malay is also the official language of Brunei, so has national language status in four of the ten countries of the ASEAN nations — no one was prepared to take up the suggestion (Okudaira 1999: 101). When I raised this with the then director of the Southeast Asian Ministers of Education Organization (SEAMEO) in Bangkok in December 2007, he replied that accepting Malay as an official language would be 'opening Pandora's box'.

Since then there has been no official request for a language other than English to be adopted as an official or working language of ASEAN. That is not to say, however, that there are no moves being made to have other languages considered. The main candidate remains Malay. Concerned Malay linguists from Malaysia, Indonesia and Brunei continue to lobby for its adoption. In addition to the practical reasons for adopting Malay, these scholars also present historical reasons for its adoption. For example, Abas (2000) argues that a language known as Kw'enlun, operated as a Malay lingua franca two thousand years ago through the islands of the Nusantara Archipelago (an area encompassing most of present-day Indonesia, and the Philippine and Malaysian archipelagos), and that its position as a regional lingua franca is thus well-established. Abas also points out that one of the reasons why Malay was adopted as a regional lingua franca is that it posed no threat to others. Its original speakers were seafarers and represented a minority. This minority-speaker status was also a major reason for its later adoption as the national language of Indonesia (Alisjahbana 1976). However, Abas' claim that Malay is about 'to become the official language of wider communication in the region of Southeast Asia and beyond' (2000: 245) appears wildly optimistic, especially given that the new ASEAN Charter lists only English as the working language of ASEAN.

There have also been rather more strident calls for the acceptance of Malay, based on the notion of Malay becoming the working language of the 'East Asian Community', an idea long held by a minority of Malay politicians (Rashid 1993). Some argue that 'Malay must become the official language of ASEAN and an international language' (Makarenko and Pogadaev 2000: 218), but these calls remain largely unheeded. In fact, and in Malaysia itself, English remains important. While the policy to teach maths and science in English caused considerable controversy and has recently been rescinded, Dr Mahathir's current view demonstrates a significant shift from the early Malaysianization policy with which he was so closely associated. He now believes that English is the primary conduit of knowledge creation and dissemination (Gill 2007), arguing that those without knowledge will be 'slaves to those who have knowledge'. This view appears to be accepted by the majority (Rappa and Wee 2006). All this seriously weakens the case of those who are calling for Malay to be adopted as the second working language of ASEAN. The perception that English is *the* language of science and modernity means that it is becoming increasingly adopted in the regional school curricula, often at the expense of local languages. This theme is developed in greater depth in later chapters.

Is there another language that might be adopted as a working language of ASEAN? The membership of Laos in 1997 and Cambodia in 1999 means that there are now three countries with a French colonial past. Given Vietnam's earlier request for French to be considered, a renewed request for French might have been expected. In fact, however, Vietnam has been successful in fast-tracking the learning of English and the United Nations' (UN) presence in Cambodia with UNTAC (United Nations Transitional Authority in Cambodia) has also heightened the need and motivation for English in that country, as has membership of ASEAN itself (Keuk 2007). This leaves Laos, where English has also replaced French as the first foreign language. The fact that Vietnam has moved so successfully and quickly to adopting English as the second language and that Cambodia's reliance on the UN has suddenly prioritized the need for English may explain why no official request for French has been reiterated. A further reason for this may be the general decline of the role of French as an international language (Phillipson 2008), although, as will be shown in Chapter 3, the French francophone agency, AUPELF, is now teaching French to more Vietnamese than during the time when Vietnam was a French colony. Nevertheless, it remains highly unlikely that ASEAN would accept French as a working language, which no doubt disadvantages some, especially Laotian and Cambodian delegates. Anecdotal evidence indicates that many Laotian and Cambodian delegates remain silent in various ASEAN fora because of their relatively low proficiency in English.

The likelihood of ASEAN moving towards the EU model and accepting all member languages as official languages, is also highly unlikely. ASEAN officials are only too aware of the complexity associated with the need for the translation and interpretation service in the EU to say nothing of the cost. Tagliabue (2006) has estimated the annual EU translation and interpreting bill to be US$1.3 billion. Thus ASEAN bureaucrats identify the use of English as the sole official and working language of ASEAN as offering great advantages. It saves enormously on costs and labour, it allows direct dialogue between member states (although, as we have seen, some member states are more equal than others here), it allows easy dialogue internationally and it facilitates technology and knowledge transfer (Okudaira 1999). The assistant to the secretary general of ASEAN at the time of the drafting of the ASEAN Charter, Termsak Chalermpalanupap, sees the adoption of English as the sole working language as representing a great advantage which ASEAN has over the European Union (2009: 132). The ASEAN Charter is unequivocal: 'The working language of ASEAN shall be English.'

What about Putonghua?

One language which might come to work alongside English as a working language of ASEAN is Mandarin Chinese (Putonghua). While the only ASEAN country where it is an official language is Singapore, there is a significant ethnic Chinese presence throughout the countries of ASEAN. Chinese languages are spoken in all the countries of ASEAN and Putonghua is becoming increasingly spoken as the lingua franca among overseas Chinese communities. The establishment of the ASEAN + 3 grouping, where the '+3' are Korea, Japan and China, simply adds to the outreach of Putonghua with the realization that Southeast and Northeast Asia are interdependent (Curley and Thomas 2007: 12).

The Chinese government is also actively promoting the teaching and learning of Chinese internationally. For example, an increasing number of Confucius Institutes are being established around the world — some five hundred are planned by 2010 — with several in the ASEAN region. The aims of the Confucius Institutes are similar to those of the British Council, namely, they aim to spread language and culture in such a way to make people sympathetic towards the culture and make them want to learn the language. At the same time, there has been a dramatic increase in the number of other Putonghua training centres throughout the ASEAN region and Putonghua is also becoming an increasingly common school subject. Finally, it represents one of the world's great civilizations and the fastest growing economic and political power. On the face of it, then, it would seem a strong candidate for a working language of ASEAN.

The major — perhaps the only — disadvantage that Chinese has is a linguistic one, namely the complexity of its script. This complexity is well understood by the Chinese themselves. Indeed, the low levels of literacy occasioned by the complexity of script is often cited as one of the major reasons for China's backwardness at the beginning of the twentieth century, where scholars at the then Beijing Imperial University seriously argued for the development of an alphabetic script, if not the complete abolition of the language itself (Ramsey 1987: 3).

Literacy in Chinese is usually measured by the number of characters a learner has acquired (Chen 1999: 136*ff*). Primary school leavers are expected to know about 2,500. The actual figure in Hong Kong is 2,600 compared with 2,834 in China itself (Taylor and Taylor 1995: 136). University graduates are expected to know at least 3,500, while the highly educated may know up to 10,000 characters.

Learning to read and write Chinese takes time. It has been estimated that the Chinese spend two years more on learning to write Chinese than people who use alphabetic systems (Chen 1999). To this, however, must be added the extra curriculum (and homework) time devoted to learning how to read and write. For example, 30% of class time is spent on learning the language — most of it in learning to read and write (Chen 1999; Taylor and Taylor 1995).

Recognizing the inherent difficulty associated with learning to write Chinese, the post-1949 government of China introduced a series of language reforms designed to make the language easier to learn. Two such initiatives, the use of an alphabetic language, *pinyin,* as an aid in primary schools, coupled with the development of simplified characters, have significantly increased the national literacy rate in China (Taylor and Taylor 1995). Attempts to make Chinese an alphabetic language have been abandoned, however, as the huge number of homophones in Chinese means that these cannot be adequately distinguished in an alphabetic script. For example, the Putonghua sound *ji* in the first tone can have some thirty-five different meanings. Another major reason why the Chinese government will resist moves to alphabetization is that they understand this will inevitably lead to a significant undermining of what it means to be Chinese. The written script has been the primary tool in giving the Chinese people a sense of common inheritance and kinship. It has for millennia acted as a bridge between the mutually unintelligible Chinese dialects, as, with certain exceptions, the written form is common to all. 'Ethnolinguistic cohesion would have been impossible if somewhere in the linguistic history of China, written Chinese had gone down the road of alphabetisation' (Li 2006: 152).

Despite the recent reforms introduced by the Chinese government, learning to read and write Chinese remains a time-consuming process. This raises questions concerning whether children would have enough time to learn how to read and write Chinese. Would there be enough time in the school curriculum for children to acquire Chinese literacy? As will be illustrated in later sections of the book, the school language curriculum in ASEAN countries is already under significant strain, and part of this is indeed due to the increasing popularity of Putonghua.

In any event, there is, in my view, little likelihood that Putonghua will join English as a working language of ASEAN in the near future.

English and other languages

In closing this first chapter, I shall briefly foreshadow some of the issues concerning the relationship between English and other languages in the context of education and the school curriculum which will be dealt with in detail in later chapters.

Without exception, the amount of English in the school curriculum has increased over the past decade in each of the ten ASEAN countries. All countries now teach English as part of the primary curriculum, with Brunei and the Philippines also teaching content subjects — typically maths and science subjects — through English. In Singapore, English is *the* medium of instruction. The other languages associated with the Singaporean government's bilingual policy — Chinese, Malay and Tamil — are taught only as subjects. In Cambodia, Vietnam and Laos, where schools used to teach French, Russian and German along with English, English has now become the major second language. As one commentator reports for Vietnam:

> when Vietnam embarked on economic reforms in 1986 ... it prompted a nation wide rush to learn English ... English classes were crammed with not just students but also professionals such as doctors and engineers as well as retired government officials, senior police, army officers and diplomats (cited in Ho and Wong 2004: 1)

English has been introduced into the primary curriculum in Indonesia and Thailand, although only as an optional subject in the case of Indonesia. As will be argued in Part III, it is hard to see how this policy can lead to successful language learning, given the shortage of qualified language teachers and suitable teaching materials. In the bleak assessment of the situation in Indonesia, Dardjowidjojo lists a whole catalogue of linguistic and non-linguistic reasons for the 'failure' of English language teaching there (2000: 28). In an attempt to solve the problems of the acute shortage of qualified and proficient teachers of English, the Thai government recently went on a mass recruitment campaign for 10,000 native speakers of English to teach in primary and secondary schools throughout the country. Perhaps fortunately, as these teachers required no qualifications or vetting, this was extremely unsuccessful. Yet this blanket-like employment of unqualified and unvetted native speakers in itself gives rise to serious ethical and professional issues. It is impossible to estimate how many of these native speakers of English are teaching English through East and Southeast Asia at the moment, but China alone hires some 150,000 'foreign experts' a year, many of whom fall into this category (Jeon and Lee 2006).

The shortage of qualified English teachers is mirrored in other East Asian countries. China has introduced English as a primary school subject and the number of teachers required for this alone is incalculable. And a recent policy announcement from South Korea includes a five-year plan for all subjects to be taught in English (Card 2008). Although this plan has since been considerably watered-down, English remains a priority in Korean primary schools. In Part III, the privileging of the native speaker over local multilingual teachers is discussed in depth, where it will be argued that local governments need to place their resources in the training of local multilinguals rather than in the employment of native speakers, especially monolinguals with no relevant qualifications.

This rush towards English also comes at the expense of local languages. Where people can afford it, it is not uncommon for them to send their children to private English-medium schools. They are therefore prepared to sacrifice fluency or literacy in their child's first or national language for proficiency in English. This is common even in Hong Kong. 'To actually forsake the public school system that teaches in your own language for the private one that teaches in English is an increasingly common phenomenon' (Wang 2007: xiv).

At the same time, despite the principle enshrined in Article 2 of the new ASEAN Charter 'to respect the different cultures and languages of the region', there is little evidence that ASEAN countries are teaching each other's languages. With the exception of Putonghua, which, as reported above, is becoming increasingly popular and taught in more and more schools, no Asian languages (other than the first language) are taught as part of the core curriculum. A recent study of the Vietnamese curriculum helps bring this home (Baker and Giacchino-Baker 2003). They report that while some 98% and 95% of children at primary and upper secondary schools respectively study a foreign language, English accounts for a staggering 97.9% while French accounts for 1.69%, Russian 0.32% and Chinese 0.03% (2003: 8). What this suggests is that it is the linguistic capital of languages that is being bought and sold in the linguistic marketplace. The political impetus for promoting the teaching and learning of specific languages is almost entirely instrumental (cf. Rappa and Wee 2006). Signs of integrative or humanistic motivations are absent, despite Article 2. These issues and their implications for language education are discussed in much greater detail in the final part of the book. In the next two chapters, more detailed accounts of the historical development and current roles of English in each of the member states of ASEAN is provided. The development of the respective national language is also considered. The focus of Chapter 2 is on the so-called 'outer circle' countries, namely, Brunei, Malaysia, Singapore and the Philippines. Chapter 3 focuses on the so-called 'expanding circle' countries of Cambodia, Indonesia, Laos, Thailand and Vietnam and it will be argued that the increasing role of English within these countries suggests that 'expanding circle' may not be an appropriate classification for these countries any more. Burma is also included here.

2 Malaysia, Singapore, Brunei and the Philippines: Linguistic context and the role of English

This chapter will provide a historical description and comparison of the roles of English in those ASEAN countries that were previously colonies of English speaking empires and which, following Kachru (1992c) can be classified as 'outer circle countries', namely Brunei, Malaysia, the Philippines and Singapore. While Burma was once a colony of the British empire, its decades of closure to the outside world means that the role of English is radically different from the other countries of the colonial enterprise, and it will thus be considered in the next chapter. The different and changing roles of English in the four outer circle countries will be highlighted and critically considered, with the issues of the medium of instruction and the role of language(s) in education receiving special treatment. The major focus will be on Malaysia and the Philippines. In Malaysia, I shall suggest the major motivation for language education policies has been ethnicity and race (see Lee 2007). In the Philippines, however, I shall argue that the major motivation has been class (see Tupas 2007, Rappa and Wee 2006), with the need to modernize acting as a powerful motivator for English in all countries.

Shared concerns

The dramatically increasing importance and roles of English in today's globalizing world has brought similar concerns to many countries, including those in ASEAN. The roles of English as the major language of modernization, knowledge and globalization make it important, if not compulsory, for governments to adopt language education policies which are designed to ensure that their citizens become sufficiently proficient in English in order to be able to use it to access knowledge and contribute to the development and dissemination of knowledge. The urgent and widespread parental demands for their children to learn English also make this a very significant political issue which governments cannot ignore. All governments are thus faced with decisions over when to introduce English into the school curriculum and whether to introduce it as a subject and/or medium of instruction. If it is to be introduced as a medium of instruction, then the question arises over at which grade and/or for which subjects should it be introduced.

At the same time, there is the concern that the increased presence of English will threaten not only local languages but local cultures. How then can an equitable and practical balance be struck between English and other languages? This has become perhaps the most crucial (and difficult) educational question facing governments today, and governments' attempts to provide answers to this question invariably raise much controversy and emotion. As will be illustrated below, while many of these problems are shared, governments' responses to them have differed. Each of the countries has tried to answer these questions in its own way, and each has had to deal with the consequences of the language education policies it has implemented. Of none, however, can it be said that the policies have been uniformly successful. On the contrary, the implementation of policy has occasioned anger and dissent among significant sectors of the population, often leading to the very divisiveness that the policy hopes desperately to avoid. This can certainly be said of Malaysia's language and language education policies and it is to these I now turn.

English and language education in Malaysia

The British established the colony of the Straits Settlements of Penang, Malacca and Singapore in 1824 and established English-medium schools in all three settlements. British control over the Malay States was extended and formalized with the Treaty of Pangkor, signed in 1874, whereby a British 'Resident', as the office was somewhat coyly called, was installed as the official advisor to the Sultan of Perak. The first British Resident was J.W.W. Birch whose term of office was cut short by his assassination the following year.

While English-medium schools were established, the official position was that these would be only for a very small elite. The policy with regard to education of the locals was well encapsulated in a statement made by Maxwell, who was, between 1920 and 1926, the chief secretary of what had come to be known as the Federated Malay States. This statement is commonly quoted, but it is worth repeating, as it clearly outlines the British policy at the time as being more concerned with the training of the majority in practical skills and in maintaining the status quo, than in providing a general all-round education through which people might expect to achieve some form of social mobility,

> The aim of the government is not to turn out a few well-educated youths, nor yet numbers of less well-educated boys; rather it is to improve the bulk of the people and to make the son of fisherman or peasant a more intelligent fisherman or peasant than his father had been, and a man whose education will enable him to understand how his own lot in life fits in with the scheme of life around him. (Maxwell 1983: 408)

This view was shared by Dussek, who was both the assistant director for Malay Schools and principal of Malaya's first teacher training institute, the Sultan Idris College. In a talk given in 1937, he argued for the importance of vernacular schools on the grounds that their curriculum was designed 'to meet the needs of the rural community, special stress being laid upon gardening and handicrafts' (Dussek 1983: 447). In a remark which may explain the perceived need to separate ethnicity and occupation which is reported later in the discussion of the New Economic Policy, Dussek pointed out that introducing carpentry into the curriculum of the Malay schools was a waste of time, as the Chinese would not let Malays enter the trade. Maxwell's ideas that education should merely help the Malay fisherman and peasant become a more intelligent fisherman and peasant are relevant here also. In this context, it is worth recalling that Malaysia was a trade or exploitation colony. Mufwene has distinguished these from 'settlement colonies' (2001: 8–9) of which Australia and New Zealand are examples. The role of an exploitation colony was to provide wealth to the colonizer. 'Colonial possessions which drained the imperial purse were anathema' (Kratoska 1983: 3). The British needed people who would help the colony become wealthy. In the context of Malaysia, this meant not only Malay fishermen and peasants, but also workers for the tin mines and rubber plantations. The Chinese were brought in to work the mines and the Tamils were brought in to work the plantations. Thus were sown the seeds of Malaysia's current multicultural and multilingual society which has had an extraordinarily profound effect upon Malaysia as a whole, not least in its language and language education policies.

The arrival of so many migrant workers led to the establishment of vernacular schools. During Maxwell's time, the Malay vernacular schools were free and were run by the government. The Tamil vernacular schools were mostly established in rubber plantations and were a mixture of government and aided schools. The Chinese vernacular schools were different in that they were established and run by the Chinese community and pupils paid monthly fees. Figures presented by Maxwell (Maxwell 1983: 405) show that, in 1925, about half of all Chinese and Malay boys were in school (compared with the figure of one in every twenty Malay girls). Only one in about three Tamil boys were enrolled. Table 2.1 shows the overall numbers of children enrolled in different schools at this time.

Table 2.1 School enrolments (1925)

School Type	Numbers Enrolled
Malay vernacular schools	26,000 boys; 3,000 girls
Chinese vernacular schools	15,000 (boys and girls)
Tamil vernacular schools	8,000 (boys and girls)
English-medium schools	14,000 (boys and girls of all nationalities)

That 14,000 students of all nationalities were enrolled in English-medium schools illustrates how highly sought after such schools were. Despite the British aim to restrict English-medium education to a highly select elite, parental pressure saw the establishment of private English-medium schools. Most were run by missionaries (Wong and James 2000) and remain highly regarded and prestigious today. For example, the Victoria Institute in Kuala Lumpur, which was established in 1893, was the country's first English-medium secondary school. It is still considered to be one of the best schools in Malaysia. The cachet associated with the original name of the school can be seen from the recent decision to rename the school the Victoria Institute after being called the Sekolah Menengah Victoria for many years. The trend of preferring to see one's children educated privately through English rather than through government schools and the local language is even more pronounced today. Reiterating Wang Gungwu's observation about this which was cited in the previous chapter helps underscore this, '[t]o actually forsake the public school system that teaches in your own language for the private one that teaches in English is an increasingly common phenomenon' (2007: xiv).

The arrival of so many migrant workers also affected the population balance, so that, at the time of Malaysian independence in 1957, the Malays made up less than 50% of the people. Being a minority in their own country caused Malays and many Malay politicians deep concern. The relative number and status of the Malay population is crucial in understanding subsequent language policy. Not surprisingly, Malays felt that their language and culture was under threat in their own country. In 1957, the Institute of Language and Literature, or Dewan Bahasa dan Pustaka, was formed. Importantly its tasks included not only the preservation of the language and culture, but also the development of Malay into a world language by 2020 (Rappa and Wee 2006: 36).

Two unexpected major political events of the early and mid-1960s altered the balance of the population in favour of the Malays. The first was the decision of Sarawak and Sabah to join the Federation of Malaya. Sarawak had been run by the Brooke family for some one hundred years (the so-called 'White Rajahs') until the Japanese invasion, and then became a British colony in 1946. Sabah had been the colony of British North Borneo.

In 1962, a team headed by Lord Cobbold and which included Sir Anthony Abell, a former governor of Sarawak, went over to Sarawak and Sabah to find out whether the people would be interested in joining Malaya. The Cobbold Commission duly reported that they were in favour of so doing. The work of the Cobbold Commission remains murky, but the result of it was that 'Malayans woke up one morning in September 1963 to find themselves Malaysians, with a host of new fellow countrymen from the other side of the South China Sea' (Rashid 1993: 59). Malaya became Malaysia and the Malays, together with the indigenous peoples, became a majority in their own country.

The second political event which was to alter the population balance further in favour of the Malays was the expulsion of Singapore from the Federation in 1965. As the population of Singapore was about 80% ethnic Chinese, this reduced the number of ethnic Chinese in the Federation. Today, Malays now make up about 65% of the population, Chinese 30% and Tamils 8% (Gill 2007: 107).

That the Malays made up less than 50% of the population until the mid-1960s is one reason why Malay has been seen as so important for preserving the identity and culture of the Malays (Ganguly 2003). The British were also sensitive to this, and the Barnes Commission of 1951 recommended that Malay should become the medium of instruction in all primary schools. This was just the first of a series of education reports and acts over the next decades, all of which had to deal with the contentious issues of language and media of instruction. The subsequent policies have also seen several changes of direction.

As might have been expected, the non-Malays were not supportive of the recommendations of the Barnes Commission, preferring to retain the Chinese and Tamil vernacular schools. The Fenn and Wu report of 1952 took their side and argued that schools should be allowed to adopt different languages as media of instruction. This was to little immediate avail, however, and the 1952 Education Ordinance adopted the recommendations of the Barnes report. This became 'the cornerstone of language education policy in post-colonial Malaysia' (Ganguly 2003: 243).

Language and ethnicity became increasingly important political considerations over the next few years leading up to the country's independence in 1957. The United Malay National Organisation (UMNO) had been formed in 1948 and it successfully promoted the Malay language as the sole national language. While few objected to this, many non-Malay groups objected to the Malay medium of education policy. The Malay Chinese Association (MCA), which supported mother tongue education, was particularly influential, as UMNO realized that it needed MCA support in the 1955 elections (Lee 2007). Thus the Razak Report of 1956, which in effect became the Education Ordinance of 1957, made concessions, many of which remain in force today. The 1957 Ordinance saw the creation of the two different primary school systems, the 'national' schools and the 'national-type' schools. National schools used Malay as the medium of instruction and were staffed by Malay teachers and attended by Malay students. National-type schools could choose whether to use English, Chinese (Mandarin) or Tamil as media of instruction. Secondary schools were all 'national' schools, although Chinese schools were allowed to teach through Mandarin as long as they also taught Malay (Lee 2007). This has led to the inevitable consequence of a racially segregated school system in a multiracial and multilingual country whose greatest boast is its racial harmony and diversity.

The years since the Razak Report of 1956 and the Education Ordinance of 1957 have seen several further acts, including the Talib Report and Education Act of 1960 and 1961 respectively, and the universally unpopular National Language Act of 1967, which ruled that Malay was the official language, but that other languages 'could be used in all unofficial matters' (Ganguly 2003: 248). The late 1960s saw inter-ethnic tensions rise, especially between the Chinese and the Malays. The national elections of May 1969 resulted in the majority of the ruling coalition being drastically reduced. A major cause of this was the desertion of many Chinese from the Malayan Chinese Association in reaction to what they felt was the obsequious and acquiescent behavior of the MCA to UMNO (Rashid 1993: 86–7). Tensions became inflamed and resulted in the racial riots of 1969, the subsequent suspension of parliament and the establishment of a National Operations Council (NOC). Malaysia's first prime minister, the popular and collegial Tunku Abdul Rahman, soon resigned and Razak, who was to become the second prime minister (and father of Najib), took over the NOC and the lead in setting out the New Economic Policy (NEP). This had two major aims, namely the elimination of the idea that race and occupation were linked, and to eradicate poverty (Ganguly 2003: 249). Malays were to be lawyers and engineers, not just farmers and fishermen. What it also did, however, was to provide a host of measures which would positively discriminate in favour of Malays under the general name of the *bumiputra* policy, which gave special privileges to Malays and 'sons of the soil'. Thus Chinese and Indian Malaysians who had lived in Malaysia for generations now saw themselves as second-class citizens. This must have been particularly galling in the case of the *bumiputra* of the newly acquired provinces of Sabah and Sarawak, as they had been Malaysians for less than a decade. Thus has Malaysia been called a nation of paradoxes with the traditional Malay concepts of *kesetosaan* (tranquility) and *keharmonian* (harmony) now operating alongside the *bumiputra* policy (Rappa and Wee 2006: 34).

The linguistic side to the NEP was realized in the elimination of vernacular schools and the gradual implementation of Malay as the medium of instruction in all primary and secondary schools. This was given twelve years to be completed, when the universities would follow. The first government Malay-medium university, the Universiti Kebangsaan Malaysia (UKM), or the National University of Malaysia, was established in 1970, some fifty years after the idea of a Malay-medium university had first been proposed by the Malay literary scholar, Abdul Kadir Abadi (Gill 2005). UKM includes as part of its agenda 'the nurturing of Bahasa Malaysia as an intellectual language at the national and international level' (Gill 2005: 35).

Not only would the universities adopt Malay as the medium of instruction, there would also be a quota system for Malays. This meant, in short, that it would be far harder for non-Malays (that is to say, *non-bumiputras*) to gain entry into local universities. Not surprisingly, many non-Malays voted with their feet and enrolled their children in English-medium universities in places such as Britain and Australia, marking the start of the dramatic increase in international students in Australian universities.

The position of Malay was further strengthened by the Constitution Amendment Act of 1971. Under this act, the place of Malay 'may no longer be questioned, it being considered that such a sensitive issue should be forever removed from the arena of public discussion' (Rappa and Wee 2006: 38).

After some two decades of this pro-Malay language policy, there was a general understanding among ruling politicians that it had been a failure. For example, many of the graduates from Malaysian universities were now basically monolingual in Malay and unemployable in many walks of life, especially in the private sector (Gill 2007). Thus in 2002, the policy was overturned. Much of the initiative for the new policy came from Dr Mahathir himself, who had been prime minster since 1983 and who had been a prime instigator of the 1979 Education Act which reaffirmed the policy of Malaysianization. The new policy called for the gradual re-introduction over a five-year period of English as the medium of instruction for maths and science from Primary 1. In addition, universities would be given far more freedom to choose the medium of instruction. Indeed in 1993, there had already been significant relaxation of this, with certain science and engineering subjects along with medicine being taught through English (Ganguly 2003), although the National University (UKM) rejected this proposal and continued to teach science and technology through Malay until the government policy mandated the switch of medium of instruction in these subjects from Malay to English in 2002 (Gill 2005). A further motivation to allow the emergence of private universities has been globalization. The 1996 private Higher Education Institutions Act led to an increase in private institutions and universities. Private universities could choose their medium of instruction on the condition that Malay was made a compulsory subject. Dr Mahathir himself officially opened the Chinese-financed English-medium Tunku Abdul Rahman University in 2002.

The creation of the private universities system has led to an unfortunate result. Generally speaking, graduates of the government universities come from the lower classes and are mostly Malay. Despite the switch to English medium for science and technology, the level of English proficiency for graduates from other disciplines may not be high. Graduates from the private universities, on the other hand, are from the middle and upper classes, are mostly Chinese and their overall proficiency in English is higher (Gill 2005). Graduates of private universities are therefore more employable, especially in the private sector.

While the overall relaxation of the Malay-only policies of the past has been generally welcomed, the policy of teaching maths and science through English from Primary 1 has been heavily criticized on a number of grounds. People have complained on purely practical grounds, pointing out that there are simply not enough local primary teachers of maths and science who have sufficient levels of English to teach the subjects in it, especially in rural areas. The shortage of qualified English teachers and of teachers with high levels of English proficiency is indeed acute, as many had left the profession when the medium of instruction switched to Malay (Wong and James 2000). Another criticism comes from language professionals who have argued that Primary 1 is too early to start teaching subjects through English, especially as the children's own level of English is poor. The Chinese schools are angry, as they argue that they successfully teach these subjects through Chinese and, if they do have to adopt English, then Chinese will be reduced to being taught solely as a subject. They have thus presented a host of different proposals which would allow them to teach a percentage of these classes in English and a percentage in Mandarin (Gill 2007: 116–7). Malay nationalists also oppose the policy, seeing it as a revival of the colonial era in its undermining of the place of Malay and, as a consequence, Malay nationalism itself (Puteh 2006). The Malay Language Academy is also naturally strongly opposed to this policy, arguing, with justification, that maths and science can be taught through Malay, especially at the primary level. A group opposed to this policy organized mass rallies to protest against it, an action that the editorial of 19 February 2009 in the pro-Malaysian government paper, the *New Straits Times,* poured scorn upon. First claiming that the widespread use of English in schools and literature 'can only be good for the nation', the author continued:

> But as far as the defenders of the Malay language are concerned, their fighting words may yield yet another case of "*yang menang menjadi arang, yang kalah menjadi abu*" (winners turn into coal, losers into ashes). Which is why it would be far better for them to get over their post-colonial hang-up over the English language.

Two further quotes from a debate recorded in the *New Straits Times* of 21 March 2009 capture the differing viewpoints. Ng Chai Heng wants the policy of teaching maths and science through English dropped as:

> They (the students) can't even understand English, how can you make them study Science and Maths in English?

His opponent in the debate, Datin Noor Azimah, used the argument that Malay was not an international language — unlike Mandarin — and this was why the policy of using English as the medium of instruction for maths and science (PPSMI) should be retained:

> Mandarin is an international language, that's where the Malays are at a disadvantage. Because *Bahasa* is not an international language. That's why we are fighting and want PPSMI to be retained, because it is an advantage to the Malays.

At the same time, the then minister of education, Hishamuddin Hussein, hoped that the new policy would help attract children of all ethnic backgrounds to the national schools and create, for the first time, an ethnically diverse student body in Malaysia's government schools. But he has admitted that this will be difficult, not least because it will require the staff of these schools to become ethnically mixed (Gill 2007: 120). An alternative way of achieving an ethnic mix is through the establishment of 'vision' schools where Malay, Mandarin and Tamil schools are sited in the same compound to 'promote integration and unity among students of various races' (Rappa and Wee 2006: 48).

In the event, the government took the decision in July 2009 to gradually rescind the policy. The teaching of maths and science through English will gradually be phased out from 2012 because the government, according to the deputy prime minister Muhyiddin Yassin, has now recognized that far too many children, especially those from the lower socio-economic classes and rural areas, were failing in maths and science, and that there were not enough suitably qualified teachers with adequate proficiency in English. This is not to say that the current government does not recognize the importance of English. Instead, however, of using English as a medium of instruction, the government proposes to increase significantly the amount of time given to teaching English as a subject in both primary and secondary schools. The decision has not been welcomed by the middle classes. Dr Mahathir, who has expressed his dismay at the decision, even set up a poll on his blog (http://chedet.co.cc/chedtblog/) asking people to cast votes in favour or against the government's decision. He closed this once the total vote reached 100,000, with more than 80% of the voters indicating they were opposed to the new policy.

The above account has summarized the major milestones in the development of language policy and language education policy in Malaya and Malaysia. These provide ample evidence for the claim that educational and pedagogic issues are less important than political, social and economic ones in the forming of such policies (Tsui and Tollefson 2004). Three major issues can be identified: the preservation and development of Malay; the role of Mandarin and Tamil in the education system; and the role of English.

Despite the efforts of the Language Academy, Malay remains as a language of Malay identity and culture. The 2002 decision to teach maths and science through English was a serious blow to the Academy's attempt to develop Malay as a world language by the year 2020. Malay has simply been unable to keep pace with scientific and technological developments, while to provide translations into Malay of the thousands upon thousands of scholarly reports published each year has proved impossible (Gill 2007). Instead, Malay remains associated with traditional culture. In a world where the importance of languages is increasingly judged by their instrumental value, Malay has lost out to English and Mandarin. As Rappa and Wee have elegantly argued, a crucial aspect of Asian modernity is to 'manage' English and find ways in which English and local languages can operate in a complimentary way (2006: 23). Yet, by being a language associated with tradition, Malay can be seen as reactionary and 'old-fashioned'. To paraphrase Fishman (1973), English provides the road from the rural local village to the high-tech global metropolis. Malay provides the village road maps, English the global ones. In addition, however, English also provides a form of linguistic glue within Malaysia itself. While Malay is undisputed as the national language, it is not always used for inter-ethnic communication nowadays, especially among the better educated. Many Chinese prefer to speak Mandarin for intra-ethnic communication, but English for inter-ethnic communication, although the relationship between language and identity in Malaysia is tortuously complex (Lee 2007). Many monolingual Malays created by the policies associated with Malaysianization have found themselves unemployed and unemployable.

In the Malay King's recent address at the Opening of Parliament (*New Straits Times*, 17 February 2009) he said, speaking in Malay,

> Our multiracial and multicultural characteristics should be synthesized and turned into the nation's strength.

It may be that English will prove a more effective medium for this than Malay. I now turn to discuss the situation in Singapore.

English and language education in Singapore

While the general histories of Malaysia and Singapore have many similarities, the language and language education policies in Singapore are quite different from those of Malaysia's and provide a cautionary example of how important it is to study local contexts and situations when considering language and language policy (Sonntag 2003). While I have suggested that the main issue in the construction of language policy in Malaysia has been the relationship between the races, in Singapore the main issue has been intra-racial, especially between the Chinese themselves, with the major struggle taking place between the Chinese-educated and the English-educated Chinese (Tan 2007). In Singapore, the debate has also been dominated by economic concerns and the recognition of the need to modernize. This economic imperative has played a stronger role in Singapore than in Malaysia, while the need for language as an identity and cultural marker has played a smaller role in Singapore than in Malaysia.

Singapore's introduction to English was, however, comparable to Malaya's, as Singapore was, along with Penang and Malacca, one of the three settlements which comprised the Straits Settlements when these were established in 1824. While Singapore shares the same ethnic mix as Malaysia, the relative numbers of the different ethnic groups are significantly different. In Singapore, the ethnic Chinese make up the great majority and constitute over 70% of the population. Malays (about 14%) and Indians (about 8%) thus represent much smaller percentages of the population than they do in Malaysia. In addition, there is a sizeable Eurasian community in Singapore, along with the large expatriate workforce of nearly half a million — a sizeable number in the population of less than five million — although this has been dropping dramatically since the beginning of the recent global economic crisis.

While Singapore was a British colony, education in English and the vernacular languages (Chinese, Malay and Tamil) was provided. As was the case in Malaya, however, there was great parental pressure for English-medium schools, as that was seen as the way to success.

In this, Singapore's first prime minister, Lee Kuan Yew concurred. Disagreement over the relative importance of relative languages was a major cause of Singapore's expulsion from the Federation in 1965. Lee Kuan Yew wanted to promote English and saw no need to promote Malay, especially in a country with such an overwhelming majority of Chinese. Yet, Lee Kuan Yew also understood the need to respect the languages of the various ethnic communities and the need to find a delicate balance. He managed this by establishing Malay as the national language of the now independent Republic of Singapore, but making Malay, Mandarin, Tamil and English official languages. The first two items of Article 153A of Singapore's Constitution read (Tan 2007: 75):

(i) Malay, Mandarin, Tamil and English shall be the four official languages in Singapore
(ii) The national language shall be the Malay language and shall be in the Roman script

The present language policy centres around the bilingual policy, whereby each person learns English and their mother tongue, although the definition of mother tongue is specially constructed as 'the symbolic language of the group of one's paternal ancestry, rather than the language of one's primary socialisation, or one's "native speech"' (Tan 2007: 79). Despite this definition, Mandarin has been adopted as the 'mother tongue' of the ethnic Chinese, and there has been a long-standing campaign against other Chinese languages, termed 'dialects' by the Singapore government. In contrast, Indians whose mother tongue is not Tamil can learn other Indian 'mother tongues' such as Bengali, Hindi, Punjabi and Gujerati, but the local community is responsible for establishing and running the particular language centres where these languages are taught (Tan 2007: 90).

As indicated above, the major controversy has been among the Chinese themselves. In the early years immediately before and after independence, Chinese-educated Singaporeans were, or were perceived as being, associated with Mainland China and communism, and thus treated with great suspicion by their English-educated counterparts. The political upper hand was always held by the English-educated Chinese, however. These dominated the People's Action Party (PAP), the political party which has been in virtually complete control of Singapore since 1965. Since the elections of 1968 when it won all the seats, the PAP has lost a total of twelve seats in nine elections. In the 2006 election, the PAP won all but two of the eighty-four seats. The PAP is thus able to exercise real power and in 1971 the government decided to close the leading Chinese-language newspaper, the *Nanyang Siang Pau,* when the paper foolhardily demanded more Chinese education in its editorial pages (Ganguly 2003: 257). The Chinese-medium university, Nanyang, which had been established in 1951, was also viewed with suspicion as a breeding ground for those with communist sympathies, and this too was effectively closed in 1981, by being 'merged' with the newly established National University of Singapore (NUS). As NUS is an English-medium university, Nanyang University actually represented the last of Chinese-medium tertiary education in Singapore (other than in Chinese studies). The relatively new Nanyang Technological University, established in 1991, is English-medium, as are all other tertiary institutions.

In 1979, the then deputy prime minister, Goh Keng Swee, released the Goh Report, which was very critical of the state of bilingual education. There were also government concerns about the use of Chinese dialects and their apparent contribution to divisions among the ethnic Chinese. One of the outcomes of the Goh Report was thus the 'Speak Mandarin' campaign of 1979, which encouraged the use of Mandarin as the lingua franca among Chinese dialect groups. This has been remarkably successful in that Mandarin has become the lingua franca of the younger generations of Singaporean Chinese. This very success has, however, led to a number of negative consequences. First, it has become racially divisive. Ethnic Chinese now speak Mandarin to each other, whereas before, English or Bazaar Malay was the common lingua franca among the Chinese, and they were thus able to mix freely with the Malays and Indians. Ethnic Chinese now tend to stick together more than they did. Second, it has become generationally divisive as the younger ethnic Chinese can no longer communicate in the Chinese dialects of their parents and grandparents.

The current bilingual policy is more accurately classified as an 'English + 1' policy, with every Singaporean being required to learn English and their 'mother' tongue. The aim here has been to ensure that Singapore can maintain its place as an international city in the era of globalization, while ensuring that its citizens remain in contact with their original culture. The policy has been a success with regard to the first aim. The adoption of English as *the* medium of instruction has meant that most Singaporeans are highly proficient speakers of English, with an increasing percentage listing English as their first language. Tan quotes the then deputy prime minister Lee Hsien Loong, giving a 2001 figure of 44% of primary school students saying that they speak English as a home language (2007: 86). In 2004, the number of Primary 1 children giving English as their home language became the majority for the first time. The *Straits Times* of 18 March 2009 reported the latest figures which show that 60% of Singaporean Primary 1 children now speak English as their home language, with a mere 40% speaking Mandarin. But this very success with English has meant that the second aim has not been successfully met. For example, while the 'speak' part of the 'Speak Mandarin' campaign has been successful, the Chinese literacy of Singaporean students is poor. Lee Kuan Yew appears to have recognized this as a cause for concern and recently encouraged parents to speak Mandarin with their children at home (*Straits Times,* 18 March 2009). With English as the medium of instruction, Chinese is taught as a subject, as are Malay and Tamil. This means that there has not been enough curriculum time available for ethnic Chinese students to learn how to read and write Chinese. As explained in Chapter 1, acquiring literacy in Chinese takes significantly more time than acquiring literacy in an alphabetic language such as English (Chen 1999). The government has recognized this and has two major concerns. The first is that Singapore needs people highly literate in Chinese and highly familiar with Chinese 'high' culture, as China becomes an increasingly strong political and economic force. The Singaporean government has introduced a series of measures to try and produce an elite group of Chinese Singaporeans 'who are steeped in the Chinese cultural heritage, history, literature and the arts' (Tan 2007: 83). The so-called Special Assisted Plan (SAP) schools aim to produce this elite group of Chinese-English bilinguals.

The second concern is that many Chinese Singaporeans are losing touch with their Chinese cultural roots. In an attempt to reverse this, the government has introduced a new Chinese syllabus, Syllabus B, which is far less challenging that the original syllabus, but which is aimed at helping students learn at least something about Chinese and Chinese culture. But this has not been successful, as taking Syllabus B is seen as 'a badge of dishonour' (Tan 2007: 86). The relatively low levels of Chinese literacy among the majority of ethnic Chinese Singaporeans thus remains a great concern. Despite recent government initiatives to increase levels of Chinese proficiency, 'the overall CL (Chinese language) level is declining', especially in terms of literacy in Chinese (Goh 2009: 189). In a speech given in November 2009, Singapore's minister mentor Lee Kwan Yew admitted that the bilingual policy had been a mistake in that it demanded too much of children.

> We started the wrong way. We insisted on *ting xie* (listening), *mo xie* (dictation) — madness! We had teachers who were teaching in completely-Chinese schools. And they did not want to use any English to teach English-speaking children Chinese and that turned them off completely. (*Temasek Review*, 18 November 2009)

The successful adoption of English as the major language of the majority of Singaporeans has led to an unforeseen result, which is the adoption of a local variety of English as the identity marker for Singaporeans. It will be remembered that the two aims of the bilingual policy were to ensure that Singapore would be able to participate in globalization on the one hand (through English) and keep a sense of local identity on the other (through the mother tongue). What has happened, however, is that English has taken over both roles with the development of Singaporean English, a local variety marked by influence from local languages at the levels of phonology, lexis, syntax discourse and cultural conventions. Part II of the book provides specific linguistic illustrations of local varieties of English along with its use as a lingua franca, so none will be provided here. However, the Singaporean government has proved extremely unwilling to recognize this Singaporean variety of English, rather fearing that its use in international contexts will render Singaporean unintelligible and make them a laughing stock. It has thus been promoting the 'Speak Good English Movement'. In this, however, the government seems keen to stamp out Singaporean English as an identity marker, fearing that this will further reduce the roles and domains of the 'mother' tongue. Alternatively, it misunderstands the different functions that all languages play. The informal, colloquial varieties of languages are often used for intra-ethnic, intra-community communication and function strongly as identity markers (Kirkpatrick 2007a). It does not matter if outsiders cannot understand this variety. It is not for them, it is for insiders within the local speech community. These colloquial identity-marker varieties are not used in out-group or international communication, where more formal and standard varieties are used. Singaporeans, in much the same way as Australians and others, will use a localized colloquial variety when talking with each other in informal contexts (and in the Singaporean context, this variety will inevitably be characterized by code-mixing), but will use a more standard and educated variety in more formal contexts or when communicating with speakers from other linguistic and cultural backgrounds. If the government's motivation in promoting the Speak Good English Movement is to try and prevent English from taking over as the Singaporeans' linguistic identity marker, it is almost certainly too late. If the government's motivation is to encourage Singaporeans to use a more standard form of English in international communication, it is almost certainly unnecessary. The bilingual policy has succeeded in making English the common language of Singapore. It has failed in helping people retain their links to their traditional cultures. This includes not only the issue of literacy in Chinese but also the decreasing ability to use Chinese dialects. Ironically, the government now seems to realize that its lack of support for dialects may have been misjudged, as these, along with their associated clan memberships, continue to play an extremely important role in intra-Chinese relationships, within Chinese communities, both within China itself and overseas (Tan 2007). But Lee Kuan Yew remains convinced that learning dialects is wasted effort. In a speech reported in the *Straits Times* of 18 March 2009, he said, 'If you speak Hokkien or Cantonese, you reach some 60 million in Fujian or Taiwan, or about 100 million in Guangdong and Hong Kong. With Mandarin, you can speak to 1,300 million Chinese from all provinces in China.' In this, a comparison with the language education policy in Hong Kong is instructive. The Hong Kong government has retained Cantonese, the mother tongue of the great majority of the Hong Kong population, as the medium of instruction in primary schools, where English is taught only as a subject. As a result, all Hong Kong school children who go through the government system become literate in Chinese while retaining Cantonese. While the levels of English in Hong Kong are not as uniformly high as they are in Singapore, its people are literate in

Chinese, fluent in Cantonese and increasingly proficient in Mandarin. Singaporeans are highly proficient, if not fluent, in English. Singapore is becoming an increasingly English-speaking society where English is also acting as an identity marker. Singaporeans' expertise in English will, of course, be highly advantageous in certain international settings, but their lack of expertise in other languages may prove disadvantageous in others, especially those where a proficient knowledge of Chinese would be helpful. I now turn to the situation in Brunei.

English and language education in Brunei

Brunei became a British protectorate in 1888, fourteen years after the Treaty of Pangkor. The familiar question of how to modernize and become part of the international arena through English while retaining the local culture through Malay was originally to be answered by adopting the Malay policy of the use of Malay as the sole medium of instruction. Indeed, this was the recommendation of the Baki-Chang Report of 1959 (Jones 2007). Despite this also coinciding with the 1959 constitution which specified Malay as the national language, the policy was not implemented for a number of reasons, including a civil insurrection in 1962 and then, in the 1970s, political disagreements with Malaysia. Among other things, this led to the recall of Bruneian students from Malaysia.

Brunei gained independence in 1984 and the following year saw the introduction of the National Education System and the birth of the bilingual or *dwibahasa* policy (Jones 2000). This is still in effect today and involves Malay being used as the medium of instruction in the first three years of primary school, after which English becomes the medium of instruction for maths, science, geography, history and technical subjects. Malay remains the medium of instruction for Malay literature, Islamic knowledge, civics, arts, handicrafts and physical education (Omar 2007: 358).

The year 2009 saw some changes to the policy, with adoption of the *National Education System for the 21st Century* (SPN 21) (http://www.moe.edu. bn/web/spn21). In a striking contrast to the Malaysian government's recent shift back towards the use of Malay for the teaching of maths and science, Brunei has decided to increase the role of English by making English the medium of instruction for these subjects from Primary 1. Remarkably, no explanation of the reasons behind this decision is provided in the new curriculum document (Brunei Ministry of Education 2009). This new policy is scheduled for full implementation in primary schools in 2011.

Initially many resisted the bilingual policy, some for pedagogic reasons, some for national ones. Those with pedagogic concerns argued that becoming bilingual was cognitively too demanding. Those with national concerns argued that giving so much curriculum time to English would undermine the position of Malay on the one hand, and introduce harmful 'Western' concepts on the other. Today, however, most of these pedagogic and political concerns have dissipated and the bilingual education system has become accepted. Rather, today's concerns centre around the socially divisive effect of the elite schools, where wealthy parents send their children and where the teaching and resources are superior to the normal government schools. It has become more an issue of resources than anything else, as the government schools are poorly equipped and there is a lack of proficient bilingual teachers. As Jones has pointed out, it is now not a question of whether a bilingual system should be implemented, but how it should be implemented in an equitable way to ensure that all do indeed graduate bilingual (2007: 257). In short, the majority accept the importance of English while still being confident that the role of Malay will not be undermined, especially as it is the language underpinning the three pillars of the country's philosophy, namely *Melayu, Islam, Beraja*, or Malay, Islam and Monarchy (Omar 2007). Generally speaking, Brunei's bilingual language education policy has probably been the most successful of all the ASEAN member states, even though access to English in many rural areas remains extremely limited (Martin and Abdullah 2002).

To date in this chapter, the situations in Malaysia, Singapore and Brunei have been summarized and considered. All three of these countries share a British colonial heritage and Malay as a national language. While all are multilingual and multicultural, the major ethnic groups are similar. I now turn to consider the Philippines, a country with a quite different colonial heritage and a country in which a far greater number of languages are spoken. Another fundamental difference, at least between the Philippines and the Muslim countries of Brunei and Malaysia, is that the Philippines is 92% Christian, the great majority of whom are Catholics.

English and English language education in the Philippines

The population of the Philippines is around seventy-six million spread over some seven thousand islands. As indicated above, over 90% of the population is Christian. As Filipinos are ethnically related to the Malays, this makes the Philippines the largest Malay nation on earth and the largest Christian nation in Asia (Rappa and Wee 2006: 62). It is a country of extreme linguistic diversity with eight major indigenous language groups comprising more than one hundred languages (Galang 2000).

The Philippines was a Spanish colony from 1565 (the name of the country commemorates King Philip II of Spain) until 1898, whereupon it became an American colony with the Spanish defeat by the United States in the Spanish American War (Thompson 2003). The Treaty of Paris of 1898 gave Cuba — another Spanish colony — its independence, but pressure from President McKinley resulted in the Philippines simply shifting colonial masters from the Spanish to the Americans. It became an independent nation in 1946.

The Philippine Commission of 1898 headed by Governor Taft had planned to provide basic education either through Spanish or local languages, but it first discovered that very few people spoke Spanish, and second, that the local languages had no literary tradition and this made them unsuitable as media of instruction (Thompson 2003: 19). Here we see one immediate difference from the situation in Malaya, where Malay was the national language and spoken by all Malays. In stark contrast, the multilingual nature of the Philippines meant that no one local language was the obvious choice for the national language. Indeed, it was not until 1941 that Tagalog was made the national language, a decision that still evokes controversy, as will be shown below, even though it has since had its name changed to Filipino.

The findings of the Philippine Commission led to the Second Philippine Commission and the decision in 1901 to adopt English as the medium of instruction. This decision to adopt English rather than Spanish was supported by Apolinario Mabini, one of the ideologues behind the Philippine revolution against the Spanish (Gonzalez 1996a). The adoption of English also appealed to the colonizers, as they felt that English would help the locals 'imbibe and internalize democratic principles' (Gonzalez 1996a: 27). In this, the American policy was significantly different from the British policy in Malaya, which was to provide an English education only to a small and privileged elite.

The adoption of English as the medium of instruction meant that there was a great need for English teachers, and five hundred were duly dispatched from the United States in 1901. As the ship that brought them was called *The Thomas*, these early English teachers are known as *Thomasites*. Even with teachers being sent from the United States on a regular basis, they never constituted more than 30% of the teaching force, and by 1921, this had dropped to 9%. This has meant that, in the Philippines, English has been taught mainly by Filipinos (Gonzalez 1996a). The same is true of the other countries of the region. The overwhelming majority of English teachers have been locals. This has made the development and dissemination of local varieties of English inevitable, a topic which is discussed in greater detail in Part III of the book.

The decision to adopt English as the medium of instruction was successful if the numbers of Filipinos who reported being able to use English are reliable. The census figures of 1918 show that over 50% of Filipinos of ten years old or more said they could speak English and

55% said they could read and write it (Gonzalez 1996a: 27). English remained the sole medium of instruction until 1938. In 1939, the use of native languages as 'auxiliary media of instruction' was mandated (Galang 2000: 271) and, in 1941, Tagalog was made an official language. These developments followed on from the promulgation of the National Language Law and the founding of the National Language Institute in 1936, some twenty years before its Malaysian counterpart was established.

The choice of Tagalog as the national language was unpopular with the majority of Filipinos. Tagalog is spoken around Manila — Tagalog literally means river dweller, the river in question being the Pasig, which flows through Manila — and has about four million native speakers. But, as mentioned above, the Philippines is multilingual and many speakers of other languages were naturally angry at the choice of Tagalog (Gonzalez 1996b). Particularly strong resistance came (and, to a certain extent, still does) from Cebuano speakers, who can be numbered at over six million, if the dialects related to Cebuano are included (Thompson 2003: 29).

In order to deflect these criticisms of a local language becoming the national language solely because it was spoken in and around the capital, Manila, the National Language Institute (Komyson sa Wakang Filipino) was given the task of creating a new language to be called Pilipino, which would use Tagalog as the base, but invest it with features from other local languages. To quote from the 1973 Constitution, the 'language needed to be formed from all existing Philippine languages' (Gonzalez 1996b: 328). This was clearly an impossible task and the result has been a language that appears to be Tagalog with a few 'ethnic' additions. In an attempt to convince doubters that the new language was indeed Pilipino and not Tagalog wearing make-up, the 1987 Constitution renamed it Filipino. The change of the initial sound from a 'p' to an 'f' was significant, as Tagalog has no 'f' sound. This then represented a further attempt to persuade people that the new language was indeed Filipino, not Tagalog. The Constitution also promises that the work will continue: 'the national language of the Philippines is Filipino. As it evolves, it shall be further developed and enriched on the basis of existing Philippine and other languages' (Rappa and Wee 2006: 73). The addition of 'and other languages' is important as it allows the borrowing of words from English and Spanish. Indeed, many contemporary critics now claim that colloquial Filipino has become 'Taglish', a code-mixed variety of Tagalog and English.

The development of a national language meant that the Philippines could implement a bilingual education policy, with P/Filipino and English as the two languages. The Bilingual Education Policy (BEP) duly came into effect in 1974 with a timetable for the policy to be fully implemented in primary schools by 1982. Starting in 1974, maths and science and 'English Communication Arts' were taught in English from Grade 1. All other subjects were to be taught in Filipino. The BEP would take effect in high schools in 1981–82. But as Benton (1996: 309*ff*) has pointed out, the BEP represents two quite different systems. Tagalog-speaking children in and around Manila learn through a standardized version of Tagalog and English. But children whose first language is not Tagalog have to learn through two 'foreign' languages. And for many children, Tagalog and English may well be their third and fourth languages, as they speak their mother tongue and a regional lingua franca as their first and second languages.

The Linguistic Society of the Philippines has carried out a survey into the effectiveness of the BEP. The findings indicated that the BEP favoured only Tagalog-speaking students from Manila. Socio-economic status was found to be the main predictor of achievement among these students, followed by the teachers' proficiency. Non-Tagalog-speaking Filipinos were accepting Filipino as the national language, but did not agree that this meant it should automatically become a universal medium of instruction (Gonzalez 1996b). The lead author of the report, Brother Gonzalez, cautioned that in a bilingual scheme where one of the languages is not at the 'same level of cultivation' as the other, and if the two languages do not share the same social prestige (as is the case with English and Filipino), the indigenous language is bound to suffer and the less advantaged may end up in a state of 'semi-lingualism' (1996b: 332).

In recognition of the particular difficulties faced by non-Tagalog-speaking children, there have been several attempts to introduce vernaculars as media of instruction in the first three years of primary school. For example, a commission headed by Senator Angara recommended the use of local languages as auxiliary media of instruction (Thompson 2003, Galang 2000), as did Brother Gonzalez himself when he was minister for education in 1999. More recently a Multilingual Education and Literacy Act has been proposed. But these recommendations had, until late 2009, been blocked by those who insist that Filipinos need more English on the one hand, and nationalists who strongly support the use and spread of Filipino on the other. An interesting personal perspective comes from Tupas, himself a speaker of two Visayan languages (Aklanon and Ilongo), but who now speaks Filipino. He writes that, realistically, Filipino is the national language, and 'it is now more of an issue of attitudes, not inability, to speak the national language' (2007: 32).

The recommendations to use local languages as media of instruction are also opposed by those who feel that science and maths must be taught in English, as English is the language of modernization and technology. These are familiar arguments and I shall return to a critical review of them in Part III of the book, but I would simply quote an alternative view here, expressed by the Filipino scholar, Bernardo: 'There seems to be no theoretical or empirical basis so far to obligate the use of English in teaching mathematics' (2000: 313).

Much in the same way that the Institute of Language and Literature was set the task of making Malay a modern world language, the National Language Institute of the Philippines was similarly tasked with 'intellectualizing' Filipino, a task embraced by the prestigious University of the Philippines, when the university president introduced a five-year programme starting in 1989–90 in which Filipino would be introduced as the medium of instruction. However, this was not successful, with most staff preferring to lecture in English and most students electing to take the subject 'Communication Arts' though English rather than Filipino (Garcia 1996). The policy 'met with great difficulties' (Sibayan 1996: 240) and the hope that other universities would adopt a similar policy was not fulfilled. The hesitation in accepting Filipino as an intellectually modernized language is seen even in government circles. A decree issued by President Aquino that all government documents be issued in both English and Filipino was followed only for a year and was then 'completely ignored' (Garcia 1996: 82), obviously being especially unpopular in non-Tagalog-speaking regions (Sibayan 1996).

Making Filipino an intellectually modernized language appears a formidable task, as it has yet to develop the appropriate range of vocabulary and registers. And in calling for Filipino to become the tertiary medium of instruction as soon as possible, Garcia argued that '[i]n the universities and colleges the most convenient way for intellectualizing Filipino in the professions and different disciplines is to convince those who are experts in the field to use Filipino in their lectures and more importantly in their publications' (1996: 83–84). Yet this remains more dream than reality. In particular, academics will only publish in Filipino when they receive equal reward and recognition as when publishing in English. It is hard to see any Filipino academic choosing to publish an article in Filipino — especially in the fields of science and technology — when the alternative is to publish in English.

The BEP has been described as a compromise between the pro-English group who wanted the country to modernize and globalize and the pro-Filipino group who wanted a more inclusive and democratic society (Hau and Tinio 2003). This is also a class conflict between the English-speaking elite and the others. There is agreement, however, that the results of the BEP have not been satisfactory, with many Filipinos being proficient in neither English nor Filipino. The BEP also privileged Filipino at the expense of other Filipino vernaculars. It needs to be stressed again that both media of instruction, English and Filipino, are languages that most Filipino children meet for the first time on their first day in school.

In responding to criticism of the BEP, in 2003, President Gloria Macapagal-Arroyo ordered the return to English as the main medium of instruction. This announcement was naturally supported by the elite, as it was recognized how important English was for international trade and modernization. Her announcement was also supported, however, by non-Tagalog groups (Hau and Tinio 2003: 24). For all the efforts to convince people that Filipino is made up of all the languages of the Philippines, people still consider Filipino to be Tagalog under another name.

The need for English is also recognized beyond the elite and by those of low socio-economic status. Perhaps one of the most striking phenomena in the Philippines is the number of Overseas Contact Workers (OCWs). The 2008 Survey on Overseas Filipinos reports that some two million Filipinos were working overseas in 2008, primarily because there is an acute shortage of work in the Philippines itself. For example, in Hong Kong alone, several thousand Filipinas are employed as domestic assistants. And while, on the face of it, this does not look like a job which would require English, Filipinas are preferred as their English skills can be used to teach English to the children of their employees. The foreign exchange which these OWCs remit is also crucial for the Philippines economy, with the 2008 Survey reporting a remitted income in 2008 of 140 billion pesos (US$3 billion). A major demand for English in the Philippines is thus to develop a workforce of English-speaking Filipinos who can be exported to work overseas so that they can remit foreign exchange.

Much needed opportunities for employment at home has recently been created by the success of the call centre industry (Bolton 2010). High proficiency in English is a fundamental requirement for employment in these call centres. Thus many non-Tagalog-speaking Filipinos from a range of socio-economic classes now see English as a far more useful language than Filipino.

At the beginning of this chapter, I listed a number of the difficult questions which governments have to face when deciding on language and language education policy. Maminto (2005: 335–7) presents a number of such questions in the context of the Philippines, which I paraphrase below:

> As four languages can be involved (the mother tongue, the regional lingua franca, Filipino and English) how can the curriculum be best aligned to ensure success?
>
> How can languages develop a complementary rather than competitive relationship?
>
> When should the regional language take over or work alongside the mother tongue?
>
> When should English be introduced and how?

Should Filipino be used from Primary 1?

Should flexibility be allowed according to specific regional and local conditions?

As we have seen, the Bilingual Education Policy advantages Tagalog-speaking children from the higher socio-economic circles of metro Manila and disadvantages the others, which represent the great majority of the population. While there have been recommendations on several occasions for the adoption of vernacular languages as the media of instruction, at least for the lower levels of primary schools, these recommendations have only recently received official support. Other suggestions include:

> the abandoning of the BEP, the establishment of Filipino as the medium of instruction with local vernaculars as auxiliary media of instruction, and the teaching of English as a subject (with the promotion here of the educated variety of Filipino English) (Hau and Tinio 2003: 350)

> the adoption of Filipino as the medium of instruction in primary schools and English in secondary schools (Tupas 2007: 31)

> the use of vernaculars as media of instruction at the lower levels of primary school, with the gradual adoption of Filipino in upper primary and then English in secondary (Tupas 2007: 31)

The first and third of these look as though they should be at least trialled, but there seems little prospect of that in the current situation, where the focus remains so heavily on the national language and English. Tupas (2007: 31) considers the Philippine experience provides ample evidence for Tsui and Tollefson's claim (2004: 2), which he quotes:

> Medium of instruction policy determines which social and linguistic groups have access to political and economic opportunities, and which groups are disenfranchised. It is therefore a key means of power (re)distribution and social (re)construction, as well as a key arena in which political conflicts among countries and ethnolinguistic, social and political groups are realized.

The Philippine government finally announced a radical change of policy in the later part of 2009, when the Department of Education issued an order entitled *Institutionalising Mother Tongue-Based Multilingual Education* (MLE) (http://mothertongue-based.blogspot.com/).

Article 1 of the Order validates the 'superiority of the use of the learner's mother tongue or first language in improving learning outcomes ...' and Article 2 of the Order describes MLE as 'the effective use of more than two languages for literacy and instruction'. Significantly, Article 4 of the Order points out that top performing countries in the Trends in

International Mathematics and Science Study (TIMMS) are those that teach and test students in science and maths in their own languages. This official promotion of MLE is seen as a triumph for all those who have been promoting the use of vernaculars as media of instruction in the early years of primary school.

The Order requires its 'immediate compliance', but it will take some years before the level of its implementation and its efficacy can be adequately evaluated. Supporters will hope, however, that the sobering formula for success for a Filipino child identified by Bautista in 1996 will soon be able to be recast: be born in metro Manila; be a native speaker of Tagalog; and study in an excellent private school (1996: 225). In short, be a rich and well-connected Tagalog speaker.

Summary

This chapter has reviewed the development and role of English in the four 'outer circle' countries of ASEAN. The main focus has been on the role of English in education and its relationship with other languages. It has been argued that, while these countries may share similar histories, the language education policies in each are distinctive and conditioned by local concerns. Dominating the debates in all these countries, however, is the view that English is *the* language of modernization and knowledge dissemination, and thus has to represent a major part of the school curriculum. In the next chapter, the situation in the remaining six member states of ASEAN will be reviewed.

3

Burma, Cambodia, Indonesia, Laos, Thailand and Vietnam: Linguistic context and the role of English

The previous chapter summarized the development and roles of English with a particular focus on language in education in those ASEAN countries that had a colonial history from which they inherited an institutional role for English. In this chapter the development and roles of English and the national language in the remaining countries of ASEAN will be considered. Again, the focus will be on language education.

Three of these countries — Cambodia, Laos and Vietnam — were once part of the French Protectorate of Indo-China. Indonesia was a colony of Holland. Thailand is the only country of the ASEAN group that was never colonized. This means that the history of English is significantly shorter in these countries and that the major concerns have centred on the development of the respective national languages. Problems associated with the accommodation of English into the school curriculum are thus more recent.

This leaves Burma. Although this was a British colony, its history since independence, and especially since 1962 when the military dictator, U Ne Win, assumed power and its subsequent international isolation means that the institutional role of English was lost. In this, at least, it has more in common with these countries than those described in the previous chapter.

The case of Indonesia

Indonesia is the largest country in the ASEAN group and is the largest Muslim nation in the world. It is also even more ethnically and linguistically diverse than the Philippines. Its population of more than 200 million comprises some two hundred ethnic groups which speak some four hundred languages. Javanese has, with 75 million speakers, the most mother tongue speakers, representing just less than 40% of the total population. The next most populous mother tongue is Sundanese, but whose speakers constitute only about 14% of the population (Montolalu and Suryadinanta 2007). Yet, partly because it was the language with the most speakers, Javanese was not adopted as the national language. A second reason for its being overlooked as the national language is its innate difficulty and concern with hierarchy (Bernard 2003). Javanese comprises a number of social dialects, so learning Javanese actually means learning a number of languages along with complex cultural rules of when to use which variety with whom (Alisjahbana 1976). It was thus considered unsuitable for a national language at the time when Indonesia was struggling to gain independence from the Dutch. The people wanted a more 'democratic' language and one which was not spoken by a powerful group. Malay fitted the bill perfectly. It was already being used as a lingua franca in the region — indeed, as reported in Chapter 1, an old form of Malay called Kw'enlun had served as a regional lingua franca several hundred years previously (Alisjahbana 1976), so people were used to this role of Malay. At the same time, in the 1930s, the number of Malay speakers represented less than 2% of the population, so privileging Malay as the national language was not seen as a threat to other ethnic groups. It was also considered relatively easy to learn, another potential reason for its success as a lingua franca (Ostler 2005). Its other great advantage is that it had become 'the language of unity against the Dutch' (Bernard 2003: 273). It had become the lingua franca for groups such as the Serakat Islam and other Muslim anti-Dutch groups (Bernard 2003: 272). Thus the Second Congress of Indonesian Youth which was held in 1988 formally adopted Malay as their language, renaming it Bahasa Indonesia or the Indonesian language (Alisjahbana 1976).

The Japanese occupation further promoted the use of Malay, as the Japanese banned the use of Dutch. Dutch had previously been seen as an important language of education for the same reasons that English had been in the colonies of Brunei, Malaysia and the Philippines. It was the language of upward social and economic mobility. By the 1920s, some Dutch felt that too many locals were now able to speak their language as these people started clamouring for more privileges and better positions, a possibility foreseen by Maxwell in Malaya in the same period when he justified the teaching of useful skills to the Malay fishermen and farmers, as we saw in the previous chapter.

With the end of the war and the defeat of the Japanese, Indonesia proclaimed independence. The Constitution of 1945 enshrined Bahasa Indonesia (BI) as the national language. 'The language of the state shall be the Indonesian language.' This met with little resistance.

> It appears that the selection of the Malay language as the Indonesian national language was quite smooth as other languages ... were not widely used by other ethnic groups ... there has never been any opposition to the language. (Montolalu and Suryadinata 2007: 41)

The proponents of BI were now faced with similar problems to those faced in Malaysia and the Philippines in trying to develop BI into a modern language. As we saw earlier, both the Philippines and Malaysia established national language academies to undertake this task. Indonesia proved no exception and in 1942 — while still under Japanese occupation — the Indonesian Language Committee was set up. Its task was to write a grammar of BI and to provide BI with an 'adequate, uniform, technical and scientific terminology' (Alisjahbana 1976: 69). Remarkably, the committee was initially overseen by a Japanese, seconded from the Ministry of Education. According to a member of the committee and the head of the Working Committee on the Indonesia Language, which was set up in 1947, the Japanese soon lost interest in the proceedings, so the committee was also able to take on the role of promoting BI as the language of Indonesian unity and resistance to the Japanese. In the first fifteen years of the existence of the National Language Institute (Lembaga Bahasa Nasional) which was established a little later and which is now known as the Pusat Pembinaan dan Pengembangan Bahasa, 321,710 new terms were coined (while the Malaysian equivalent, the Dewan Bahasa dan Pustaka, coined 148,442 new terms). Many of these are old Malay words pushed into new service, some are new words and some are loan words and 'all of them pushed aside many other old words and concepts of the Malay language' (Alisjahbana 1976: 26). The respective national language institutes also worked to create a unified Malay and Indonesian orthography, a task which was completed in 1972.

Despite the work of these committees and language institutes, Alisjahbana remains pessimistic, feeling that the task of BI in replacing Dutch as the language of modern culture has not been successful. Modern culture is a culture of universities, banks and factories, not one of temples, churches and mosques (1976: 116). In further arguing that there are simply not enough modern books in BI and that the task of translating modern scientific and technological texts into BI is insurmountable, he concludes that, if BI cannot modernize quickly enough, then English must be used in secondary and tertiary education (1976: 118).

The view that BI remains inadequate as a language of modernization is shared by Montolalu and Suryadinata. BI and the vernacular languages are

> not sufficient to catch up with the rapidly developing world. Foreign languages, especially English, are the keys to the gate of the scientific and modern technological world and other world civilizations. (2007: 43)

While attempting to make BI a modern language, the Indonesian Language Institute was also occupied in making it the national lingua franca. It is worth remembering that, at the time of independence, Malay was spoken as a mother tongue by less than 2% of the population. The development of BI as the national lingua franca has been remarkably successful. For example, in the ten years between 1980 and 1990 the percentage of people who reported using BI daily rose from 49% to 68%. During the same period the percentage of those reporting that they did not understand BI dropped from around 40% in 1980 to around 17% in 1990 (Montolalu and Suryadinata 2007: 47). This figure will have decreased further, not least because the medium of almost all education is Bahasa Indonesia.

The language education policy in Indonesia has thus focused on the teaching and learning of the national language, BI. In the early years of the Sukarno regime, local languages were promoted, as Sukarno needed the support of their speakers. This policy was to change after Suharto's coup of 1965 and his assumption of the presidency the following year. It will be remembered that these were the years of the war in Vietnam and the Cultural Revolution in China. There was the real concern of communism spreading throughout Southeast Asia — indeed, as was reported in Chapter 1, this fear was one of the motivating factors for the establishment of ASEAN itself in 1967. As was the case in Singapore, local Chinese — especially the Chinese-educated — were viewed with suspicion. Suharto's coup involved a violent strike against the Indonesian Chinese. Not only were thousands of so-called communists killed, but the Chinese language was banned (Bernard 2003: 278). Suharto made the promotion of BI the priority and it became, and remains, the medium of instruction from primary through to tertiary education. Certain local languages, however, can be used as the media of instruction for the first three years of primary (Bernard 2003: 278).

In 1987, the government moved to allow more instruction in local languages in the hope of 'preserving the values and cultures of local ethnic groups' (Bernard 2003: 279). In reality, however, only five languages were allowed and these included the two major languages, Javanese and Sundanese, along with Batak (with about six million speakers) and Balinese and Buginese (each with about four million speakers). Textbooks are only available in Javanese, Sundanese and Balinese.

The Fifth Language Congress held in 1988 saw the publication of the first BI grammar. But this was by no means the first grammar of Malay. The first glossary of Malay was compiled as early as 1521. The author, Pigafetta, was a member of Magellan's fleet and he worked on the glossary while the fleet was anchored in Tidore (Alisjhabana 1976: 33). The Dutch produced several Malay grammars and the first 'non-Dutch' grammar of Malay was written in 1884 by Lie Kim Hok (Budianta 2007: 53).

With the fall of Suharto in 1998, the government has followed a policy of decentralization and allowed more regional autonomy. This has helped revive some ethnic languages. Table 3.1 is slightly adapted from Montolalu and Suryadinata (2007: 48).

Table 3.1 Vernacular language speakers in 1980, 1990, 2000

Language	1980	1990	2000
Javanese	40.44%	38.08%	34.70%
Sundanese	15.06%	15.26%	13.86%
Madurese	4.71%	4.29%	3.78%
Batak	2.12%	1.97%	1.91%
Minangkabau	2.42%	2.23%	2.06%
Balinese	1.69%	1.64%	1.42%
Buginese	2.26%	2.04%	1.91%
Indonesian (BI)	11.93%	17.11%	34.00%
Others	17.48%	17.11%	4.57%

While the table shows that the percentages of the Indonesian population who speak the seven ethnic languages listed have declined slightly, the figures appear remarkably stable over a twenty-year period. However, these are relatively major languages, so this is perhaps not so surprising. What is noteworthy is the increase from almost 12% to 34% of the population who now say they are L1 speakers of BI, along with the very significant drop from 17.11% to less than 5% of the population who now say they speak 'other' vernaculars. This would suggest that BI is displacing the smaller languages with fewer speakers. Even where the local language provides a strong sense of identity, as is the case of Achenese, the language of the small province on the westernmost tip of Sumatra, where there have been regular calls for more Achenese autonomy and independence, BI remains strong, as people recognize its national importance (Bernard 2003: 285).

As indicated earlier, however, official support is available only for five of the major languages. Without official support for the smaller languages, their future would seem to be under threat, a phenomenon that can be seen throughout the region. In the absence of official national support, ASEAN itself shows no sign of providing support for these local regional languages. Help in preserving the language of the Cia-Cia tribe, who live on Buton Island in southeast Sulawesi, has not come from an ASEAN organization, but from the South Korean Hunminjeongeum Research Institute. According to the Research Institute's website, the written version of the language has been developed using the Korean phonetic script, Hangul, in what is thought to be the first time Hangul has been used in this way outside Korea. The first textbook includes traditional Cia-Cia and Korean stories (http://www.hani.co.kr/arti/english_edition/e_international/369998.html).

With regard to Bahasa Indonesia itself, however, it is clearly a great success story. The current absence of the significant presence of a Western language has been helpful, as Indonesian has been able to take on the position of the language of modernity and progress (Simpson 2007b: 334), although, as Alisjahbana has indicated above, much work remains to be done. English has yet to make significant inroads into the education system. Indonesia is the only country in ASEAN which has not made English a compulsory part of the primary curriculum. However, it is commonly taught in primary schools as an optional subject (Siti 2008). Although it has been regarded as the first foreign language since the 1950s (Dardjowidjojo 2000), the number of people who can use it with any real fluency remains low. Interestingly, and perhaps significantly, this does not seem to have hindered Indonesia's progress towards becoming a modern democratic state. The success of the recent elections and the smooth re-election of President Yudhoyono, along with the increasing influence and role that Indonesia is playing regionally and internationally, would suggest that English is perhaps not the *sina qua non* of modernization many in the region believe it to be.

The case of Thailand

Along with Indonesia, Thailand was one of the founding members of ASEAN, but, uniquely among all the ASEAN member states, was never a colony. English was brought to Thailand, not by a colonial power, therefore, but by the modernizing Thai king, Mongkut, or King Rama IV (r. 1851–68). Keen to ensure that Thailand modernized itself before having modernization thrust upon it (Luangthongkum 2007), he encouraged Western learning and the learning of English. One episode from this period of Thai history has become extremely well-known. King Mongkut appointed an English governess, Anna Leonowens, to teach English at court. This was described in Margaret Landon's novel, *Anna and the King of Siam,* later much romanticized in the musical, *The King and I.* Thus, English was being taught at the Thai court (although the country was still known as Siam at the time) through the invitation of the king himself, not too long after British imperial expansion had seen its arrival in neighbouring Malaysia.

Rama IV was not the first or only Thai king to have had significant influence on language and language development, although it was Rama IV, who, while still a monk, discovered the stele of Ramkhamhaeng, a king of the thirteenth century. On this stele is inscribed the history of the period. If the stele is authentic, it shows a standardized alphabet as early as the thirteenth century (Diller 1991). More recently, Vajiravudh (Rama VI) was the first member of the Thai royal family to be educated in the West and he brought back a host of modernizing ideas, not all of which were received with warmth by his people (Simpson and Thammasathien 2007). His work on language has been significant, however, and the volume *Principles of the*

Thai Language stemmed from work done by Rama VI in the early 1900s. This book provided the basis for later Thai language textbooks (Keyes 2003).

This linguistic standardization represented just one strand in Rama VI's desire to establish a national Thai identity. Rama VI died in 1925 and the person most closely associated with promoting the goal of a national Thai identity was Phibun Songkhram, who became prime minister in 1938. A year later, the name of the kingdom was formally changed from Siam to Thailand and the government announced that all inhabitants of Thailand would be called Thais and would be required to study Thai (Simpson and Thammasathien 2007). A series of decrees to this effect were promulgated from 1939. Thais were required to become literate in Thai, which became the sole medium of instruction. Thus, for example, Chinese schools now had to teach through Thai (Keyes 2003).The Thai language has thus been a major tool in the creation of national unity and identity.

As well as being the only country of the ASEAN group not to have undergone a period of colonialization, Thailand is also distinctive in that its population is less diverse than the populations of other ASEAN nations. This is not to say that it is completely homogeneous, but, out of a population of over sixty million, the great majority of more than fifty million report themselves as monolingual speakers of Thai (Luangthongkum 2007: 183). In addition, 99% of the population are Thai nationals. Thai identity has thus been related to the concept of *ekkalak*, or one characteristic. Until relatively recently, the Ekkalak Thai Office campaigned for national unity and security on the basis of 'one language and one culture in Thai society' (Luangthongkum 2007: 181). A significant switch occurred in 1997, however, when the concept of *ekkalak* was officially replaced by *pahulak*, or pluralism, but the shift appears to be more rhetorical than real.

This homogeneity is only relative, of course. Some sixty other languages are spoken in Thailand, but the total number of speakers of these languages at four million represents less than 5% of the overall population. One would therefore predict that many of these languages will come under threat, especially as the perceived need for all to learn English becomes increasingly felt. As is the case in all countries under discussion here, the role of English as the international lingua franca and language of modernity has resulted in an enormous demand for it. Currently English is taught as a foreign language in all Thai government schools, starting from primary. Yet the lack of qualified teachers and resources, especially in the countryside 'has caused a disaster as far as English language teaching and learning is concerned' (Luanthongkum 2007: 189). As reported in Chapter 1, one response to the lack of English teachers was for the Thai government to advertise in 2006 for thousands of native English speakers to apply for jobs as English teachers in the Thai schools. Perhaps luckily for the government, the salary offered was not very attractive and they received only eleven applications.

English is spoken well by only the educated elite, especially those involved in business. Prime Minister Abhisit Vejjajiva, with his Eton and Oxford education, is an exception among politicians whose linguistic needs are to be able to speak in various dialects of Thai to show that they and their constituents are as one. Not surprisingly, given the instrumental motivations that dominate language learning, the other language which is in demand is Mandarin. Mandarin has a long history as a school subject in Thailand, first being taught in the eighteenth century. As was noted above, the teaching of Chinese was proscribed in the middle of the twentieth century, but is now taught in increasing numbers in government high schools. As also noted earlier, the Chinese government has opened several Confucius Institutes in Thailand.

The result is predictable. While Thai remains entrenched as the medium of instruction, the major languages that are taught in schools are English and Mandarin. Local and regional languages are neglected. Religious schools have, until recently, provided the only exception to this, with Pali and Arabic being learned in Buddhist monasteries and private Muslim schools and mosques respectively (Luangthongkum 2007: 191). However, in recent years, the study of 'local wisdom and local culture' has become a part of the school curriculum, perhaps reflecting the government's confidence that Thai identity has now been firmly established (Simpson and Thammasathien 2007: 406) and this has meant local languages can now be taught as subjects. How secure this concept of national Thai identity is can be open to question. Not only has the country been politically unstable for decades, seeing ten successful coups and seven aborted ones since 1932, the current political situation suggests deep divisions among the Thai. Since the 2006 coup which ousted the then prime minister, Thaksin Shinawatra, regional and class division has become apparent. The south of the country is battling a separatist movement which is being driven by powerful elements of the Muslim minority. The north and northeast feel increasingly sidelined and disadvantaged as the centralization policies introduced by earlier governments take effect. This northern disaffection was exploited by Thaksin who promoted his own 'northernness' by deliberately choosing not to use standard Thai but the distinctive northern Thai script in his campaign publications (Lintner 2009). Many observers feel that any Thai unity is being fragilely preserved only by the Thai reverence for their current king, Bhumibol Adulayev, who is the world's longest serving monarch. The fear is that his death will further expose the current fault lines and lead to serious unrest (Lintner 2009: 112).

The case of Burma

Burma, or Myanmar as the current military regime re-named it in 1989, is mainland Southeast Asia's largest country (Callahan 2003) and is an ethnically and linguistically diverse country. Accurate figures are hard to come by, but estimates of the number of languages spoken vary from seventy to more than a hundred (Watkins 2007). The three main language families represented are Tibeto-Burman, Tai-Kadai and Mon-Khmer.

After a series of Anglo-Burmese wars, the first of which ended in 1826, the British finally annexed Burma as a whole in 1886. This was some fifteen years after the Treaty of Pangkor saw Malaya under British control and more than a decade before the United States colonized the Philippines. English was the language of government and administration during the colonial period. Use of English was welcomed by many, including the local Indians and Chinese. At the same time, Burmese was promoted and local people were permitted to study in their respective languages. Christian missionaries developed orthographies for several indigenous languages, including Kachin and Lahu (Kyaw 2007: 151).

Opposition to British rule and the official use of English developed in 1920s and 1930s was orchestrated by a student organization entitled Do Bama Asiayone, or Our Myanmar Association. This organization was dominated by the Burmese elite and they promoted the notion of Burma as 'our country, our language and our literature' (Callahan 2003). Its policies included a universal system of Burmese education with Buddhism at the 'core of cultural, religions and personal identity' (Watkins 2007: 271). The movement ultimately failed as it was unable to develop 'a strong, convincing and all encompassing Myanmar' identity (Kyaw 2007: 153) and was thus seen to be exclusive and anti-'foreign'. Indeed, British rule was popular among many of the ethnic minorities precisely because they feared oppression by the majority Burmans after independence. The current regime's change of the name to Myanmar signals the goal of the regime as being one of Myanmarization at the expense of the minority groups, and as an attempt to distance the country from the colonial and pre-military era (Watkins 2007).

The war years of 1942–45 saw the Japanese occupation. Independence came in 1948 under the leadership of Burma's first prime minister U Nu. Aung San (father of Aung San Su Kyi), the founder of the Burmese independence movement and the one person seen as able to unite the disparate Burmese tribes, had been assassinated by political opponents in 1947. U Nu, a Buddhist scholar and literary figure, became his reluctant replacement when the time came to appoint the prime minister. Aung San had earlier successfully persuaded the initially resistant minority groups to be part of the new Union of Myanmar. They agreed on the condition that they could choose to secede from the Union after ten years. This gives some idea of the fragmented state in which Burma was at the time. Language was also a sticking point, but the minority groups finally accepted Burmese as the official language, considering it easier to learn than English. It was also made the medium of instruction in primary and secondary schools, with English being taught as the major foreign language. Foreshadowing reasons for the promotion of Malay in Malaysia, one reason for making Burmese the official language was to weaken the power of Indian and Chinese merchants (Kyaw 2007). The various states also received promises that they would be able to use their own languages. In the event, the 1947 Constitution only granted this linguistic right to the Shan and the Kachin States (Kyaw 2007).

U Nu remained prime minister until 1958, when he was deposed by General U Ne Win. However, he stood up against the military and successfully lobbied for a further round of elections, which he won handsomely, thus becoming prime minister for a second time in 1960. On this occasion, however, he only lasted two years before Ne Win toppled him in a second coup. In a strange accident of history, U Nu was to be appointed prime minister once more in 1990, when the National League of Democracy (NLD) won an overwhelming victory in the polls, but he was promptly placed under house arrest by the military junta (as was the leader of the NLD, Aung San Su Kyi). He died in 1995.

The years 1962–88 were dominated by U Ne Win, the army and the 'Burmese road to socialism' under the Burmese Socialist Programme Party (BSPP). During this period, Burmese remained the official language and the role of English was significantly weakened, as Burmese was made the medium of instruction in all university subjects. The government attitude to minority languages was initially liberal, however, and the 1966 Education Act required the teaching of minority languages up to Grade 2. Textbooks were published in some of the minority languages, including Mon, Shan, Karen, Chin and Kachin (Kyaw 2007: 162). However, the current military regime provides no support for the maintenance or development of any language other than Burmese itself (Watkins 2007: 286).

U Ne Win, whose behaviour was becoming increasingly erratic and reliant on his fortune-tellers, was ousted from power in a violent military coup in 1988, which saw the deaths of several thousand in Rangoon alone. The coup was led by General Saw Maung, who then allowed democratic elections to take place in 1990. However, when the results showed that the National League of Democracy (NLD) had triumphed, with more than 80% of the vote, he declared the results null and void and promptly arrested the leaders. Aung San Suu Kyi, the leader of the NLD, remains under house arrest at the time of writing.

The strength of the army has increased exponentially over the years to a total of about half a million today, the great majority of whom are Burmans and this has had a significant linguistic consequence (Callahan 2003). The increase in the number of Burmans in the army has seen the need for members of the minority groups to learn Burmese in order to negotiate with the army. This, together with the policy which closed all minority language newspapers and forced all publishing to be done in Burmese, has meant that the minority groups now all have proficiency in Burmese. Indeed, the opposition National Council for the Union of Myanmar now uses Burmese as its lingua franca. Ironically, therefore, Burmese has thus become the language of rebellion as well as of control (Kyaw 2007: 171), especially as the minority groups are now able to communicate with the monolingual Burman opposition. 'Karen tribesmen can only co-ordinate their resistance to the Myanmar government through the use of Burmese' (Ostler 2009: 194). In more recent times, therefore, the current junta has once more promoted the use of minority languages, but the aim is to divide the groups. General Saw Muang's re-classification of the minorities into as many as 135 separate groups was for this express purpose (Callahan 2003: 166).

It took the failure of one of U Ne Win's daughters to be accepted into university in England because of her poor English that led to a re-think of the Burmese-only language policy and the revival of English. The author was one of the first of five academics to enter Burma in 1984 in response to the Burmese governments' request for English language experts. Despite the government's apparent wish to revive English, however, this has proved to be a difficult task for a number of reasons. First, at least one generation of Burmese has not studied English. Second, the 1988 coup saw the schools and universities closed for several months and the removal of all foreign teachers. Third, since 1988 the State Law and Order Restoration Council (SLORC) (later renamed the State Peace and Development Council or SPDC) has also seen frequent disruptions to schools and universities, including their regular closure for significant periods of time. These disruptions have meant that education as a whole has suffered under the SLORC regime. Fourth, many educated Burmese who speak English have left the country, some at considerable personal risk. There are thus very few qualified and proficient English teachers left in the country. Finally, resources and materials are poor. The role of English in Burma is thus restricted to the elite and to a small number of domains, mostly involving the few NGOs and aid programmes which remain. Instead, Burmese has become the language of the regime *and* the resistance and provides an example of a 'foreign' language providing an effective language of resistance even when it is also the language 'of a political and military opponent' (Watkins 2007: 284).

The case of Laos and Cambodia

The next three ASEAN countries to be considered, Laos, Cambodia and Vietnam, experienced significantly different colonial histories from those countries considered above and in Chapter 2. Most notably, in the context of language education and language education policy, the colonial language each inherited was French. Each country also had a period of Soviet dominance when Russian was the major common language. Common to all three countries has been the choice each has had to make concerning the relative position of French and English within the school curriculum. All three have, to a greater or lesser extent, chosen English as their country's major foreign language.

Laos joined ASEAN in 1997, the same year as Myanmar. It had previously been part of the French Protectorate when the French colonized the Kingdom of Luang Prabang as Laos. Laos officially gained independence in 1948, although this was really only fully achieved in 1954 with the French defeat at the hands of the Vietnamese in Dien Bien Phu in 1954 (Keyes 2003). Laos has a population of six million, but, in contrast to Thailand, Laos is not as united by language. An attempt to convince the population that they all derive from the same ethnic group resulted in the division of the country into three so-called 'Lao' areas, namely Lowland Lao, Midland Lao and Upland Lao. But, as Watkins (2007: 409) points out, these three groups are linguistically quite separate. The Lowland Lao, who make up about 65% of the population, are speakers of Tai. The Midland Lao, who comprise about 25% of the population speak Mon-Khmer languages and the remaining 10% of Upland Lao are speakers of Tibeto-Burman languages. These languages are not mutually intelligible and many dialects of them can themselves be subdivided into several smaller mutually unintelligible groups.

Although the French developed a standard Lao based on spoken Lao, it did not really become the national language until the communists, the Pathet Lao, took power in 1975 (Keyes 2003: 199). Lao was also viewed with suspicion by those who did not support the Pathet Lao. It is worth noting that when the Pathet Lao took power in 1975, as many as 10 % of the population fled the country. A large number of the Lao ethnic group remain in Thailand and now see themselves as Thai. While Lao acts as a lingua franca within Laos (Keyes 2003), it does not act as a language of unity, as Thai does in Thailand and Bahasa Indonesia does in Indonesia. Nor is it a language of cultural identity, as Malay is, for example, for ethnic Malays. Indeed, certain minority groups, including the Hmong, refuse to learn Lao.

In recent years, English has become the first foreign language and is now taught in schools. The most recent ministry pronouncement rules that English will be introduced from Primary 3 (Phommanimith 2008), despite the desperate shortage of qualified teachers and suitable materials. This, along with the overall shortage of resources, means that only a small minority of the elite have proficiency in English. This in turn has meant, among other things, that those who have proficiency in English, rather than those with the relevant expertise, are selected to represent Laos at ASEAN meetings.

Cambodia was the last of the current member countries to join ASEAN, becoming a member in 1999. While both Vietnam and Laos had undergone extremely harsh times during the Vietnam War, few countries can have suffered at the hands of foreign incursion and local despotism as much as Cambodia has since independence in 1953. The political situation has been fluid since independence, to say the least, and a brief account of this is necessary in order to contextualize the current position of English in Cambodia.

The first years after independence were, in fact, relatively stable years when Cambodia operated as a monarchy, with Norodom Sihanouk as king (Clayton 2006). Sihanouk owed his position to the French who, believing he would be agreeable to their policies, elevated the young prince to the monarchy, hoping that by so doing they would be able to counter the influence of pro-independence factions. In the event, in 1953, at a time when French control in the region was almost at its end, Sihanouk dissolved parliament, announced martial law and declared independence (Neau 2003). In 1960, he also renounced the throne in order to become head of state, a position of real political power.

The relative calm was disturbed by the Vietnam War. The Americans had been providing aid and support to Cambodia. In 1963, Sihanouk sided with the North Vietnamese and allowed them to enter Cambodia. This led to the American bombing of the country, and Sihanouk being deposed in 1970 in favour of the more pro-Western Lon Nol, who gained initial popularity for his anti-Vietnamese stance. Through a combination of repatriation and massacres, he halved the Vietnamese population in Cambodia (Heder 2007). Once people sickened of his 'virulent ethnonationalism' (Heder 2007: 300), Lon Nol's popularity quickly waned and this period saw the rise of the Cambodian Communist Party, the Khmer Rouge, culminating in their succession to power under the leadership of Pol Pot in 1975. Four years of brutal repression and subjugation of their own people by the Khmer Rouge followed. As many as a million fellow Cambodians may have been put to death by the Khmer Rouge. Pol Pot's reign was ended by the Vietnamese invasion of 1979 and the installation of a Vietnamese-backed government in Cambodia, which lasted for ten years (Clayton 2006).

The 1991 Paris Peace Accords opened a new chapter in recent Cambodian history with the arrival of the United Nations Transitional Authority in Cambodia (UNTAC) and several thousand personnel associated with UNTAC (Anderson 1999). Their major task was to organize the first parliamentary-style elections. These were duly successfully held in 1993. In 1997, however, the communist party, under the leadership of Hun Sen, orchestrated a coup against their coalition partners, and once more Cambodia was under virtual martial law. To the surprise of many, however, further elections were held in 1998, resulting in a clear majority for Hun Sen. Since then, Cambodia has moved to rejoin the international community, as exemplified by its membership of ASEAN.

Linguistically, Cambodia is relatively homogeneous. The great majority of the population (more than 90%) are Khmer. Khmer is indisputably the national language and successive governments of all political hues have aggressively promoted the policy of Khmerization (Heder 2007). When the French withdrew in 1953, Cambodia re-introduced Khmer into the school curriculum and Khmer gradually replaced French as the medium of instruction in primary and secondary schools (Clayton 2006).

French remained the first foreign language until the years of the Pol Pot tyranny, when no foreign languages were taught. Indeed, nothing was. It has been estimated that, during the Khmer Rouge years, 90% of school buildings were destroyed and 75% of teachers, academics and administrators were murdered (Neau 2003).

The ten-year rule of the Vietnamese-backed regime saw Vietnamese and Russian as the two foreign languages. These were replaced by French and English in 1989. The arrival of UNTAC and Cambodia's subsequent and continuing move to rejoin the international community including their membership of ASEAN, has meant that French is being relentlessly squeezed out in favour of English. Clayton (2006: 1–2) relates a telling account of a 1993 student demonstration at the Institut de Technologie du Cambodge (renamed from the 'Kampuchea-Soviet Friendship Higher Technical Institute' as it had been known during the Soviet period). The dispute arose over the Institute's medium of instruction. As aid for the Institute was being provided by the French francophone agency, AUPELF, not surprisingly, AUPELF insisted that the medium of instruction be French. This was not what the students wanted. 'Rather, they wanted to study in English' (Clayton 2006: 1). In the end, a compromise was reached; French would be the medium of instruction but special classes in English as a foreign language would also be provided.

In the years since this dispute, English has increasingly gained ground. When the Royal University of Phnom Penh allowed students to select which foreign language they wanted to study, over 80% chose English (Clayton 2006). A ministry official interviewed by Clayton argued that 'teaching

French instead of English is in fact an indirect punishment for students because it so clearly limits their opportunities' (2006: 222). In a thoughtful analysis, Clayton suggests that Cambodia represents a good example of where the role of English is not simply post-imperial but 'post-Anglophone' (2006: 246). Within Cambodia itself, English is essential for most jobs with foreign agencies. NGOs and aid organizations from all over the world currently operate in Cambodia and all require English. Only a minority of these agencies are Anglophone. Even French agencies require their employees to speak English. Membership of ASEAN is also a significant factor in the promotion of English. Clayton (2006: 230–1) quotes several government officials emphasizing this:

> If we don't know English, how can we participate?

> We need to know English so that we can defend our interests. You know, ASEAN is not a kissy-kissy brotherhood. The countries are fiercely competitive, and a strong knowledge of English will help us protect Cambodian interests.

This post-Anglophone role of English is also understood by other ministry officials interviewed by Clayton. The following is a typical quote: 'You know, when we use English, we don't think about the United States or England. We only think about the need to communicate' (2006: 233). This attitude was also captured by a Cambodian English teacher I recorded in 2005 (see Chapter 6):

> In the future I hope that more and more Cambodians will speak English because we understand about [*sic*] the advantages of English. We cannot live without English because we have to (make) contact (with) the world. We have to do business with the world. We have to develop our country with the world ...

This is not to say that the increase in the use of English has not led to concerns. Following the example of many other countries of ASEAN, Cambodia established a National Language Institute in 2000. Its major task is to strengthen and modernize Khmer. While Khmer remains the medium of instruction in the universities, it is recognized that Khmer lacks technical vocabulary in many domains. The rector of the institute is thus concerned that Khmer will be displaced by English in higher education (Clayton 2006).

Within the school system, Khmer is the medium of instruction. English or French — but it is mainly English — is taught from Primary 5 for two to five hours per week 'according to the school availability of local resources' (Ministry of Education, Youth and Sport 2004: 10). The 2000 Country Report on English language teaching identified many problems, all of which are familiar and include the low level of teachers' salaries (who therefore moonlight on a regular basis), the poor English proficiency of many English teachers, a lack of resources and the lack of adequate teacher training (Neau 2003). Overall school drop-out rates are also a concern. While 80%–90% of all children enter primary, only 20% go on to secondary, and only 10% of the original Primary 1 cohort will graduate from secondary school (Heder 2007: 304). Retention rates are, however, said to be gradually improving.

Until recently, indigenous groups were disadvantaged in the education system, as Khmer was the sole medium of instruction. This meant that most children of minority groups either did not attend school or dropped out early (Clayton 2006, Thomas 2002). In 2002, however, some experimental schools were established in which indigenous students can study in the vernacular before gradually switching to Khmer medium of instruction (Thomas 2002). Allowing students to study in their vernaculars is crucial in attracting them to school in the first place, and then in keeping them there, a point which will be emphasized again in Part III.

In a repeat of what is happening throughout ASEAN, the language other than English which is being increasingly studied in Cambodia is Chinese. Chinese has an interesting recent history in the country, as it was banned in 1970 by the Lon Nol government, for the same reasons that it was banned in many other countries of the region: it was the language of communism. The ban was lifted in 1992, since when the number of Chinese primary, secondary and private schools has mushroomed. Most students entering the Chinese primary schools are Chinese Cambodians who speak Khmer. The curriculum also includes English as a subject (Clayton 2006). One significant difference between the modern Chinese schools and those which were in operation before the 1970 ban, is that the medium of instruction is now Mandarin, while, in the past, Chinese dialects had been the media of instruction (Clayton 2006).

In summary, English has become Cambodia's first foreign language, with Chinese also in demand. The role and influence of French has declined dramatically. Khmer itself is under no threat, although its domain use in higher education is likely to become increasingly challenged. Some indigenous languages are acting as media of instruction in experimental bilingual schools. In general, however, the linguistic repertoire of Cambodians will be Khmer, with English and then Mandarin Chinese as learned languages.

The case of Vietnam

While Cambodia has suffered the harshest conditions in recent years, Vietnam's long history has also been punctuated by war and hardship. It was ruled by China for a thousand years up to the tenth century before becoming independent (for the first time) in 938 (Wright 2002). The Vietnamese inherited Chinese and the Chinese script (Chu Nho), but in the thirteenth century developed a new script, Chu Nom, which rendered Vietnamese in Chinese characters.

The country was 'torn by strife' during the sixteenth and eighteenth centuries (Wright 2002: 226). Contact with the West started at this time, with the Portuguese arriving in 1515, bringing in their wake a host of missionaries. As has so often been the case, the missionaries proved to be catalysts and agents of linguistic change. In the seventeenth century, Alexandre de Rhodes developed an alphabetic script for the language which was called Quoc Ngu (national language) (Wright 2002: 227). At the time, however, its use was restricted to missionary schools and it was not until the French gained control of the country in 1862 that Quoc Ngu slowly started to become more widely used. The first schools to use Quoc Ngu as a medium of instruction were established in 1864 (Lo Bianco 2001).

On gaining power in Vietnam, the French divided the country into three parts: the southern part they called Cochinchina, the central part was called Annam and the northern part Tonkin. In 1884, the Indo-Chinese Union was established, which included Cambodia. The strength and role of the various languages and scripts differed according to geographical location. Quoc Ngu became more popular in the south, but Chinese remained important in the north. The Chu Nom script operated only in restricted domains throughout. In 1918, Chinese characters and Chu Nom were both formally abolished, with documents written in only French and Quoc Ngu.

The French aim was assimilation, and they saw Quoc Ngu as an aid to this, not least because the adoption of Quoc Ngu would weaken Vietnam's ties to China (Thaveeporn 2003). Eventually it prevailed over Chinese and Chu Nom. Quoc Ngu was easier to learn than Chinese, became associated with modernization, and, crucially and ironically, with Vietnamese liberation and independence from the French. All this hastened its success. Today, it is used throughout all administration and education.

French colonial rule was marked by 'active defiance, revolt and resistance' (Wright 2002: 232). At the end of the Second World War and the defeat of the Japanese, Ho Chi Minh took control of the north and declared Vietnam independent. Vietnamese and the Quoc Ngu script became symbols of unity and independence (Thaveeporn 2003) and Vietnamese became the medium of instruction across all levels of education. Ho Chi Minh's declaration of independence was not, however, accepted by the French who entered into a long campaign to try and regain control of the entire country. This ended in their defeat in 1954 at the decisive battle of Diem Bien Phu.

The Geneva Conference (1954–56) divided Vietnam into north and south, a division only erased in 1975 with the American defeat in the Vietnam War. The Americans had, of course, brought English to Vietnam, especially the south. With the American defeat, those who had learned English 'found it expedient to forget it quickly' (Wright 2002: 235). Ho Chi Minh and the north were, not surprisingly, extremely antagonistic to American culture and influence (and thus English) and French. The languages of the enemy were not to be promoted. This makes the contrast with the language policies of today even more striking.

Today, Vietnam has a population of around seventy-five million, of whom the great majority are Vietnamese, comprising nearly 90% of the population. There are fifty-four other ethnic groups (Thaveeporn 2003: 212). As we have seen, after independence there was a move to establish Vietnamese and Quoc Ngu as the sole national language and script respectively, and Vietnamese was made the medium of instruction. At the same time, however, Ho Chi Minh recognized how much he depended on other ethnic groups for support, so, in the north at least, minority languages were promoted.

Vietnamese comprises a range of dialects. One of the major tasks of the Institute of Linguistics, which was established in 1968, is to standardize the language and develop a Vietnamese lexicon. The goal is for the lexicon to be national, popular and scientific. That is to say, the lexicon should avoid the adoption of foreign imports wherever possible and the terms adopted should be easily understood (Le and O'Harrow 2007: 431). As a result, '[t]he complex Confucian/Chinese and Catholic styles of writing gradually disappeared' (Thaveeporn 2003: 227). At the same time, the use of Quoc Ngu script by Vietnamese authors greatly added to its prestige and aided its popularization (Le Minh-Hang and O'Harrow 2007).

In the 1960s, the minority languages that had scripts were taught in primary schools and this was the policy after re-unification in 1975. In 1980, the government decreed that Vietnamese would be the lingua franca for all ethnic groups. The government also endorsed bilingualism and asked for more proficiency in Vietnamese and ethnic languages. Studies to support the romanization of ethnic languages were supported. The Education Law of 1991 states that ethnic minorities have the right to use their own languages in primary schools as auxiliary media of instruction alongside Vietnamese. Twenty-six of the fifty-four ethnic languages now have a writing system (Thaveeporn 2003: 237).

Despite these forward-looking government policies, however, by the early 1990s only 13 out of the 201 provinces were teaching the minority scripts. One major reason for this was that the policy was to use the scripts of the minority languages to teach the children Quok Ngu rather than their own language. Thaveeporn (2003: 231) reports that this policy had three negative results:

(i) Many ethnic minority children simply stopped going to school. School attendance rates among certain ethnic minorities had never been high, but Thaveeporn reports that less than 7% of Yao and Hmong children attend school.
(ii) The number of children who dropped out of school has increased.
(iii) The number of children having to repeat classes has increased.

Using literacy in the L1 with the express purpose of teaching literacy in Vietnamese is unlikely to be successful. 'If efforts are not made to promote minority languages, preservation will only slow the degradation of dying languages' (Diffloth 1994: 52–53). In this context it is important to consider the Vietnamese government's motivation behind the initial promotion of ethnic languages and scripts. This was not really to maintain and preserve the minority languages. Ho Chi Minh had been heavily influenced by Stalin's policy towards minorities, which was first to accommodate them, but with the ultimate intention of assimilation. In other words, the support provided to local languages was designed only to accommodate them in the first instance so that they could be assimilated into mainstream Vietnamese culture (Le and O'Harrow 2007: 436).

A second reason for the declining interest in local languages is that all understand the importance of Vietnamese. Many parents would rather their children learn Vietnamese than their mother tongues. A third reason is the increasing demand for English and languages which are seen to provide opportunities for socio-economic benefit.

Some ten years after unification, the Vietnamese government decided to open up the country to the world and to participate in globalization. Thus the Doi Moi policy was introduced and this unleashed the demand for English. As was reported in Chapter 1,

> when Vietnam embarked on economic reforms in 1986 ... it prompted a nationwide rush to learn English ... English classes were crammed with not just students but also professionals such as doctors and engineers as well as retired government officials, senior police, army officers and diplomats. (cited in Ho and Wong 2004: 1)

As indicated above, it is ironic that the languages that were, until recently, associated with the enemy, Chinese, French and English, are now the three languages most in demand. The foreign language curriculum is now dominated by English with over 90% of children learning it (Baker and Giacchino-Baker 2003). I described in Chapter 1 how the Vietnamese had unsuccessfully requested that French be adopted as a working language for ASEAN in preparation for its joining the organization in 1994. The role of English as ASEAN's only working language is one obvious factor in increasing the demand for English. However, there is also increasing demand for both Putonghua (Mandarin) and French. The AUPELF has the ambitious goal of 5% of Vietnamese secondary school students graduating through a French-Vietnamese bilingual system by 2010 (Wright 2002), and the agency now has more Vietnamese students studying French than at any time during the colonial period.

The Vietnamese government is also 'opening up' in another way, as it is trying to reconnect with the Vietnamese diaspora, which number some three million people (Carruthers 2007). The major reason for the government's interest in the overseas Vietnamese is economic. Vietnamese overseas remit about US$3 billion annually, a figure comparable to the sum remitted by Filipino overseas workers in 2008. It is also realized that overseas Vietnamese who speak Vietnamese remain in closer contact with their country of origin (and thus remit more money) than those who no longer speak it. This explains why Vietnam has started broadcasting programmes in Vietnamese language and culture, targeting overseas Vietnamese. The Vietnamese government is spending substantial sums on transmitting Vietnamese language and culture to overseas Vietnamese, while providing relatively small amounts to promote ethnic languages and cultures within Vietnam itself.

The Vietnamese school curriculum provides a good example of how pressures to learn the national language along with regional and international lingua francas mean that local languages are in serious danger of dying out. Typically, Vietnamese children will learn through Vietnamese as a medium of instruction. English is a compulsory subject from Grade 3 in primary school and will be the first 'other' language learned. Either Putonghua or French will be the next most popular languages. Given that these languages are not cognate and, while Vietnamese now has an alphabetic script, it is different from the English/French scripts, and given that Putonghua has a logographic script, the linguistic demands placed on the L1 Vietnamese child are challenging, to say the least. If the child comes from one of the ethnic minorities, the challenge is even greater. The chances of ethnic children retaining their mother tongues once they enter school are remote. The chances of them finding the linguistic demands of learning in, what is for them, a foreign language may well lead to many dropping out of school early. This is a scenario that can be painted for almost all the countries under discussion here, and I shall return to consider the implications of this and to offer possible solutions in Part III. Table 3.2, adapted from Ho and Wong (2006: 385), summarizes the current place of English and the national language in the education systems of the member states.

Please note, however, that the recently announced changes in government policy described above mean that, in Brunei, English will become the medium of instruction for maths and science from Primary

1 from 2011; that Malaysia will revert to the use of Malay as the medium of instruction for maths and science in 2011; and that the Philippines will allow the use of vernacular languages for early primary in some areas.

Table 3.2 The national language and English in education in ASEAN in 2010
(MoI = medium of instruction)

Country	Medium of Instruction	First Foreign Language (Year of Introduction)
Brunei*	Malay and English	English (Primary 1, from Primary 4 as MoI)
Burma	Burmese	English (Primary 1)
Cambodia**	Khmer	English (Primary 5) (French also offered)
Indonesia**	BI	English (Secondary 1)
Laos	Lao	English (Primary 3)
Malaysia	Malay and English	English (from Primary 1 as MoI)
Philippines	Filipino and English	English (from Primary 1 as MoI)
Singapore	English	Malay/Mandarin/Tamil (Primary 1)
Thailand	Thai	English (Primary 1)
Vietnam**	Vietnamese	English (Primary 3 in selected schools)

* The Arabic script, *jawi*, is introduced from Primary 3.
** Some bilingual education for minority groups in early primary.

Summary

In this chapter the role and development of local languages and the place of English in six member states of ASEAN has been described. These are all countries in which English has played few institutional roles, as they were either colonized by non-Anglophone countries or, as in the case of Thailand, were never colonized at all. Burma has been included in the chapter because Burmese replaced English as the language of administration with U Ne Win's takeover of the country in 1962.

As English is now playing an increasingly prominent role in all these countries — and not least because English is the sole working language of ASEAN — we can now query their classification as 'expanding circle' countries. In all but Burma and, possibly Laos, English is playing an increasingly important role, especially as a language of communication between them. It is, however, perhaps instructive to note that English does not appear to be a *sine qua non* of either economic or political development. While it is true that countries such as Burma and Laos are stagnating, this has more to do with their repressive political systems than with their lack of proficiency in English. Two countries which have been successful are Vietnam and Indonesia. Both countries have strong national languages which are spoken or understood by the great majority of the population. In Vietnam's case, this is the language of the great majority of the Vietnamese people. In Indonesia's case, in contrast, Bahasa Indonesia was originally a language spoken by a small minority group and has only relatively recently developed into the national lingua franca. While English is becoming more widely used in Vietnam, it is still only spoken by a small minority of the population. This is also true of Indonesia. It would appear, then, that economic progress and political development can be successfully achieved without mass recourse to English.

One measure of economic growth is the amount of foreign direct investment (fdi) into a country. Table 3.3 shows the foreign direct investment figures from countries outside ASEAN into Vietnam and Indonesia for the years 2006–08. The figures for Singapore, Malaysia and the Philippines are also given. While it would be unwise to make too much of these figures, it is interesting to note that the figures have increased significantly for both Vietnam and Indonesia, while dropping slightly for Singapore and alarmingly for the Philippines. The trends and rates of increase for Vietnam and Indonesia would also suggest that it will not be long before they both overtake Malaysia.

Table 3.3 Foreign direct investment inflows (from outside ASEAN) 2006–08 (in US$ million)

Country	2006	2008
Indonesia	3,559.9	4,963.4
Vietnam	2,218.0	5,776.8
Singapore	26,913.0	22,801.8
Malaysia	5,591.9	6,196.0
Philippines	2,963.9	1,520.0

(Adapted from the ASEAN Secretariat Statistics; http://www.aseansec.org/Stat/Table25.pdf)

In Part II, the focus shifts to a description of selected linguistic features of English when used as a lingua franca by speakers from ASEAN countries. Chapter 4 provides examples of phonological and lexical features. Chapter 5 describes a selection of grammatical and discourse features and pragmatic norms. Chapter 6 considers and illustrates the communicative strategies exhibited by ASEAN speakers of English as a lingua franca.

Part II
Linguistic Features of English as a Lingua Franca in Asia

Introduction to Part II

In Part I, the history of ASEAN, the development and roles of English in the ASEAN member states were compared and contrasted. In Part II, the focus shifts towards a description of the linguistic features of English in ASEAN, especially when it is used as a lingua franca. The need for or indeed the possibility of describing English as a lingua franca is in itself controversial, as some scholars believe that, by definition, lingua franca English cannot be realized as a single variety on the grounds that its speakers come from different linguistic backgrounds and have different levels of proficiency. However, the role of English as a lingua franca has become the major role of English in today's world, and the situation in ASEAN is simply an example of this. There are currently more non-native speakers of English than there are native speakers (Graddol 2006). In the Asian context, most speakers of English in the Asian region are 'English-knowing' multilinguals (Pakir 2000) for whom English is not a first language and who are more likely to use English with fellow English-knowing multilinguals from within the region than with people who speak native-speaker varieties (Kirkpatrick 2007a). English is thus increasingly used as a lingua franca within the Asian region (Krasnick 1995; Okudaira 1999). Bolton (2008: 7) estimates that the extraordinary recent growth of the use of English in Asia has resulted in 812 million English users. Speakers in the countries included in the ASEAN + 3 grouping comprise some 450 million English-knowing multilinguals. To paraphrase Mauranen, if we want to understand the use of English in today's world, 'ELF must be one of the central concerns in this line of research' (2006: 147).

As alluded to above, however, there is currently controversy over the definition and existence of English as a lingua franca. Opponents argue that the language used by non-native speakers of English in reciprocal conversation is in fact learner English, and deficient in that the language use deviates from native speaker norms (cf. Elder and Davies 2006). Others argue that ELF describes a language function rather than a form and that

ELF cannot therefore be classified as a distinct variety (cf. James 2005, Mollin 2006b, Modiano 2006).

While these arguments appear supportable, recent work on the development of ELF is showing shared linguistic features, especially in the area of syntax. For example, Seidlhofer's research into European ELF (cf. Seidlhofer 2004, 2007; also see below) shows a remarkable number of shared but distinctive linguistic features, as does work by other scholars (cf. James 2000, Cogo and Dewey 2006, Ranta 2006). This would suggest that ELF, despite being used by speakers of different linguistic backgrounds, shares a range of linguistic features. As Ranta suggests, these 'tendencies' can be described (2006: 97).

Perhaps the earliest significant study into the linguistic features of ELF is Jenkins' work into the phonology of international English (2000). She distinguishes between a lingua franca core (LFC) and non-core. The LFC comprises phonological features which have been empirically shown to be important for intelligibility when English is being used as a lingua franca among non-native speakers. Jenkins argues that it is these core features that need to be included in the language teaching curriculum. This reduces the syllabus to a manageable size, while making it teachable (Jenkins 2007). Other less problematic phonological features (in terms of ELF intelligibility) are classified as non-core. ELF proficiency levels are thus not determined by their degree of closeness to native speaker norms, but are derived from ELF speakers themselves. I return to the notion of the LFC in the context English as a lingua franca in ASEAN in Chapter 8.

Seidlhofer and her team at the University of Vienna (cf. Seidlhofer 2001, 2004, 2007) have collected a corpus of English as a lingua franca in Europe. This is the Vienna-Oxford Corpus of English (VOICE). To quote from the VOICE website (http://www.univie.ac.at/voice/voice.php?page=corpus_description):

> VOICE comprises naturally occurring, non-scripted face-to-face interactions in English as a lingua franca (ELF). The recordings made for VOICE are keyboarded by trained transcribers and stored as a computerized corpus. Currently VOICE comprises 1 million words of spoken ELF interactions, equaling approximately 120 hours of transcribed speech.

The ELF interactions cover a range of domains, functions and participant relationships across a range of speech event types. To date the linguistic features of European ELF lexico-grammar which have been identified (cf. Breiteneder 2009; Hülmbauer 2007; Breiteneder 2005; Seidlhofer 2005) include features such as:
(i)   the non-marking of the third person singular with '-s';
(ii) interchangeability of the relative pronouns, 'who' and 'which';
(iii) flexible use of definite and indefinite articles;

(iv) extended use of 'general' or common verbs;
(v) treating uncountable nouns as plural;
(vi) use of a uniform question tag;
(vii) use of demonstrative 'this' with both singular and plural nouns;
(viii) use of prepositions in different contexts.

These linguistic features also occur in many vernacular varieties of English, both traditional and new (Britain 2007; Mesthrie and Bhatt 2008). This leads to the question of whether vernacular universals exist (cf. Filppula, Klemola and Paulasto 2009). In other words, are there linguistic features that differ from standard and codified varieties of English but which exist in all vernacular and spoken varieties of English? As this debate about the existence of vernacular universals is mostly concerned with features of syntax and morphology, it is taken up in more detail in Chapter 5.

A second major ELF corpus is being compiled by Mauranen at the University of Tampere in Finland. This is the corpus of English as a lingua franca in academic settings (ELFA (http://www.uta.fi/laitokset/kielet/engf/research/elfa/). This currently comprises a million word corpus of academic lingua franca English (Mauranen 2003, 2006). She sees two sets of potential results. First, at a theoretical and descriptive level, the results will tell us what linguistic features lingua franca speakers share and how these differ from those of native speakers. The results will also provide insights into the existence of universal vs. culturally specific communicative features. Second, at a practical level, the results will legitimize ELF as a language learning goal. The importance of complementary work in this new field is recognized by Mauranen, 'Discovering regularities (and irregularities for that matter) in lingua franca English invites international co-operation' (2003: 524–5).

In addition to these linguistic descriptions of English as a lingua franca in European contexts, there are also a number of corpora of Asian varieties of English. The best-known of these comprise a part of the International Corpora of English (ICE) and include corpora of Hong Kong, Indian, the Filipino and Singaporean English (Greenbaum 1996; Nelson 1996). Each corpus comprises a million words made up of written and spoken texts.

Part II provides a description of certain linguistic features of English as a lingua franca within ASEAN. Chapter 4 describes a selection of phonological and lexical features. Chapter 5 looks at grammar, discourse and pragmatic norms. Chapter 6 provides examples of the communicative strategies adopted by ASEAN speakers of ELF. The primary data includes recordings of six semi-formal conversations, each comprising between three or four speakers. All ten ASEAN countries were represented (see below for details). This data is referred to as ASEAN ELF. The make-up of the six groups is provided below:

Group 1:
FBrun (female from Brunei; ethnically Chinese)
FViet (female from Vietnam)
FPhil (female from the Philippines)
MThai (male from Thailand)

Group 2:
FSing (female from Singapore, ethnically Indian)
FLao (female from Laos)
FMyan (female from Burma)

Group 3:
MIndon (male from Java, Indonesia)
MCamb (male from Cambodia)
FSing (female from Singapore, ethnically Malay)

Group 4:
FBrun (female from Brunei, ethnically Malay)
FMal (female from Malaysia, ethnically Malay)
FThai (female from Thailand)
FViet (female from Vietnam)

Group 5:
FIndon (female from Java, Indonesia)
FMyan (female from Burma)
FCamb (male from Cambodia)

Group 6:
MMal (male from Malaysia, ethnically Chinese)
MLao (male from Laos)
FPhil (female from the Philippines)

The data also includes a South East Asian Ministers of Education Organisation (SEAMEO) Centre Directors Meeting held over two days in Bangkok in July 2008, which I was fortunate enough to attend and be allowed to record. This meeting was attended by representatives from the specialist training centres which SEAMEO operates throughout Southeast Asia.[1] The meeting was also attended by native speakers of English, including representatives from UNESCO, the British Council, Bangkok, and the Australian Embassy in Bangkok. This data is referred to as SEAMEO. Where relevant, I shall make reference to the other corpora and work outlined above and to the work of other scholars who have described the linguistic features of Asian varieties of English.

Before moving onto the descriptions themselves, two caveats need to be made. The first concerns the English proficiency of the informants. A key issue in the description of new varieties of English and in the description of English as a lingua franca concerns how to draw the line between a learner of English and a fluent speaker of it. In other words, how can the researcher be sure that a distinctive feature which does not occur in standard British or American English is a feature of a new variety of English or is a mistake? In this connection, the inclusion of native speakers in corpora of lingua franca English has been questioned. In the ASEAN context, it makes little sense to try and restrict the data to so-called non-native speakers as many speakers of Southeast Asian varieties of English can be classified as native speakers. For example, as we saw in Chapter 2, recent figures from Singapore show that more than 60% of primary school children report that English is their primary home language. It would therefore make no sense to exclude speakers from any ASEAN ELF corpus on the grounds that their level of English was thought to be too proficient. With regard to data obtained from the semi-formal conversations referred to above, all informants were English language teachers and all had been provided scholarships by their respective governments to undertake a professional development course for English language teachers at the Regional Language Centre (RELC) in Singapore. The great majority of the twenty informants were highly proficient users of English. However, there were two or three whose level of English could be described as intermediate. Perhaps significantly, they came from Laos or Cambodia.

The second caveat concerns the data itself. While we know something about the linguistic backgrounds of the informants listed in the six groups above, we do not know enough about the relative frequency of the features used in the context of English as a lingua franca use throughout ASEAN. The author and a team are collecting an ASEAN ELF corpus which will be comparable to the VOICE European corpus, but this will not be available for some time yet. Linked to this is the ability of many educated multilingual users of English to use different varieties of English along a continuum between the informal and colloquial basilect and the more formal acrolect. Generally speaking, the data here comes from the more formal end of the continuum. When the data is of basilectal usage, this is indicated. The notation conventions used in the description of the data are provided in Appendix 1.

4
Pronunciation, intelligibility and lexis

This chapter describes a selection of the phonological and lexical features of ASEAN speakers of English. As described and illustrated in Part I, ASEAN comprises ten nations which have had different histories with regard to their exposure to English. Those countries which were colonized have developed their own varieties of English and some of these have been codified (cf., for example, Platt and Weber 1980; Deterding, Low and Brown 2003; Deterding, Brown and Low 2005; for Singaporean English). The varieties of Bruneian, Malaysian and Singaporean English share a number of features, not least because the inhabitants of these nations speak, albeit to different degrees, a similar selection of languages as their first languages, including several varieties of Chinese and Indian languages as well as Malay. They were all also colonies of Britain and thus a British model was considered to be the desired target. The English of the Philippines, on the other hand, has distinctive features (cf. for example, Gonzalez 1996a and Thompson 2003). The preferred target model has traditionally been standard American English.

Cambodia, Indonesia, Laos, Thailand and Vietnam, either because they were never colonized (Thailand) or were colonized by the French (Cambodia, Laos, Vietnam) or the Dutch (Indonesia), did not develop their own varieties of English. Thus, when ASEAN speakers use English as a lingua franca, some will be speaking an established variety whose features have been described and codified, while others will be speaking varieties that have not yet become established and, as indicated earlier, may have somewhat lower levels of English proficiency. All this would suggest that the pronunciation of these speakers would be characterized by variation caused by the speakers' different linguistic and educational backgrounds. However, as will be shown later, there are a surprising number of shared phonological features.

At this stage, it is worth briefly reviewing the stages through which English has progressed on its way to becoming a world language and one that is represented by so many different varieties of English. Kachru, Kachru and Nelson (2006) describe four diaspora of English: the first saw English in Scotland, Wales and Ireland; the second was the movement of British migrants to the USA, Canada, Australia, New Zealand and South Africa; the third diaspora took place during the colonial era when English was taken to and developed in countries such as India, Nigeria and Malaysia. This third diaspora has resulted in the development of new varieties of English. As we have seen, these have developed in the 'outer' circle countries of ASEAN, namely, Brunei, Malaysia, the Philippines and Singapore. Many of these new varieties of English have reached Schneider's final stage of development (2007) whereby they have developed sub-varieties. Thus we need to talk, not about Singapore English in the singular, but about Singaporean Englishes in the plural. The fourth diaspora has seen English become a truly global language as a result of which we can move from talking about 'post-colonial' varieties to a post-Anglophone stage, where the major international role of English is as a lingua franca and where native speakers of English are not necessarily present. As we saw in Chapter 3, Cambodia in particular and ASEAN in general provide a good example of this post-Anglophone phase (cf. Clayton 2006: 246). And as this post-Anglophone English is primarily used as a lingua franca for communication between people of different linguistic and cultural backgrounds, the lingua franca use of English can be analyzed to see whether it will develop into a systematically different variety of English. Part II is a preliminary attempt to explore this issue in the context of English as used as a lingua franca in ASEAN.

In the first part of this chapter, the major interest will be on describing a selection of phonological features identified in ASEAN English lingua franca speech which appear to be *shared* by speakers from different countries, despite the differences in the speakers' L1s and the local contact languages. Where relevant, reference will be made to the phonological features of specific varieties. After describing and illustrating a selection of shared features, the question of mutual and international intelligibility of ASEAN English as a lingua franca will be considered.

Pronunciation and intelligibility

Consonants

As is common with many new varieties of English, including native speaker varieties (Fabricius 2002), speakers of ASEAN ELF regularly do not produce word-final consonant clusters. This is not altogether surprising, as consonant clusters are difficult to pronounce, especially if they do not exist in the speaker's L1. Examples from the data include the single consonant sounds in final position of words. Thus, 'firs', 'Eas', 'wol' (world), and 'expec' are typical examples from the ELF conversations and 'mon' (months), 'produc' (product), and 'draf' (draft) from the SEAMEO meeting.

Mesthrie and Bhatt (2008: 128) report three ways in which speakers reduce word-initial consonant clusters, namely: drop one of the consonants; insert an epenthetic vowel; and when the initial consonant is an [s] sound, add a vowel in initial position so that, for example 'start' becomes [is-stat]. I suspect that the second two options are more likely to be found in the speech of basilectal speakers. Only the first option — the dropping of one of the consonant sounds as illustrated above — is found in this ASEAN ELF data. It should also be stressed, however, that several speakers *do* sound consonant clusters. For example, a Thai speaker at the SEAMEO meeting produced /tapt/ (tapped) and /linkt/ (linked).

Another common phonological feature of ASEAN ELF is the replacement of voiceless and voiced TH with a plosive. This is common in the data where dental fricatives are regularly realized as [t]. Examples illustrating the use of [t] for TH in the speech of ASEAN ELF speakers are:

(1) FSing: and I think [tɪŋk] er anyway you all may er join in the… celebration
(2) FLao: new many thing [tɪŋ] from Singapore
(3) FViet: I don't have to teach theories [tirɪz]
(4) FPhil: we have er seven thousand [taʊzən] by the way we have seven thousand [taʊzən]… er seven thousand [taʊzən] one hundred islands in the Philippines
(5) MMal: and English is like a third [tɜːd] language, we have they ss– have to study three [tri] languages
(6) FMyan: er, three [triː] times

(Deterding and Kirkpatrick 2006: 395)

Speakers of many varieties, including so-called native speaker varieties such as Irish and New York English use some form of dental sound where standard RP uses a fricative (Wells 1982: 429, 515). Indeed, varieties which use /θ/ and /ð/ are a minority and thus these sounds are excluded from Jenkins' lingua franca core. It is perhaps not surprising therefore to note that the data set above indicates that speakers from Singapore, Laos, Vietnam, the Philippines, Malaysia and Burma do this. This is, of course, not to say that they always realize word-initial TH with a dental, but that this occurs. Hong Kong provides an interesting exception, as speakers of Hong Kong English commonly use [f] or [v] in this position (Bolton and Kwok 1990; Hung 2000). This is supported by research which analyzed the speech of fifteen English majors from a Hong Kong tertiary institution who were recorded during interviews. All were first language speakers of Cantonese. Tables 4.1, 4.2 and 4.3 report the pronunciations of voiceless TH in initial, medial and final positions.

Table 4.1 Pronunciation of voiceless TH in initial position (Hong Kong speakers)

Word	Pronunciation of TH		
	[θ]	[f]	[t]
think	18	7	
three	2	5	1
theme(s)	4	1	
thing	2		
thirteen		1	
thank	1		
Total	27	14	1

Table 4.2 Pronunciation of voiceless TH in medial position (Hong Kong speakers)

Word	Pronunciation of TH			
	[θ]	[f]	[t]	zero
something	4		2	2
everything	1			
methods	1			
Total	6	0	2	2

Table 4.3 Pronunciation of voiceless TH in final position (Hong Kong speakers)

Word	Pronunciation of TH			
youth		4		
both		2		
fourth	1			
month	1			
months				1
Total	2	6	0	1

Source: Deterding, Wong and Kirkpatrick 2008: 154.

This tendency to use [f] for voiceless TH is nicely exemplified in an advertising slogan used by a popular chain of tea houses in Hong Kong. On the walls in these tea houses is the cyber-speak invitation 'RU34T' or 'Are you free for tea?', where the pronunciation of '3' is considered a homophone of 'free'.

Another shared feature of most Southeast Asian varieties of English — and this is also true of many other varieties of English — is that vowel length is not distinctive (Mesthrie and Bhatt 2008). For example, the Englishes of Brunei, Malaysia, Hong Kong, the Philippines and Singapore merge long and short vowels (Deterding 2007; Gonzalez 1996b). In other words, the distinction between minimal pairs such as 'ship and sheep', 'baht and but', 'caught and cot' and 'pool and pull' is not realized in these varieties of English.

It has become customary not to talk in terms of the sounds of standard British English (or RP) and use these as a benchmark, but rather to adopt the lexical set developed by John Wells (1982). This labels the vowels of English with sets of words and their aim is to provide example words in which the relevant monophthongs occur in a wide range of varieties (but not all).[1]

As Mesthrie and Bhatt (2008: 119) explain:

> Wells thus speaks of the KIT vowel rather than the vowel /i/. The KIT class comprises all words that have the same vowel as the word *kit* in ... many varieties of English.

Table 4.4 below is taken from Deterding (2007: 13) and shows Wells' lexical set — with the addition of POOR — and their realization in Singapore English.

Table 4.4 Vowels of Singaporean English

FLEECE	i	NURSE	ə	GOAT	o	GOOSE	u
KIT	i	*lett*ER	ə	THOUGHT	ɔ	FOOT	u
*happ*Y	i	*comm*A	ə	FORCE	ɔ	PRICE	ai
FACE	e	START	ʌ	NORTH	ɔ	MOUTH	au
DRESS	ɛ	PALM	ʌ	LOT	ɔ	CHOICE	ɔi
TRAP	ɛ	BATH	ʌ	CLOTH	ɔ	NEAR	iə
SQUARE	ɛ	STRUT	ʌ	CURE	ɔ	POOR	uə

This lack of a distinction between long and short vowels is common among many Asian varieties of English and in ASEAN ELF. This tendency to shorten sounds extends to the monophthongization of certain diphthongs. For example, Deterding and Kirkpatrick (2006: 397) report the monophthongal realization of the FACE and GOAT vowels in ASEAN ELF.[2] This has also been recorded for Malaysian English (Baskaran 2004), Vietnamese (Honey 1987) and Thai (Smyth 1987). The ASEAN ELF examples are:

(7) FPhil: you learn the language in a natural way [weː]
(8) FIndon: we can go to another place [pleːs]
(9) FBrun: it's not the type of food that you usually take [teːk] yeah
(10) MThai: a three-day holiday [hɒlideː] right

(11) FSing: I better not say [seː] things that I don't [doːn] know [noː]
(12) FMyan: they [ðeː] can go [goː] to the monastery

The tendency to reduce vowel length is also evident in making triphthongs bisyllabic. This can be seen in RP also where the vowels in words like 'tyre' and 'tower' may become homophones and pronounced [aːə] (Crutterden 2001: 139), rather than as triphthongs as in [taɪə] and [taʊə]. In the ASEAN data these would be pronounced with a [w] between the syllables, as in these examples of the pronunciation of 'our' and 'hour'.

(13) FMyan: in our [aʊwə] time we have to memorize some er most of the vocabulary in our [aʊwə] mind
(14) MCamb: we have to develop our [aʊwə] country with the world
(15) FBrun: for our [aʊwə] high school we get good results
(15) FIndon: an hour [aʊwə] in the airport
(16) FCamb: two hours [aʊwəs]

I discuss issues of intelligibility below, but I suggest that the ELF realization of 'our' as [aʊwə] is easier to understand than RP [a].

Lack of aspiration on initial plosives is also found, although there is no suggestion that this occurs with all initial plosives. Examples include a lack of aspiration on initial [t] and [p] (Deterding and Kirkpatrick 2006: 396–7):

(17) FPhil: this is my second time [daɪm]
(18) FViet: so they will teach [diːtʃ]
(19) FMyan: pardon? [baːdən]
(20) MCamb: I find most car in Singapore ... pretty [brɪtɪ] new
(21) FSingM: I do not really have that much patience [beɪʃəns]

A further distinctive feature which is shared by many of these speakers is the lack of reduced vowels. This was very common in the ASEAN ELF data. Examples include:

(22) FSing: the communicative [kɒmjuːnɪkeɪtɪv] approach
(23) MIndon: it's officially [ɒfɪʃəlɪ] launched
(24) FBrun: can't compare [kɒmpeə] now
(25) FPhil: and from the text we prepare the grammar lessons [lesɒnz]
(26) FMyan: from [frɒm] there we can [kæn] continue [kɒntɪnjuː]

Extract 26 shows that this use of a full vowel also occurs in function words such as *from* and *can*, where RP speakers would use a schwa. This is also exemplified in Extracts 27 and 28.

(27) FPhil: or to become proficient in the language, you have to [tuː] spend a lot of money
(28) FIndon: er and then I tried to [tuː] look for the officer but...

The lack of reduced vowels is reported in many new varieties of English (Deterding 2010) and is almost certainly caused by contact-induced change from influence of the many Asian and African languages which show a tendency towards syllable-timing. As Mesthrie and Bhatt (2008: 129) point out, 'the number of new English varieties which exhibit tendencies towards syllable timing is impressive'.

Speakers of stress-timed languages — and many native speaker varieties of English are stress-timed — will naturally use unstressed vowels in normal speech. This is why the schwa is so common. Speakers of syllable-timed languages, on the other hand, tend to give equal prominence to each syllable and this leads to a lack of reduced vowels. As will be further discussed below, this tendency towards syllable timing may constitute an aid to international intelligibility for these new varieties of English, with clear implications for English language teaching.

Linked to this and possibly also to the linguistic typology of many Asian languages allowing null subjects and thus being classified as pro-drop (Li and Thomson 1976; Kirkpatrick 1993; Mesthrie and Bhatt 2008), pronouns often receive stress when in subject position as illustrated below:

(29) MIndon: I bought in the Muslim mmm restaurant
(30) FMyan: and HE has been in Singapore er three times
(31) MThai: when I have to speak
(32) MCamb: when we er conducted lesson or teach them er THEY cannot perform very well

Object pronouns also often receive stress:

(33) FSingM: and it's difficult for you to actually teach THEM and all that
(34) FIndon: OK, I just er waited for HIM an hour in the airport
(35) FBrun: so I had so m-, I grew up with a lot of languages around ME

Finally, heavy-end stress is also common, as exemplified in Extract 35 above and in the following examples:

(36) FSingI: er we do not er teach grammar the incidental WAY
(37) FLao: ah, yes we can follow the ... er ... teaching plan that we HAVE
(38) FViet: I I mean this for the er for the sub er for the grammar subject itSELF, it's not for interpreter SKILLS

Heavy-end stress also frequently occurs on repeated words:

(39) MMal: because there are a lot of students who are weak in English and they go to such schools just to learn ENGLISH
(40) FMyan: I love teaching and I enjoy TEACHING
(41) MThai: it was meant for only a h- a holiday a three-day HOLIDAY
(42) MCamb: erm English is very new and very few people speak ENGLISH

Deterding and Kirkpatrick (2006: 400) suggest that this use of heavy-end stress has the communicative function of signalling the end of an utterance, especially when it is accompanied by a falling tone. This is to be compared with the function of heavy-end stress in native speaker varieties where it often signals new information (Levis 2005), who also argues that this difference in function of end stress may be features of inner and outer circle Englishes respectively. The use of heavy-end stress to signal the end of an utterance appears to be a characteristic of ASEAN ELF.

Features of pronunciation which are shared by ELF speakers are listed in Table 4.5 (adapted from Deterding and Kirkpatrick 2006: 395).

Table 4.5 Summary of pronunciation features shared by ASEAN ELF users

Feature	Example(s)
reduction of consonant clusters	first – firs
dental fricative /θ/ as [t]	many thing [tɪŋ]
merging of long and short vowel sounds	[iː] and [ɪ] to [ɪ]
monophthongization of FACE and GOAT diphthongs	
reduced initial aspiration	they will teach [diːtʃ]
bisyllabic triphthongs	in our [aʊwə] time
lack of reduced vowels	officially [ɒfɪʃəlɪ]; to [tuː] visit
stressed pronouns	and HE has been in Singapore
heavy end-stress	the incidental WAY

A key question that needs to be addressed in any discussion of distinctive phonological features of specific varieties or of English as a lingua franca is the extent to which these features may hinder intelligibility for speakers of other varieties. This is of particular importance in lingua franca communication as, by its very definition, a lingua franca needs to be intelligible across linguistic and cultural boundaries. However, intelligibility is a complex concept and has proved difficult both to define and investigate. Smith, perhaps the seminal figure in intelligibility research (cf. Smith and Rafiqzad 1979; Smith and Bisazza 1982; Smith and Nelson 2006) has distinguished three levels of understanding: intelligibility, comprehensibility, and interpretability. Intelligibility refers to the ability to recognize words and utterances; comprehensibility refers to the ability to understand the meaning or locutionary force of utterances; and interpretability refers to the ability to understand the illocutionary force — the pragmatic meaning — of an utterance.

Smith has shown in tests of *intelligibility* which involved asking subjects to note down specific words when listening to native and non-native speakers from a range of different countries that 'the native speaker was always found to be among the least intelligible speakers' (Smith and Rafiqzad

1979: 375, cited in Nelson 2008: 300). In a later study into *comprehensibility* which checked how much people understood when listening to speakers of different varieties of English, Smith and Bisazza (1982: 265) found that '[t]he American speaker was easiest ... and the Indian was most difficult'. They also found that familiarity with a speaker's variety of English was crucial as, for example, the Japanese listeners found the Japanese speakers the easiest to understand. They concluded that 'one's English is more comprehensive to those people who have had active exposure to it' (1982: 269, cited in Nelson 2008: 300).

Interpretability — Smith's third level of understanding — is particularly hard to research (Pickering 2006), not least because cultural values and frameworks often need to be understood (Nelson 2008). In studies into the overall intelligibility of Singaporean English (Kirkpatrick and Saunders 2005) and Hong Kong English (Kirkpatrick, Deterding and Wong 2008), tapes of Singaporean and Hong Kong speakers in conversation with a native speaker were played to an international audience who were required to answer comprehension questions on what they had heard and to indicate whether they found the speakers likeable and or intelligent and to say why. While these studies involved one-way communication in that the listeners were unable to provide feedback which would be normal in real-time face-to-face conversation, the results of both studies showed that the speech of the Singaporeans and Hong Kongers was relatively easy to understand (and thus comprehensible) and the messages intended by the speakers relatively easy to interpret (and thus interpretable). For example, almost all the listeners to the Hong Kong speakers scored more than 80% on the comprehension exercise after only one hearing. Most listeners were also able to justify their evaluation of the speaker's intelligence and likeability by making reference to the respective speaker's remarks. Those that fared less well were all themselves second language speakers of English and their poorer results may reflect their own lower levels of English proficiency.

One reason for the international intelligibility of new varieties of English may well be linked to their lack of reduced vowels and tendency towards a syllable-timed rhythm and this may be to their advantage in this respect. As Hung (2002: 3) has argued, most speakers of syllable-timed languages 'would in fact find stress-timed English less intelligible than syllable-timed, on account of the massive reduction and neutralisation of unstressed syllables'. He thus asks (2002: 7) why and when should teachers modify their learners' phonology of English. For example, why would it be considered important to coach learners into a stress-timed pattern when their 'natural' syllable-timed pattern is an aid to international intelligibility?

In this context, it is thus interesting that the ASEAN ELF data shows remarkably few occasions where communication was affected by the use of distinctive phonological features. While there were relatively few misunderstandings, these did occasionally occur and some examples of this and suggestions for the possible causes of the misunderstandings are provided below. It should also be noted that the speakers' communicative strategies were primarily aimed at enhancing communication and ensuring that participants did not lose face in some way. These communicative strategies are described in Chapter 6.

In this first example of misunderstanding, FMyan hears 'rooms' as 'food'. She signals that she is unsure of what MIndon is asking with an 'er' but this is misinterpreted by MIndon as being a request for more information about the 'what about' rather than the 'rooms'.

(43)

MIndon: what about your rooms
FMyan: er
MIndon: you feel OK any [problems
FMyan: I] find the taste er quite OK (ehm) but er like yours is I think er ... er ... the rice a little bit sticky (ehm) in our country we don't er eat er rice as sticky as that rice here er ehm and then ehm how shall I say er ... and then vegetables er maybe er the same vegetables we eat (ehm) in our country (ehm) but er the price for them is also expensive (laughter) I think because I prefer eating vegetables (OK) I prefer vegetables er than (OK) to meat er
MIndon: OK what I'm asking is about room ...

(Kirkpatrick 2007a: 161)

While the misunderstanding above is likely to have been caused by a mishearing, sometimes it is hard to identify the precise cause of a misunderstanding. For example, in Extract 44, the Thai participant needs the question to be asked again. This is perhaps because he himself is about to ask a question but is interrupted by FBrun and there is some overlapping speech.

(44)

FBrun: So how [how
MThai: [I I mean
FBrun: do you find the course so far? (1.3)
MThai: mmm?
FBrun: How did you find the course that we did [so far
MThai: er actually it's an a very in-intensive course

Sometimes the misunderstanding is caused by a speaker's idiosyncratic realization of a vowel sound. In Extract 45, FMyan pronounces 'pearl' as [baː] and FIndon has to ask specifically for clarification. Here then is an example of when the 'let it pass' principle (Firth 1996; Kirkpatrick 2007b) is not observed, as FIndon needs immediate clarification in order to participate in the conversation. It would appear then that the use of /aː/ for /ɜː/ has caused this problem (cf. Jenkins 2000: 145–6).

(45)

FMyan:	by the way er have you seen any er pearl [baː] beads at this shopping centre?
FIndon:	bal bead what's that?
FMyan:	er er pearl necklace
FIndon:	yeah a lot but too expensive

Generally speaking, however, the ASEAN ELF data is characterized by mutual understanding, except when a participant uses an idiosyncratic pronunciation that is not recoverable from the context. In the Extract 46 below, MLao pronounces 'holes' in such a way that MMal and FPhil are completely flummoxed. It is not until he spells out the word that the others finally understand what he means.

(46)

MLao:	you know at the time that ehm tsunami occurs there were some problem in my country
MMal:	what problem
MLao:	yeah we've got some problem we have big holes [hoʊnz] in in some areas
MMal:	horns? Sorry
MLao:	hole [hoʊn] you know hole [hoʊnt]
FPhil:	what houn
MLao:	yeah big hole [hoʊn]
MMal:	(laugh) what
FPhil:	what's a horn
MMal:	sorry
MLao:	H-O-L-E something like this
MMal:	holes?
MLao:	yeah
MMal:	holes oh you mean a hole in the ground
MLao:	yeah

The final example of misunderstanding comes when a speaker uses the wrong lexical item. MCamb does not understand so MIndon repeats the question. This time though FSing offers a more appropriate word which MIndon immediately adopts.

(47)

MIndon: so how long do do they have to sit in the junior high school and senior high school?
MCamb: ehm I've been teaching there for two years after my graduation er from er
MIndon: no I mean er er how many years do students have to sit [FSing: stay] to stay in the junior high school [MCamb: ehm] and the senior high school
MCamb: er in in in Cambodia er junior high school starts from grade seven

(Kirkpatrick 2007a: 162)

In the following extract, it would appear that the idiosyncratic pronunciation of FLao contributes to the misunderstanding, as evidenced by the second pause which persuades her to try again. FLao's pronunciation includes a final [n] on 'school', [w] instead of [l] in 'only', [ti] for 'three' and [ts] rather than [tʃ] in 'teacher'.

(48)

FLao: especially in my nn schoon here are only [onwi] three [ti:] teacher [ti:tsə] (1.0) [tri: ti:tsə]
FSing: three teachers
FLao: [yes, three teachers
FSing: trained to teach English
FLao: Yes, all trained

It is also worth noting that while FLao's pronunciation of 'three' as [ti:] causes problems, as soon as she inserts the /r/, the problem dissolves as FSing immediately understands her. This is further evidence that the use of [t] for voiceless TH does not cause misunderstandings.

Similar idiosyncratic pronunciations are the probable causes of the misunderstandings in the following two examples. In Extract 49, FViet pronounces 'sauce' as 'shors' and this is followed by a silence and then a querying 'mmm' from FMal which leads FViet to explain what 'sauce' is. Even so, it is not clear that FMal has understood, although FBrun clearly has.

(49)

FViet: Of course we have to er make er some [ʃɔ:s] (0.7)
FMal: mmm
FViet: sauce [shors] yeah erm you erm [shors] yeah it is ere r a little water a little sugar a little fish sauce [shors] some chilli and some pepper
FMal: mmm
FViet: yeah
FBrun: OK, guys, enough about food.

In Extract 50, FMyan makes 'us' sound more like 'arts' and FSing indicates that she does not understand, after a long pause of more than one second.

(50)

FMyan:	They can get, they can acquire more English than [uts] (1.2)
FSing:	[hmm-mmm
FMyan:	[but mm er in our time we have to memorize some er most of the vocabulary in our mind and
FSing:	[mmm
FMyan:	[we have to erms er r- repeat before the teachers

While Extracts 43–50 illustrate occasions where misunderstanding took place, it needs to be stressed that these were few and that communication was mostly successful, suggesting strongly that there were few problems with intelligibility. It should also be noted that where there were problems of understanding, these were primarily caused by the idiosyncratic pronunciations of individual speakers. FMyan's pronunciation of 'pearl' as [baː] and MLao's pronunciation of 'hole' as [hoʊn] are examples. That is not to say that idiosyncratic pronunciation necessarily caused misunderstanding. For example, in the SEAMEO data one Indonesian pronounced the 'g' of 'generation' and another the 'g' of 'archaeology' as /g/ but, probably because the meaning was easily retrievable from the context, this did not appear to cause any misunderstandings. Neither did the use of distinctive but shared phonological features cause misunderstanding. Thus the use of the distinctive but shared phonological features listed in Table 4.5 above did not appear to cause any problems for understanding in this lingua franca communication. The presence of these shared but distinctive phonological features suggest that an ELF variety is developing. That such a variety has to be mutually comprehensible goes without saying.

Nevertheless, this represents a small data set and it would be vastly premature to argue from this alone that ASEAN ELF users seldom encounter problems of intelligibility. We need further research into this area to include settings where the stakes are higher and where serious disagreements are likely. We also need to consider the communicative strategies adopted by speakers in these ELF situations to see if these help in reaching understanding. These are the subject of Chapter 6. I now turn to a discussion of the use of lexis.

Lexis

While phonology may be the most obviously distinctive characteristic of any variety of English — someone's accent is the first thing people notice — the use of distinctive lexis is also a core characteristic of all varieties of English. For example, the following list of words used to describe cars/automobiles and lorries/trucks in British and American English respectively, could lead an 'innocent' bystander to wonder how the respective speakers could be describing the same object.

British	American
bonnet	hood
boot	trunk
gear lever	(stick) shift (knob)
bumper	fender
exhaust (pipe)	tail pipe/muffler
windscreen	windshield
number plate	license plate
reversing lights	back up lights

There are countless examples of the use of different words to describe the same object or phenomenon across varieties of English. Further differences are caused by the need to adopt words from local languages to describe indigenous phenomena, as no 'English' word for such things exist. The three objects people routinely identify with Australia — boomerangs, kangaroos and koalas — are all words taken from Australian Aboriginal languages and which have become part of the vocabulary of not just Australian English, but international English. Other 'international' examples include the following words adopted from Japanese: sumo, kimono, sake, sushi, sashimi and karaoke. Locally adopted words which become internationally understood tend to describe flora, fauna, foods and local cultural artefacts or traditions. There are many others which may only be understood by speakers of the specific varieties of English. Thus few non-Australians might understand the word 'corroboree', an Aboriginal dance ceremony of some sort, or non-Malays the Malay-English word 'adat', which is an overarching term referring to traditional Malay cultural practice. Most people will know the Malay-English word 'satay', but fewer will know 'atap' (a palm thatch used for huts).

A third cause for differences in the meaning of words in different varieties of English is that a word with one meaning in one variety takes on a different meaning in another. A good example of this is the word 'bush' in Australian English. As Butler (2002) has pointed out, its specific Australian meaning of the Australian 'countryside in general as opposed to the towns' and its importance to Australian culture means that it collocates with many other nouns in a special way. The dictionary of Australian English, the *Macquarie,* lists ninety-seven compounds with bush, including bush ballad, bush carpenter and bush tucker and defines these three compounds as:

Bush ballad: a poem in ballad meter dealing with aspects of life in the Australian bush
Bush carpenter: a rough amateur carpenter
Bush tucker: simple fare, as eaten by one living in or off the bush

By contrast, the *New Oxford Dictionary* lists only thirty-seven compounds with bush and most of these are from Australian English.

In addition to taking on a new meaning in this way, words can also become broader or narrower in their semantic scope. Thus, in Singaporean English, the word 'alphabet' refers to an individual letter of the alphabet so that, in Singaporean terms, English has twenty-six alphabets.

An example of this semantic narrowing from Singaporean English is the use of the word 'Christians', which refers only to Protestants. An example of semantic broadening and narrowing respectively from Chinese English is the use of cadre on the one hand, and migrant workers on the other. Xu (2010) explains that 'cadre' refers to leaders in general in China rather than to 'a small group of trained people who form the basic unit of a military, political or business organization' or 'a member of such a group' as the word is defined in the *Cambridge Advanced Learners' Dictionary*. 'Migrant workers' on the other hand, refers, in China, to migrants from the countryside who have migrated to the towns. It does not mean foreign workers. 'Migrant workers' thus has a more restricted meaning in Chinese English than in many other varieties.

A new variety of English may also reflect its cultural values in the way it uses lexis. Australians value informality and this is lexically realized by 'clipping', whereby many words get shortened and end in a vowel sound. Thus 'afternoon' becomes 'arvo', 'politicians' become 'pollies' and 'journalists' become 'journos'. People's names get the same treatment. 'Martin' becomes 'Marto', Barry becomes 'Bazza' and people with surnames which begin with Mac or Mc as in McKenzie and MacNamara will be referred to as 'Macca'. Occasionally, the need for a final vowel sound can lengthen the word. For example, a 'tinnie' refers to a can of beer and the name John almost invariably becomes 'Johnno'.

Cultural values and norms can also be reflected lexically as they can determine what people choose to talk about. Moody (2007) compares occurrences of the lexical items 'to eat' and 'food' in five of the international corpora of English (ICE), namely, ICE Great Britain, ICE Hong Kong, ICE India, ICE Philippines and ICE Singapore. The results are presented in Table 4.6 (Moody 2007: 52).

It is remarkable that all the 'Asian' corpora contain many more references to 'food' and 'eat' than the British corpus does. This is perhaps even more remarkable when we remember that the Asian varieties of English have their own words for food — *makan* in Malaysian English, for

Table 4.6 'To eat' and 'food' in ICE Corpora

	ICE GB	ICE HK	ICE IN	ICE PH	ICE SI
To eat	137	202	152	312	242
Food	181	296	354	260	265
Total	**318**	**498**	**506**	**572**	**507**

example — and that these are not included in the figures. This would strongly suggest that food is a more popular topic among people from the Asian cultures represented here than it is among the British. This may not be considered all that remarkable by people who have eaten in Britain and in these Asian countries.

While new varieties of English need to coin new words or adopt words from other languages in order to describe local phenomena, it can take a long time before these new words become accepted. It is sobering to think that the first dictionary of Australian English, the *Macquarie,* was not published until 1981, more than two hundred years after Captain Cook reached Australia. Butler (2007: 34–35) nicely captures the different views of the prescriptive and descriptive grammarian to the Singaporean meaning of the word 'alphabet' by comparing the definitions given in the following examples. The first is taken from the *Times Dictionary of Problem Words* by George Jenkins (Times is a Singaporean Publishing House) and the second from Adam Brown's *Singapore English in a Nutshell:*

> The noun alphabet means all the letters used in a written language. The individual letters are not called alphabets; they are called letters of the alphabet. (Jenkins 1988: 14)
>
> abcdefghijklmnopqrstuvwxyz
> How many alphabets are there here? If you are not Singaporean you may find this a strange question, as the answer is so self-evident — one, the Roman alphabet. In that case you will be surprised to find out that Singaporeans will answer that there are 26 alphabets here ... (Brown 1999: 7)

Thus, while several dictionaries of Asian varieties of English have been published, not all users of these varieties are prepared to accept the new coinages recorded in them. A person who has striven to provide recognition for Asian Englishes through the publication of dictionaries is Susan Butler, who was also the publisher of the *Macquarie Dictionary*. Among the dictionaries Butler has been involved in include a Singaporean version of the *Macquarie Junior Dictionary,* and the *Anvil-Macquarie Dictionary of Philippine English for High School*. The *Macquarie Junior* and the *Anvil-Macquarie* were both specifically aimed at the school market. The *Macquarie Junior* included common words of Singaporean and Malaysian English, examples of which are provided on p. 89.

ang mo	a white person
ang pow	a red envelope with money in it, given at Chinese New Year
atap	a roof made from nipa
blur	(of a person) confused
daching	a set of scales
godown	a wharf
havoc	(of a person) outrageously daring
hawker centre	a food centre with an open area for eating meals
kaypoh	a busy body
kelong	a fish trap
kiasu	afraid of being disadvantaged

On the back cover of the dictionary the following claim was made:

> The *Macquarie Junior Dictionary* is therefore the ideal language reference for the students of Singapore, Malaysia and Brunei because it takes into account their needs in developing English language skills, while at the same time recognising their experience and culture.

But, as Butler herself (2007: 39–40) reports, 'that cut no ice with the teachers of Singapore, Malaysia and Brunei … teachers will not lead the charge in changing attitudes to local varieties of English'.

She reports a similar experience with the *Anvil-Macquarie*, as teachers in the Philippines were primarily concerned with examination success, and local forms of English were considered deviant in that context.

Despite this reluctance to accept local lexis as part of standard English, these words constitute a defining characteristic of all varieties of English. Locally-derived idioms and code-mixing also give many new varieties of English their distinctive flavour. One source of this is the translation of idioms from the speakers' L1 into English. Examples include these two expressions used by the Chinese writer Ha Jin: a 'flowered pillowcase' to describe someone who may look attractive, but has no depth; and 'they breathe through the same nostril' to describe people who are always in agreement with each other. A Japanese example provided by the Japanese scholar Nobuyuki Honna is 'a son will chew on his parents' shins', which means that a son may remain financially dependent on his parents for many years. Prodromou (2007b: 37) cites the Serbian expression, 'one should not mix frogs with grandmothers' (one should not mix or compare things that are incomparable). Hybrid words — words which are creatively made up of words from the local language and English — provide another rich source. Two examples from Hong Kong/Chinese English are 'Cantopop' and '*dandan* noodles' (a type of spicy noodle dish from Sichuan) (see Bolton 2003 for a wide range of such examples).

In Malay, a '*dadah* addict' is a drug addict and to 'run *amok*', or to become uncontrollable with anger or panic, is now part of the international vocabulary of English. Filipino English has these examples:

> *buco* juice (the juice of a young coconut), *pulot* boy (a ball boy) and common *tao* (an ordinary person) (see Bautista [1997: 49–72] for further examples)

This use of hybridization as a way of creating new words is a part of code-mixing, and code-mixing is very common in multilingual societies such as those of ASEAN. The following examples are taken from newspapers in Malaysia and Brunei and come from David and McLellan (2007: 93–117). As the authors point out, sometimes the 'foreign' word is flagged in some way or another and sometimes an English word is given its local equivalent to ensure that it accurately reflects the local culture. On other occasions, it is assumed that the readers will know the meanings.

> ... such as their practising *sembahyang* (prayers) (98)
>
> ... is regarded as societal obligation (*fardhu kifaya*) (99)
>
> He said that there should be a clear understanding that celebrating a 'Kongsi Raya' did not mean that matters pertaining to Islam and other religions were mixed together (101)
>
> ... because it was a way to cari makan (take bribes) ... (103)
>
> Others said the tudung-clad foreign woman who was in a baju kurung had stripped ... (105)
>
> Many ... enjoyed the muruku, tosai, dal and chicken curry (109)
>
> To end the ceremony, Doa Al-Fatihah was read, followed by the breaking of the fast and Maghrib prayers (111)
>
> Seven parang wielding robbers ... (113)

McLellan (2010) also reports a very sophisticated type of code-switching among Bruneian multilinguals which challenges 'the asymmetric matrix-language-frame model of code-switching' as proposed by scholars such as Myers Scotton. In the example on p. 91, both languages — English and Malay — appear to be on an equal footing, as both supply lexical items and a syntactic frame. McLellan classifies this as 'language alternation'. It clearly requires speakers who are highly proficient bilinguals. The forward and back slashes show that there are eleven points within this short text where the speaker switches languages.

Auction stuff:

Frankly speaking,/₁ baiktah jangan dibali barang2
　　　　　　　　good-DM NEG-IMP PASS-buy RDP-thing

yg kena\₂ *auction* /₃ atu, bukannya apa\₄, *if we buy them, in a way, we are*
REL PASS　　　　　　　DEM, NEG-3s-POSS what

helping those who have used /₅ duit ketani \₆ *for their personal interest, to*
　　　　　　　　　　　　　　money 1pi-POSS

pay for their debts./₇ Mana tia yang dulu\₈ *the famous* /₉7 org　　　atu?
　　　　　　　　Where DM REL before　　　　　　ABBR-person DEM

Inda kedengaran.\₁₀ *Has the trial started?? It's so sad, isn't it, how our beloved*
NEG hearing

country /₁₁ jadi　　cemani.
　　　　　become　like-DEM

Auction stuff: Frankly speaking, it's better not to buy the things that are being auctioned, isn't it right, that if we buy them, in a way, we are helping those who have used our money for their personal interest, to pay for their debts. Wherever are the famous seven people from before? We don't hear of them anymore. Has the trial started? It's so sad, isn't it, how our beloved country has come to this.

This use of lexical items and idioms with meanings specific to a language variety — what Seidlhofer (2001: 16) has called 'unilateral idiomaticity' — along with code-mixing of various degrees of sophistication, are characteristic of language use in multilingual societies. However, one would not expect their use to be effective in lingua franca communication, as the specific lexical meanings would often be unknown to at least some of the participants. Code-mixing would be an unlikely phenomenon in lingua franca communication because its use requires proficiency in specific languages, and in lingua franca communication one could never anticipate that all participants could possibly be familiar with all the possible languages. After all, that is precisely why the participants in lingua franca communication choose a lingua franca in the first place.

It should therefore be of little surprise to discover that there is no use of 'unilateral idiomaticity' in the ASEAN ELF data. Nor is there any use of code-mixing or the use of culturally specific lexical items. Indeed, the following example is the only instance in which speakers use a lexical item from a shared L1 when there is a participant who does not speak the same language. The three participants are a Singaporean female, an Indonesian male, and a Cambodian male. The term in question is *rojak*, a Malay word meaning mixed, but which also refers to a type of salad, and is colloquially used to refer to 'mixed' English. Even here, the Singaporean speaker checks to make sure the Indonesian understands the term. The Cambodian's lack of participation at this stage can probably be explained by his non-understanding of the term.

(51)

FSing: in school in class I will try to speak good English in fact we are supposed to speak good English ... so there's no way that I will speak Singlish to my kids not in class yeah not in class er not in school but ehm like what you said just now when we go back to our friends and all that all the English and Singlish are all mixed together like *rojak*
MInd: oh like *rojak* right like that
FSing: yes you know *rojak* right
MInd: yes it's fruits mixed
FSing: all mixed up together
MInd: all right all right

The only example of the use of a 'unilateral' idiom in the SEAMEO data was uttered by one of the native speakers present, an Englishman who used a boating metaphor when saying 'the whole organization needs to be on an even keel'. I was not able to check with all the SEAMEO delegates after the session, but none of the three whom I did consult understood the meaning of this expression. This is potentially significant in that native speakers may not be aware of how difficult local idioms and vocabulary items can be for people from outside their own speech community. In contrast, multilinguals who regularly interact with people from different linguistic and cultural backgrounds are more likely to be sensitive to this, and therefore not use culturally-nuanced words which they think other interactants may not understand.

There was, however, also one use of metaphor in the SEAMEO data, which was when a Malay speaker urged people to be on time, by reminding them how inconvenient it was if a member of a fourball in golf was late. I am not sure the extent to which this was understood by the participants.

Summary

While a great deal of phonological variation would be expected in the lingua franca English of speakers from ASEAN, due in part to their different linguistic backgrounds and in part to the different models of English to which they have been exposed, a number of phonological features are shared by many of the speakers. Many of these have also been reported in other vernacular varieties of English, both new and traditional. These features seldom caused any problems for intelligibility and understanding.

One feature that has been reported here is the tendency to avoid the use of reduced vowels along with a related tendency towards syllable timing. This is possible in native speaker varieties of English — for example, when one is spelling a message out slowly to someone, possibly in a semi-humorous or sarcastic tone as in 'Let-me-repeat-this-one-more-time-to-make-sure-we-both-un-der-stand-pre-cise-ly-where-we-stand' — but it is used for creating a special effect. In ASEAN ELF it is the normal standard way of speaking, and, far from interfering with mutual understanding may actually enhance it. This has interesting potential implications for English language teaching, which will be considered in Part III.

Lexically, it is interesting to note that the distinctive lexis of individual varieties of English — including borrowed words, neologisms, idioms, hybridization and code-mixing — do not occur in the data. This makes ASEAN ELF quite distinctive from the various varieties of Asian English spoken in the region, all of which are necessarily characterized by the use of lexis to describe local phenomena and cultural values. The reason for this is not hard to explain, however. As a lingua franca is, above all, intended for cross-linguistic communication, it is only natural that speakers would try to avoid the use of lexical items which they feel other participants in the interaction might not understand. In terms of the identity-communication continuum (Kirkpatrick 2007a), this ASEAN ELF can be placed at the communication end of the continuum, while new varieties of English occupy the identity end of the continuum. This notion is revisited in Chapter 6.

In the next chapter the focus turns to grammatical, discoursal and pragmatic features.

5

Grammar, discourse and pragmatics

In this chapter a selection of syntactic and discourse features and pragmatic norms is illustrated. The first part of the chapter will provide some examples of grammatical variation in the dialects of British English. In this way, the reader can see how common and wide-ranging grammatical variation is within a traditional variety of English. Examples of grammatical variation in new varieties of English will also be illustrated, as this will help demonstrate that the type of variation and non-standard forms that are emerging in Asian varieties of English and in the use of English as a lingua franca are not particularly surprising. Rather, they represent natural language development and a consideration of the possible causes of these developments will be given. Examples of distinctive grammatical features identified in the SEAMEO and ASEAN ELF data will then be provided and discussed.

The second part of the chapter will consider and illustrate examples of discourse conventions and pragmatic norms common to Asian cultures. Their actual or potential realization in Asian varieties of English and/or ASEAN ELF will then be discussed.

Variation in British English

Crystal (2004) provides an informative and detailed account of historical variation in British English. One series of changes which is of particular significance to this study is that the inflectional system of English has gradually become less complex over time. For example, a complex system of declension on nouns has all but disappeared. The declension of the masculine noun from Old English (450–1150) '*stan*' (stone) showed inflections for case and number (Blake 1999: 65).

Case	Singular	Plural
Nominative	stan	stanas
Accusative	stan	stanas
Genitive	stanes	stana
Dative	stane	stanum

With the exception of the 'whom' accusative and the '-en' plurals in words like 'oxen' and brethren', standard British English retains only the plural marker '-s' (stones) and a possessive marker (stone's/stones'), although even the possessive marker is being used less frequently, especially with inanimate nouns.

Standard English has also seen the simplification and regularization of verbal morphology. Regularization traditionally takes place over a significant period of time, but changes due to these factors may be taking place more quickly in new varieties of English. In Old English (OE), as today, past tense was marked in one of two ways. One way was to change the internal vowel. Verbs which do this are known as strong verbs. The second way was to add a suffix. Such verbs are known as weak verbs. Examples of strong forms were:

> Findan – fand (find/found)
> beran – baer (bear/bore)
> sprecan – spraec (speak/spoke) (Blake 1996: 67–68)

Examples of the weak forms include:

> Endian – endode – endod (end/ended/ended)
> cysson – cyssede (kiss/kissed)
> cepan – cepte – ceped (keep/kept/kept) (Blake 1996: 69)

Gradually there has been a change as weak forms have become increasingly common and replaced the strong forms, while the system has also become simpler. For example, the past tense of today's 'help' had, in Old English, both a singular form 'healp', a plural form 'hulpon', and the past participle was realized by yet a third form 'holpen'. These three forms have been simplified and regularized into the single form 'helped' (Chambers 2009: 20). A similar motivation has seen the original past tense form of 'work', 'wrought', which still exists in its original meaning as 'worked' in 'wrought iron', being replaced by 'worked'. Today, nearly all new verbs take '-ed' as their past tense marker (Burchfield 1985: 43). Lieberman and his colleagues (2007) have even developed an algorithm which they claim can predict which strong form will be the next to regularize and become a weak form. 'Irregular verbs regularize at a rate that is inversely proportional to the square root of their usage frequency'

(2007: 714). In other words, the less frequent the use of the verb, the more likely it is to regularize. Their prediction is that the next verb to regularize will be 'wed', so that 'wedded' will replace 'wed'. 'Now is your last chance to be a newly wed. The married couples of the future can only hope for wedded bliss' (2007: 715).

Regularization and simplification can also account for some of the variation which exists between the past tense systems of non-standard dialects and standard English. Chambers (2009: 19) has suggested that the principle 'make past tense and past participle the same' reduces the number of irregular forms and, as irregular forms have to be memorized, the move to regularization reduces cognitive load. Thus reducing cognitive load is one possible explanation of regularization. Examples from non-standard dialects of the past participle form being the same as the preterit form are (Britain 2007: 89):

I draw   I drawed   I've drawed
I do   I done   I've done

Strong standard verb forms may be realized as weak forms in the non-standard:

I grow   I growed   I've growed

The same move towards simplification and regularization can be seen in the marking of the present tense in standard English. Today, only the third person singular form is marked, as in 'he works'. No other marking is needed for person or number. Traditionally, present tense in standard English was marked as follows (King 1997: 176):

First person singular: zero
Second person singular: -e(st)
Third person singular: -(th)
Plural: zero, or -(e)n

However, as with past-tense markings, non-standard dialects of British English display variation in the marking of the present tense (as well as across other grammatical features). The dialects of England vary in respect to how and whether they mark present tense verbs (Britain 2007: 86). And while '-s' represents the standard form of the third person singular, there is considerable variation in its use in British dialects (Ihalainen 1994: 228), as many dialects preserve older uses. One famous example is the so-called northern subject rule (McCafferty 2003), where present tense '-s' is used on verbs when their subjects are plural nouns and plural pronouns. Verbs adjacent to plural pronouns, on the other hand, receive no marking. Thus the following sentence is grammatical, following this northern subject rule:

> Cooks washes the potatoes and then they peel and boils them

Present tense marking for plural nouns is also seen in the English of the Southern United States, so that 'folks sings' is a grammatical formulation in this variety (Bailey 1997: 259–60). Note also the use of variable '-s' marking in the following example of African-American Vernacular English (Cukor-Avila 2003: 98). The instances of '-s' usage and non-use are bolded. There is also an instance of 'zero BE' here, in 'She a real young girl'.

> What's her, what's her name that coo**ks** them? She a real young girl. She bri**ng** 'em in every mornin'. An' they, an they sel**ls** 'em, an' they sel**ls** 'em for that girl there in that store.

In the dialect spoken in East Anglia in the Southeast of England, present tense verbs were not marked at all. Trudgill (2002) explains this through the large number of non-native migrants who moved to Norwich causing the need for the use of a lingua franca for communication between them and the locals. There is evidence, however, of some speakers now beginning to mark the third person singular with '-s' in this dialectal variety (Britain 2007: 87).

Other types of linguistic variation in non-standard dialects of British English include the examples below, which, unless otherwise indicated, are taken from Britain (2007: 75–104).

The double comparison (i.e., the comparison being marked by the use of both the inflectional ending and the analytic marker) is common in a number of varieties:

> it's a lot more easier than it used to be
> the most wonderfulest trip I've ever been on

The tendency to use 'less' instead of standard 'fewer' with countable nouns is also common. The examples below comes from an Australian speaker.

> The chief is saying that we have to run on less resources than what we have before. (Kirkpatrick 2007a: 75)

Multiple negation is extremely common, as is regional variation in the use of negated forms:

> they canna walk any further
> he diven't do it

There are a wide range of non-standard prepositional uses:

> I'm going *up* my friend's house
> My dad needs to go _ the opticians

The announcer on the Oxford to Banbury train advises: 'We will shortly be arriving *into* Banbury. Banbury is our next station stop.'

Finally, the invariant tag question, 'innit?' is becoming increasingly common.

These examples of non-standard forms represent only a small fraction of the non-standard forms that exist. Britain (2007: 78) suggests the grammatical features listed below represent a core of non-standard features which are common across many dialects of British English:

'Them' as demonstrative ('fetch me them eggs from the cupboard' — and notice also the non-standard use of 'fetch')

Absence of plural marking on measurement nouns ('that's three mile away from here')

'Never' as past tense negator ('I never did')

'There's'/'there was' with notional plural subjects. (A related example comes from the recent BBC documentary about the destruction of the city of Carthage by Rome. The historian Richard Miles says, 'I tell you who was busy. That was the undertakers.')

Present participle using preterit rather than continuous form ('I'm sat at a desk all day and I don't even have a window')

Adverbs without '-ly'. This is also seen in the irregular form, as in 'he does not play as good as before'. (Kirkpatrick 2007a: 74)

The use of 'ain't' and 'in't'

Non-standard uses of 'was'

These examples all serve to show that variation and the use of non-standard forms is endemic in varieties of British English. Below, examples will be given of comparable variation in new varieties of English.

Variation in new varieties of English

In a study of forty-six non-standard varieties of English from different parts of the world, Kortmann et al. (2004–07) noted that the following grammatical features were frequently realized as non-standard forms:

Pronouns, noun phrases, verb phrases (tense and aspect, modal verbs, verbal morphology), adverbs, negation, agreement, relativisation, complementation, discourse organisation and word order.

For example, half of the forty-six new varieties they surveyed frequently did not mark the third person '-s'. In a study of English as a lingua franca being used by Europeans with a wide range of different linguistic backgrounds, Breiteneder (2009) found that ten of the twenty-five speakers used zero marking for the third person singular at least once, but that all these speakers also used the '-s' marking on certain occasions. Through studying the context in which marking did occur, she pointed out that it is often retained in set phrases such as 'this means' and 'it depends', but that it is often not marked when the noun is grammatically singular but semantically plural, as with 'community' and 'minority'. Whether to treat these nouns as grammatically singular or plural has been the subject of long-standing debate among grammarians and English teachers. Breiteneder also makes the interesting observation that, as English is a non-pro-drop language and therefore requires a subject in subject position, the use of '-s' to mark the third person singular is redundant. This would suggest that those new varieties of English which developed in contact with pro-drop languages would have more need of marking the third person singular, especially if they do not require explicit subjects. As many of the speakers in the ASEAN ELF and SEAMEO data speak L1s which are pro-drop (Chinese and Malay, for example), we might therefore expect regular and consistent marking of this '-s'. However, as we shall see, this turns out not to be the case, even though the use of non-marked forms is not prevalent.

Mesthrie and Bhatt (2008), using data from sub-Saharan African, Amerindian and Irish Englishes as well as from the Englishes of South and Southeast Asia, identified a range of grammatical features which commonly occurred in these Englishes, but were not found in standard English.

The possible causes of non-standard forms and their apparent frequency of occurrence in many varieties of English are questions which are the centre of significant recent research. Mesthrie and Bhatt drew a distinction between the new varieties of Englishes which they classified as 'deleters' — with Singaporean English the best example of such a variety — and those that they classified as 'preservers' — with Black South African English as the best example (2008: 90–92). As the terms suggest, 'deleters' describes those varieties whose speakers commonly leave out grammatical elements, and 'preservers' describes those that 'disfavour the deletion of elements' (2008: 92). Their explanation for the 'deleter' — 'preserver' dichotomy is that it is 'usually dependent on the characteristic syntax of the substrate languages' (2008: 90), and that those varieties of English with Chinese substrates — such as Singaporean English — are the most prone to favouring the deletion of grammatical elements. However, the examples Mesthrie and Bhatt give to illustrate features of the 'preservers' suggest that these add rather than preserve features, and then only in specific contexts. For example, there are examples of the addition of the 'to' where the bare infinitive would be expected in standard English along with a number of examples of pronoun copying. This is common in Asian varieties of English. Mesthrie's and Bhatt's examples, all of which are taken from Black South African English, are (the 'preserved' items are italicized):

> Come what may *come*
> He made me *to* do it
> The fact has made me *to* conclude
> As you know *that* I am from the Ciskei
> My standard time, I have enjoyed *it* very much
> The man who I saw *him* was wearing a big hat
> As I made *it* clear before, I am going to talk about solutions not problems
> As *it* is the case elsewhere in Africa, much can still be done for children.
>
> (2008: 91)

The occurrence of so many comparable non-standard grammatical features across so many varieties of English has led some scholars to suggest that a set of vernacular universals exist. Chambers (2004: 129) has proposed the following candidates for Vernacular Universals:

> (ng) or alveolar substitution in final unstressed 'ing' (walkin')
>
> (CC) or morpheme final cc simplification (pos'office)
>
> Final obstruent devoicing (hundred — hundret; cupboard — cubbert)
>
> Conjugation regularization or leveling of irregular verb forms (yesterday John seen the eclipse; Mary heared the good news)
>
> Default singulars or subject-verb nonconcord (they was the last ones)
>
> Multiple negation of negative concord (he didn't see nothing)
>
> Copular absence or deletion (she smart; we going as soon as possible)

In calling these Vernacular Universals, Chambers is arguing that they exist in all vernacular varieties of English (and that they have their counterparts in other languages). This claim has been disputed. For example, Szmrecsanyi and Kortmann argue that the morphosyntactic features found in the survey of the forty-six varieties of English referred to above may be caused for different reasons in different languages (2009). They argue that variables such as the typology of the language and the geographical area in which the language is, and the influence of other languages may all play a part in the development of specific grammatical features. The relationship between Vernacular Universals and language contacts and the extent that these can be distinguished are key questions in contact linguistics (Filppula, Klemola and Paulasto 2009b: 8).

Mufwene (2001, 2009) has argued that all Englishes develop through the same processes, with the level of contact being a matter of degree. Thomason advises that a dichotomy between Vernacular Universals and contact-induced change should not be drawn because 'many linguistic changes involve both kinds of process — that is, various processes of contact-induced change and also universal tendencies of various kinds' (2009: 349).

More localized influences also need to be considered. Mesthrie and Bhatt acknowledge the importance of text type in this context and cite Sand's research into article usage, using the ICE corpora of Indian, Jamaican, Kenyan and Singaporean Englishes (2004). She showed that informational writing contained the most use of articles, while informal colloquial speech the least. Sand concludes, '[i]n all varieties, differences across text types are observable and genre differences within one variety are practically always more pronounced than overall variation across varieties' (2004: 294–5). This is a salutary lesson not to draw overall conclusions about the linguistic features of specific varieties of English based on data of single text types.

As Mesthrie and Bhatt themselves point out (2008: 39), a problem with the analysis and description of new varieties of English is that we often do not know enough about the speakers' linguistic and educational backgrounds, nor about the relative frequency grammatical items may appear either in the speech or writing of individuals or within the variety as a whole. Whether the data is collected from informal basilectal speech, or more formal acrolectal speech and/or written genres is likely to be significant in determining usage. Each of the international corpora of English (ICE, described in Chapter 4) comprises one million words taken from a variety of spoken and written texts. The SEAMEO and ASEAN ELF corpora are much smaller and comprise only spoken data in formal and semi-formal settings.

However, we need very large corpora before we can make firm judgements about the status and use of new and distinctive linguistic features. As Britain (2007: 76) has cautioned, we do not know answers to questions like:

> Who uses the non-standard form to whom and is there social stratification in its use?
> Where is the non-standard form used?
> What are the social, geographical and linguistic contexts in which the non-standard form is used?

We thus clearly remain some way from being able to answer the questions posed by Bamgbose more than a decade ago (1998: 13) in determining whether an innovation is a norm. These were:

> How many people use it?
> How widely is it used?
> Who are the people who use it?
> Where is the use sanctioned?
> Is the use accepted?

To underline the number of non-standard forms shared by many different varieties of English, a list of shared syntactic features of *African* Englishes is presented below. This is taken from Schmied (1991: 58*ff*). Many of these have been referred to above and will also be seen as features of Asian Englishes and ASEAN ELF.

Common grammatical features of African Englishes

(i) Inflectional endings are not always added to the verb but general, regular and unmarked forms are used instead.
(ii) Complex tenses such as the past perfect and certain conditionals tend to be avoided.
(iii) The use of Vb+ing constructions is extended to all verbs resulting in examples such as 'I am having your book' and 'I was not liking the food in the hotel'.
(iv) Phrasal and prepositional verbs are used differently. For example, 'I will pick you at 8'o clock tonight' (= 'I will pick you up at 8 o'clock tonight').
(v) Verb complementation varies freely to give phrases such as 'Allow him go' and 'They made him to clean the whole yard'.
(vi) Noun phrases are not always marked for number and case, or are treated differently to give 'informations', 'a cattle', 'an advice'.
(vii) Relative pronouns (whom, whose) are avoided to give 'Adult education which its main purpose is to help adults …'.
(viii) The use of plural is overgeneralized (luggages, advices).
(ix) Articles and determiners are often omitted ('I am going to post office').
(x) Pronouns are not always distinguished by gender.
(xi) Adjectives may be used as adverbs to give 'I can obtain the food easy'.
(xii) Pronoun copying is common ('Many of the fish, they have different colours').
(xiii) Negative yes/no questions are confirmed by responding to the form of the question so that the answer to 'He isn't good?' becomes 'Yes (he isn't)'.

(xiv) There are invariant question tags, for example, 'Isn't it?' and 'You wanted to leave for Nairobi, not so?'.
(xv) The interrogative word order is retained in indirect speech to give 'I cannot tell you what is the matter'.
(xvi) There is freer word order, so 'In my family, we are many' becomes common.

As also reported earlier, eight non-standard features were also identified as potential features of European ELF in the VOICE corpus. (The roman numerals after each example below refer to Schmied's numbering where, it will be seen, many refer to the same features and others to comparable ones.)

(a) the non-marking of the third person singular with '-s' (i);
(b) interchangeability of the relative pronouns, 'who' and 'which' (vii);
(c) flexible use of definite and indefinite articles (ix);
(d) extended use of 'general' or common verbs;
(e) treating uncountable nouns as plural (vi, viii);
(f) use of a uniform question tag (xiv);
(g) use of demonstrative 'this' with both singular and plural nouns; and
(h) use of prepositions in different contexts (iv).

Variation is common across a wide range of varieties of English. For a number of possible reasons, a large number of similar non-standard forms occur across a wide range of varieties. A wide-ranging list is provided by Hickey (2004: 586–620). I now turn to giving examples of a selection of non-standard grammatical features from the ASEAN ELF and SEAMEO data, while also providing comparable examples from relevant varieties of Asian English.

Non-standard features of ASEAN ELF

Articles

Distinctive article use is commonly found in Asian varieties of English. Bautista (2000: 151) identifies two usages which have become standard in educated Filipino English. These are 'the use of *majority* without an article and the use of *research* with an indefinite article'. Indeed the terms 'a research' and 'some researches' are both common across many varieties of Asian English, so it appears to be being classified as a countable noun. McArthur (2002) shows that articles are used less frequently in colloquial Singapore English (you have pen or not?), and Gupta (1988: 42) demonstrates that this also is evident in written texts of Singaporean English, 'mortality rate is high'. Mesthrie and Bhatt also provide examples from Singaporean English (2008: 49–50). However, as we noted above, Sand (2004) in a comparative study of Indian, Kenyan and Singaporean English, has observed a continuum whereby articles are used less in informal spoken contexts but more often in formal written contexts. Mesthrie and Bhatt also describe article usage in Irish English and cite Filppula's 1995 study in which he identifies seventeen functions of the definite article 'the'. They conclude that 'there appear to be two different classes of New Englishes in respect to article usage (2008: 52) with some, such as Irish and Other Celtic Englishes, using them more frequently and those that use them less frequently. It would also appear, however, that the great majority of varieties of new Englishes use articles less frequently than standard English. Examples of this are also found in the SEAMEO data where all the speakers are highly educated senior representatives of their respective countries' delegations. These examples are all of the non-use of articles, indicated by an underscore, _. The L1s and/or nationalities of the speakers are provided in brackets.

> A1: I know when we touch _ money issue it can be very controversial ... (Indonesian)
> A2: Each centre can send _ representative to be ... (Thai)
> A3: I just took it from _ document (Vietnamese)
> A4: We haven't addressed seriously _ on-line database (Indonesian)

Examples of non-standard article use from the ASEAN ELF data are surprisingly rare. Some can be attributed to a Laotian speaker whose English proficiency is not as high as the majority of the participants. Here, the non-standard forms are caused by the non-use of an article or by the use of a definite article rather than an indefinite one. Two examples are:

> A5: In my province lack of the teacher who —
> A6: We have the big class with sixty students

It should also be said that identifying non-standard forms of article use is difficult, not least because it is so often associated with the treatment of nouns as count or non-count nouns. And, as we have seen and as will be shown in the following discussion, many varieties of English treat standard English non-count nouns as countable and vice versa. Examples of these and non-standard forms of number are therefore provided next.

Number

Considerable variation in the marking or non-marking of plurals is found in all varieties of English, again including traditional varieties of English. This is also realized in the plural marking of uncountable nouns on the one hand and the non-marking of plural countable nouns on the other. It is worth noting that membership of countable and uncountable noun classes is dynamic in standard British English. For example, 'information', a noun routinely pluralized in many new varieties of English, is listed as having a history as a countable noun in the *Shorter Oxford English Dictionary* (1973).

> the action of informing, also with an and pl. An instruction. 1760
>
> that of which one is apprised or told; intelligence, news. Also with an and pl. 1527

The pluralization of standard countable nouns (*informations, luggages, advices*) is, not surprisingly, well documented in many varieties of English. And all of the four examples of non-standard use of articles above would become 'standard' with the pluralization of the relevant noun phrases (*money issues, representatives, documents and on-line databases*). Here are further examples on the non-standard marking of number from the SEAMEO data:

> N1: to strengthen inter-centre collaboration among the centre (Thai)
> N2: they have very good experience in establishing partnership (Thai)
> N3: to pay our regret (Indonesian)
> N4: I just want to comment on some of the question ... (Malay)
> N5: one three time or four time a years (Filipino)
> N6: in the next few slide (Vietnamese)
> N7: some strength and some weaknesses (Vietnamese)

These are examples of the use of a singular form when standard English would expect the plural. The non-marking here may be due to the phonological environment as marking these plurals would create consonant clusters. This simply serves to underline how careful we must be before assigning definite causes to specific usages. Example (N5) is interesting as 'time' is used twice (with no '-s' plural marking) while 'year' receives the '-s' plural marker. This could be explained, however, by a simple slip of the tongue in this context.

This addition of the '-s' marker occurs in other contexts that appear to have little to do with number, as these examples from the ASEAN ELF data attest:

> FCambod: I also arrived earliers than the exact time as the one that's pick me up (ehm) said but luckily I met him (laugh)

The same speaker also says:

> there are lots ofs kinds of fruits
> one days
> I will go next years

As these examples all come from the same speaker, a Cambodian, and, as her own level of English proficiency is also noticeably lower than the great majority of the other participants, it is tempting to argue that these uses are signs of a learner of English, rather than being systematic uses in a developing variety of Cambodian English. Further examples of this speaker's use of non-standard forms are provided later.

Verb forms

Table 5.1 below shows the overall uses of verb forms in the ASEAN ELF data along with the number of standard forms (SF) and non-standard forms (NSF).

Table 5.1 Verb forms ASEAN ELF

Verb form type	SFs	NSFs	Total
Present simple	1050	59	1109
Past simple	288	33	321
Present passive	43	4	47
Present perfect	40	4	44
Present continuous	23	3	26
Past passive	14	2	16
Present perfect continuous	9	1	10
Present perfect passive	4		4
Infinitive passive	3	1	4
Past continuous	2	1	3
Past perfect	3		3
Present continuous passive	1		1

The present simple verb form is by far the most commonly used verb form followed by the past simple form. It should be stressed that the verb form may not necessarily accord with the standard functions of the form. For example, as will be seen below, the present simple verb form is sometimes used to refer to past time, especially when the time is easily recoverable from the context, often through the use of a time adverbial. This use is also seen in standard English, with the historic present. The

108 English as a Lingua Franca in ASEAN

table also shows that the use of certain verb forms is relatively uncommon, as are non-standard forms. This supports Meierkord's findings in her study of the use of English as a lingua franca among speakers from many different countries and from many different linguistic backgrounds. Her data comprised twenty-two hours of informal spoken data, primarily of students from both outer and expanding circle countries who were studying in British universities. She analysed the data for syntactic variation and classified the syntax of the speakers as 'regular' (i.e., following native speaker norms), 'marked' (i.e., following nativized norms) or 'doubtful' (deviating from both native and nativized norms) (2004: 118). She found that 94% of the utterances of the outer circle speakers were regular and was surprised by this, as 'it contradicts the assumption that speakers would carry the characteristics of their nativised varieties into the English lingua franca interactions' (2004: 119). She also found that 95% of the expanding circle speakers' utterances were regular, but was not surprised by this, as they had been taught either British or American English. These findings did not take into account the utterances of less competent speakers. Among them, 22% 'diverged grammatically from British English or American English' (and presumably nativized norms also) (2004: 119). The difficulty in distinguishing between a competent speaker and a learner was considered earlier. The participants in the ASEAN ELF were all qualified and experienced English teachers with government scholarships studying a professional development course at the Regional Language Centre in Singapore. While the majority were therefore highly proficient speakers, a number of participants contributed more of the non-standard forms than the others. These are described below.

The only participants whose use of non-standard forms constitute more than 5% of their output are one of the Indonesians, both Cambodians and both Laotians with both Laotians contributing the highest use. Examples of the use of these NSFs are provided below. The NSFs are underlined (cf. Kirkpatrick 2007a, 2008).

A Laotian speaker

   FLao: last NAI (night) <u>we went there by walking</u>
   FSin: eh huh
   FLao: I enjoy walking [yeah
   FSin: you] mean all the way from [here
   FMyan: yes yes
   FLao: yeah]
   FSin: oh ok
   FLao: <u>some of my friend</u> hurt <u>his feet</u>
   FSin: oh ok
   FLao: (laugh) <u>he can't</u> {M: yes} <u>walk</u> and <u>he is just stand and sit</u>

FLao's use of NSFs in this extract include an awkward paraphrase of 'we walked there', the use of 'some of my friend' to mean 'one of my friends' and 'he can't walk and he is just stand and sit' where a present form 'can't' is used instead of 'couldn't' and present 'be' + bare imperative is used for the past tense form 'stood and sat'. Of course, a proficient speaker might have used the narrative present here to say something like 'and he can't walk so he just stands there and sits', but this is an unlikely option in this context. In the next example, the same speaker (FLao) explains that she is on her first overseas trip.

> FLao: er for me er I just follow her (laugh) because I (laugh) don't know anything <u>it's my first time to er go in</u> on another country
> FSin: oh ok so what so [what was your
> FLao: <u>it's hardly] for me to er doing</u> everything
> FSin: what was your first impression?
> FLao: yeah
> FSin: when you came to Singapore
> FLao: <u>I can't get or new meaning? from</u> Singapore yet

Here, there is the slightly awkward phrasing of 'it's my first time to go in on another country' and the use of 'it's hardly for me to er doing anything' where she combines the infinitive 'to' with the gerund form 'doing'. What is interesting in these exchanges is that, despite a frequent use of non-standard forms, the other participants appear to have no trouble in understanding the Lao speaker. This may be because they are all language teachers and are used to deciphering non-standard forms, but it may also be the overriding wish to communicate in lingua franca communication which is at work. It should be noted, however, that the Laotian herself does not understand at one stage here, as she clearly asks for clarification of the Singaporean's question (one that asks for her first impressions of Singapore). I shall return to this theme in the next chapter which focuses on communicative strategies.

A Cambodian speaker

This is the speaker referred to above who tends to use an 'epenthetic' /s/ in a variety of contexts. Her use of NSFs are underlined:

> I will go next <u>years I am</u> glad to be there ...
> how long have you <u>waits</u> for them?
> so we should <u>makes</u> any plan ...
> the one <u>that's pick</u> me up said ...

In the first excerpt, in addition to the 'epenthetic' /s/ on 'year', she also uses a present form 'am' when 'I'll be' would be standard. The /s/ in the second and third excerpts look like a learner's overgeneralizations. It is hard to be sure what the /s/ after 'that' and before 'pick' is doing. These excerpts are presented in context in the example below. The non-standard verb forms used by the Indonesian speaker (FInd) are underlined.

An Indonesian Speaker

FInd: I waited] for the official who <u>pick</u> (/pik/)me up ok er and then I tried to look for the official but because er er the plane you know landed so early so (ehm uh oh) the official hadn't come yet (C: ehm) yeah
FMyan: what a pity (laugh)   5
FInd: er er I I I had to stay in the airport and then did nothing (C: ehm) just <u>sit</u> and I <u>check</u> the placard of (ehm) RELC (M: ehm) ok and er and I couldn't see that's why I just <u>sit</u> and <u>take</u> a rest ... what about you what time
FCam: how long have you waits for them   10
FInd: just an hour
FCam: an hours (I: an hour) oh oh
FInd: ok I enjoyed the arcades you [know
FMyan: and] then how did you get here
FInd: er no the official   15
FMyan: came late
FInd: er that I met ok the er came late (laugh) yeah because the flight was earlier than the (eh) schedule (oh) so ok I just er waited for him an hour in the airport yeah er finally I met him (ehm) at one o' clock (laughter) that's it   20
FMyan: luckily you arrived [safely
FCam: I] also arrived earliers than the exact time (I: oh ok) as the one that's pick me up (ehm) said but luckily I met him (laugh)

What is interesting here is that, while the Indonesian does not mark the past tense form in some cases, she does in others. Some of the non-marking has a phonological explanation. For example, no speaker of any variety would sound the final /t/ of the past tense form /pikt/ in the context 'I waited for the official who picked me up', as the /t/ is dropped, being followed by a word which begins with a consonant. However, in lines 7–8, it becomes a serial non-marker of the past tense with her use of 'sit', 'check', 'sit' and 'take'. Yet she marks the past tense on all other occasions — 'waited', 'tried', 'landed', 'had', 'did', 'enjoyed', 'met', 'was', 'waited', 'met'. She also uses a standard past perfect form, 'hadn't come yet'. This simply underlines that the non-use of standard forms by certain speakers does not indicate that they do not know the standard from or that they never use it. On the contrary, in this short excerpt the Indonesian speaker uses the standard form far more often than she uses the non-standard form (10 versus 4, leaving /pik/ to one side). It is also important to note that the Cambodian also uses the standard form of the past simple. In lines 22–23, she says 'arrived' and 'met', in contrast to her use of non-standard 'how long have you waits' in line 10 and 'the one that's pick me' in line 23.

Many uses of these non-standard forms can be explained by non-marking of the verb form in situations where the time has already been established by the context. The verbal inflections simply are not necessary for making meaning in these contexts. Nevertheless, this appears random, as speakers use both marked and non-marked forms. Platt (1991) found that whether the action being referred to was habitual or a single action was significant in that speakers marked single actions more frequently than they marked habitual ones. Platt's findings were supportive of Bickerton (1981) who found that single events in the past were marked more often than habitual events by speakers of Guyanese and Hawaian Creoles. However, this does not seem to explain the choice of marked versus unmarked verbs in the examples above.

NSFs in the SEAMEO data

Verb forms

The Thai speaker's sounding of consonant clusters in the words 'tapped' and 'linked' were noted earlier in Chapter 4. Both these realizations are, however, part of non-standard forms in the following utterances where a past tense form is provided in place of a bare infinitive: 'you can tapped into the global theme' and 'later on we can linked ...' The Thai speaker again displays this preference for replacing the infinitive form with a past tense form when she says:

> the branding can be one of the issue that we probably have to identified ourselves

Here, there is also a non-standard form caused by number not being marked in the phrase, 'one of the issue' (and this is an example where the logic of numbering in English is opaque to say the least, as one could easily argue that this refers to one issue). She does, however, use the infinitive form where the standard form would require the past tense form, as in the following example of the passive infinitive:

> ... some of the information will need to be update.

But she also uses standard passive forms in these two utterances:

> some centres are exempted from tax
>
> this was agreed by the Centre Director

Other examples of non-standard passive forms include this one, in which an Indonesian speaker does not include 'is':

> Once this blueprint adopted

As a final example of a possible non-standard passive, a Malay speaker says:

> Thank you very much you give us the mandate which will be work on it.

There are a number of possible alternative standard forms here, one of which is 'which will be worked on'. Perhaps more plausible is an active version to give 'which we will work on'. It should also be noted that the Malay speaker would be classified as a 'preserver' in Mesthrie and Bhatt's dichotomy as 'it' is included. This would not be predicted by Mesthrie and Bhatt, as speakers of Malaysian English supposedly belong to the class of 'deleters'. This, however, could be explained by a possible third reading to give 'and we will work on it'.

The examples above all demonstrate how difficult it is to make reliable judgements about the linguistic causes of non-standard forms. They also demonstrate that speakers who use non-standard forms in one context may use standard forms in another.

Modality

Mesthrie and Bhatt report few examples of non-standard modal forms, other than the preference for 'would' over 'will' in some new varieties of English (2008: 64). While this preference for 'would' over 'will' is a characteristic of many varieties of Asian English, including Singapore and Malaysian, there are no instances of its use in the data. Indeed, there are very few examples of non-standard modal forms in either the SEAMEO or the ASEAN ELF data. The Cambodian speaker's use of 'should makes' is the only non-standard form. Indeed, the use of modals shows far less variation than it does in inner circle varieties of English, some of which allow multiple modals. For example, Bailey (1997: 260) reports 'we might can make it' in the speech of the American South, with Bernstein (2003: 117) proposing that the use of multiple modals being 'among the most salient features of southern grammar', the other two being the use of 'yall' and 'fixin' to'.

Inversion

Non-inversion in wh- main clauses is a common feature of new varieties of English. Mesthrie and Bhatt (2008: 80) record these two examples taken from Kachru (1992c: 360). The first is a speaker of Indian English, the second a speaker of Indian South African English.

> What you would like to read?
> What he'll say?

This non-inversion is well attested in many new varieties of English and is also seen in the use of interrogative word order in indirect speech. Indeed, one of Schmied's common features of African Englishes is that the interrogative word order is retained in indirect speech to give 'I cannot tell you what is the matter'. The SEAMEO data provides the following examples:

> I1: We didn't know what is it for? (Malay)
> I2: Now the third strategies is how we can ...? (Thai)
> I3: We support and then how we can collaborate with one another. (Indonesian)

Prepositions

All varieties of English use different prepositions in different contexts and some examples from British dialects were provided earlier. The 'correct' preposition can often be subject to relatively swift change even in the standard. For example, in my youth in the 1950s, I was constantly urged to use the preposition 'from' with the adjective 'different'. When I used 'different to' — which I did frequently, as this was common use too at the time — my mother would automatically correct me and say 'different from never different to'. I was therefore delighted when I first went to the United States to find that most people said 'different than'. There was also, I think, a class aspect to my mother's insistence on 'different from' as she also used to try and get to me to pronounce the words 'lamentable' and 'exquisite' with the stress on the first syllable, as this was considered the 'proper' way of pronouncing these words.

Given how common variation in preposition use is, it is surprising that there are very few non-standard (using standard British English as the reference) uses of prepositions in the ASEAN ELF data. One explanation may be that the participants were all English teachers and therefore themselves used to teaching the prepositions listed in their prescriptive textbooks. On the other hand, the participants at the SEAMEO meeting used a variety of prepositions in non-standard ways. Here are some examples, with the non-standard uses underlined:

> P1: and the second purpose is to seek <u>for</u> a discussion (Thai)
> P2: we tell <u>about</u> opportunities for each SEAMEO centres (Thai)
> P3: thanks <u>for</u> the World Bank who supports this programme (Indonesian)
> P4: I'm querying <u>about</u> the profitability issue right now (Indonesian)
> P5: Can I just add <u>on</u> to that (Singaporean)
> P6: … discuss <u>on</u> the branding (Malay)
> P7: … discuss <u>about</u> … (Malay)
> P8: Let's sleep <u>over</u> the issue of liberties because a lot of things are complex (Malay)
> P9: I can inform <u>to</u> you you need to make a research from now on to early next year (Indonesian)
> P10: I just want to know how you organize <u>about</u> membership fee (Brunei)
> P11: We can discuss <u>about</u> that (Indonesian)
> P12: We want to explore <u>about</u> the possibility of the (Indonesian)

Many speakers appear to have adopted 'about' as a general all-purpose preposition. Its frequent use with 'discuss' in new varieties of English is well documented, the usual explanation pointing to speakers making an analogy with 'talk about'. This could also explain 'tell about' in the second example above. The other uses of 'about' in the examples above could also all be deleted, as prepositions are not required in these contexts in standard English, to give 'querying the possibility', 'organize (the) membership fee', and 'explore the possibility'. Similarly the uses of 'on' with 'add on' and 'to' with 'inform to you' could be deleted. And while 'thanks for the World Bank' is non-standard, the same speaker uses 'Thanks to' later in the same utterance. As a final comment on these few examples, 'discuss about' and 'discuss on the branding' was produced by the same speaker.

In concluding the first part of this chapter, while non-standard forms exist in the ASEAN lingua franca data, generally speaking, there is relatively little syntactic variation and less that would be found in non-standard varieties of British English. In the ASEAN ELF data, for example, only 5% of the simple present and 1% of the simple past uses might be marked as incorrect by a pedantic English language teacher using standard British English as the reference. Most of the non-standard uses actually represent the way these speakers use tense in spoken interaction. Marking past is not necessary when the past is made clear by the context, for example. Similarly concord (and plurals) may remain unmarked. The simplification of syntax by not adding inflections where the time or meaning has already been established by the context is also a feature of new varieties of English (cf. Schmied 1991) and, as was discussed earlier, mirrors the way inflections have become simpler within traditional English itself (Blake 1996).

This type of non-standard use is common and is therefore not *necessarily* the sign of a learner of English, but can be part of the performance variety of expert users of English, especially of those whose first languages do not mark for tense. Recalling Thomason's advice (2009: 349) cited earlier, however, it is difficult to know whether this sort of non-marking can be attributed to universal tendencies or to contact-induced change, as the non-marking of verb forms in this way may also be part of the historical shift to syntactic regularization and simplification.

The use of non-standard forms of the type used by the Laotian and Cambodian speakers illustrated above, however, cannot be explained by either simplification or regularization and *may* signal that they are learners of English rather than proficient speakers of it.

The relative lack of the use of complex tense forms in the data needs to be noted. While more data from more contexts is needed, these findings support Mesthrie's research where he found complex tenses tend to be avoided in East African varieties of English (2004).

The pedagogical implications of these findings will be considered in Part III. In closing this part of the chapter and by way of signalling a move towards the discussion on discourse and pragmatic norms, I provide a harrowing example in the form of an excerpt from a sign written in English and displayed at the Choeng Ek extermination camp outside Phnom Penh in Cambodia. This shows how the successful transmission of a message is not dependent upon standard grammar.

> The extermination camp Choeng Ek is about 15 km from Phnom Penh in the South-West. It is implicated in the organization of the biggest security centre of Kampuchea Democratic in Pol Pot regime under the name S21. S21 has its headquarter at Tuol Sleng prison. All the victims (peasants, working, intellectuals, children) detained and tortured during interrogating at Tul Sleng were later sent to Choeng Ek for liquidation.

This was recorded by Anderson (1999: 59–60). She then describes the sign:

> The English translation, in capital letters which diminish in size in order to fit it all in, occupies the lower half with the original in Khmer script above it. In a further effort to accommodate the English words in the space available the sign-writer was evidently forced to split on to two lines the word 'peasant'. So now the sentence reads 'ALL THE VICTIMS, PEAS, ANTS, WORKING, INTELLECTUALS'. To me these adaptations add greatly to its pathos.

I now turn to considering a selection of discourse and pragmatic features.

Discourse features and pragmatic norms

Word order plays an important role in discourse, as its use identifies what is salient or marked in certain contexts. For example, what is sometimes called left-dislocation, is marked in standard English and draws attention to the item that is placed at the beginning of the utterance. Thus, the utterance 'Children, don't you love 'em' moves children to the left where it receives emphasis as the topic. This is therefore sometimes called topicalization. While this topic-comment structure is marked in standard English, it is the unmarked word order pattern in many languages. It is, for example, common in Chinese (Li and Thompson 1976) and other Asian languages, so we might expect topic-comment patterns to be common in the data. Examples of topicalization from the SEAMEO data include:

> T1: those issues, we can elaborate more ... (Indonesian)
> T2: some centres, we exempt of income tax (Thai)
> T3: talking about the product of our brand, this is one of the products of our brand (Brunei)

In the following discussion of discourse and pragmatic norms, most of the examples are taken from Asian languages rather than from the data itself. One reason for this is that the data did not elicit a large enough sample of specific discourse features and pragmatic norms. However, as the possible transfer of these from Asian languages into new varieties of English and English as a lingua franca is of great potential significance for intercultural communication, a description of selected discourse features and pragmatic norms from Asian languages is provided.

The potential transfer of these features from Asian languages into varieties of English and ELF is of significance because the transfer of these features is likely to be subconscious. As a result, listeners may not realize that the discourse features and pragmatic norms are derived from Asian cultures and misinterpret them as marked uses of discourse features and pragmatic norms of Anglo varieties of English. The examples below will help to clarify this point.

The transfer of unmarked and marked compound clause sequencing patterns from Chinese (and other Asian languages including Malay and Japanese) into local varieties of English, might cause problems and misunderstanding as the unmarked order in Chinese is the marked order in English. That is to say, the unmarked normal clause sequence in English compound sentences is main clause — subordinate clause (Quirk, Greenbaum, Leech and Svartvik 1985: 1070) so that 'The match was postponed because it was raining' is the unmarked clause order of this sentence. In Chinese, however, the unmarked clause order is precisely the opposite, so that 'Because it was raining, the match was postponed' is the normal clause order in Chinese. One reason for this is that Chinese follows natural or logical word order (Tai 1985) so that the effect normally precedes the result. This, in turn means that, traditionally at least, Chinese uses conjunctions far less than English, as the argument presented in the clauses follows a natural order and is clear as it stands without the need for explicit conjunctions to explain the relationship between the two clauses. This in turn means that, traditionally, Chinese has a preference for parataxis in clause relationships rather than the hypotaxis common in standard English. A natural Chinese translation of the sentence above would therefore be:

> Xia   yu,   bisai   gaiqi-le
> Down   rain, competition   postponed P

Note how a faithful translation of this into English will require switching the clause order of the Chinese paratactic clauses and adding a conjunction to explain the subordinate or hypotactic relationship between them.

> The match was postponed because it was raining.

Note also that Chinese is a pro-drop language which allows a null subject. Standard English requires a 'dummy' subject here, 'it'.

Another principle of sequencing in Chinese is that modifier precedes the modified (Kirkpatrick 1996). Chinese is a left-branching language, while standard English is right-branching. For example, in right-branching English, 'the man wearing the white scarf was arrested' or 'the man who was wearing the white scarf was arrested' conforms to the normal word order. In left-branching Chinese, however, the normal word order would be, however, 'the wearing the white scarf man [was] arrested'.

This modifier-modified principle extends to the level of discourse (Kirkpatrick 1991). It is also realized in request patterns where reasons and justifications for requests are normally made before the request itself is actually made. This is also referred to as the Chinese preference for inductive over deductive argument, a preference that is also seen in other Asian languages such as Indonesian (Rusdi 1999) and Japanese (Hinds 1983).

The letter on p. 118 is a translation of a Chinese letter of request which exemplifies these characteristics. It was written by a Chinese student from the north of China to the China Service of Radio Australia (see also Kirkpatrick 1991).

> Respected Radio Australia producers.
>
> I have been a loyal listener to Radio Australia's English teaching programmes and to 'Songs You Like' for several years. I consider both programmes to be extremely well produced.
>
> Let me describe myself a little: I am a middle school student, I am eighteen and my home is in —, a small border city. The cultural life really isn't too bad. Because I like studying English, I therefore follow those programmes closely. But because the Central Broadcasting Station's English programmes are rather abstruse, they are not really suitable for me and therefore I get all my practice in listening comprehension and dialogue from Radio Australia's English programmes. This practice has been of great benefit. As I progress, step by step through the course, I am keenly aware that not having the teaching materials presents several difficulties.
>
> Because of this, I have taken time to write this letter to you, in the hope that I can obtain a set of Radio Australia's English programme's teaching materials. Please let me know the cost of the materials.
>
> In addition, I hope to obtain a radio Australia calendar. Wishing Radio Australia's Mandarin programmes even more interest.
>
> (Listener's name and date)

In this letter the writer first respectfully addresses the reader and then engages in 'facework' to get the reader on her side. She then provides reasons for her request before finally making it at the end of the letter. The schema of this letter can therefore be represented in this way:

> Salutation
>
> Facework
>
> Reason(s) for request(s)
>
> Request(s)
>
> Sign Off

This schema contrasts strikingly with a preferred contemporary 'Anglo' rhetorical style that prefers to place the request towards the beginning and to soften it if thought necessary with internal modification (Blum-Kulka, House and Kasper 1989). This would give something like:

> Dear Radio Australia
>
> I'm sorry to bother you, but could you please send me some teaching materials. I really need them to help me learn English. If you could also send a calendar, that would be great.
>
> Many thanks.

Interestingly, the Chinese letter above almost perfectly follows the Ciceronian arrangement of argument and the one which is recommended in the Medieval European letter writing manuals of the twelfth and thirteenth centuries (Kirkpatrick 2007c):

> Salutation (Salutatio)
>
> Facework (Captatio Benevolentiae/Securing of Good Will)
>
> Reasons for Requests (Narratio/Background)
>
> Requests (Petitio)

This contemporary Chinese request schema is also common in Indonesian/Malay and Japanese and raises the question therefore, of whether it will become a preferred request schema in Asian varieties of English. This is an area of research much needed in both the study of varieties of English and English as a lingua franca. The issue is extremely complex, not least because of the dynamic and shifting nature of cultural norms heightened by increasing cross-cultural movements. We can draw a parallel between the linguistic features of new varieties of English being shaped by a mix of language contact-induced change and universalist tendencies, and the cultural features of new varieties of English being shaped by cultural contact-induced change and globalizing tendencies. As is always the case, however, the flow of cultural influences is multidirectional and its consequences hard to predict. For example, it seemed safe to predict that new Asian varieties of English would adopt a greeting which made some reference to food, as so many Asian languages use a food-related enquiry as a standard form of greeting along the lines of 'Have you eaten yet?' However, this has only happened in Singapore, while the common English greeting, 'Hello how are you', has been translated into Asian languages to become the default greeting. Hence, '*Ni hao?*' (How are you?) has replaced '*Ni chifan-le meiyou?*' (Have you eaten?) as the standard greeting in Modern Standard Chinese.

The use of terms of address is another area where Asian cultural values might be predicted to have an influence over Asian varieties of English. For example, all lecturers in universities in the English-speaking world will have come across a natural reluctance on the part of many international students to address their lecturers in an informal way, preferring to use their formal titles such as 'Teacher' or 'Professor', as this conforms to their own cultural norms. Even when these students know that it is culturally acceptable for them to address their lecturers by their first names, to actually do this themselves so violates their own cultural norms that they feel unable to do so. This reluctance or inability to adopt the host culture's norms because they violate one's own has been called 'pragmatic dissonance' by David Li (2002: 561). We would therefore expect new varieties of English to conform to local cultural norms in such cases of pragmatic dissonance. To a certain extent, this is confirmed. While students from some countries soon feel able to refer to lecturers by their first names, others prefer to adopt naming practices that reflect their own cultural values. Thus Muslim students will call their lecturers, not by their first names but preface the first name with a title. Not 'Andy' then, but Professor Andy. Japanese students prefer to use only the title 'Professor' or 'Teacher'.

A third area where we might expect local cultural values to influence local varieties of English is the giving and receiving of compliments. In many Asian cultures, compliments must be deflected or categorically rejected. They cannot be accepted with a graceful 'thank you'. Indeed, in Japan, compliments cause such consternation to the recipient, that it is considered polite not to compliment a person directly, but when talking to a third person. In Chinese, compliments are traditionally rejected. However, once again the changing nature of cultural norms is evident, as recent research has shown that Chinese now feel able to accept compliments in certain circumstances (Su 2008).

The extent to which local cultural values should be expressed in the local variety of English is the subject of a recent study into semantic and pragmatic conceptualizations of Persian culture in the English spoken by Persians (Sharifian 2010). The concept of *aberu* and *tarof* were just two of the Persian cultural values he considered. He defines them as follows:

Âberu in contemporary Persian captures conceptualisations of the social image and status of a person and/or their family, both nuclear and extended, and their associates and friends. This social image and face is tied to a large number of social norms in relation to financial status, behaviour, both linguistic and non-linguistic, and social relationships and networks. It is hard to find something that one does or has that would not have any implications for or impact on one's *âberu*.

Târof is a cultural schema that underlies a significant part of everyday social interactions in Persian. Its realisation in conversations may be in the form of 'ostensible' invitations, repeated rejection of offers, insisting on making offers, hesitation in making requests, giving frequent compliments, hesitation in making complaints, etc.

Sharifian argues that cultural conceptualizations of this type have to find expression in the local variety of English in order for the local variety to adequately reflect and represent the speaker's culture. This is also strongly argued by Wolf (2010) in the context of African Englishes where he says that the ability for local varieties of English to adopt local cultural conceptualizations means that these cultural values can be reflected in the local variety of English. There is, of course, a fundamental need for varieties of English to reflect their speakers' own cultural values. The extent to which this transfer of cultural values and pragmatic norms from the speaker's culture(s) into their respective varieties of English raises serious questions for cross-cultural communication.

Many Asian pragmatic norms centre around modesty. Discretion and respect for seniority — often determined by age and gender — are culturally valued and explicit criticism can be frowned upon. These cultural values lie behind the so-called ASEAN way, which relies on gentle behind-the-scene persuasion and consensus. This was given explicit form by a Singaporean delegate at the SEAMEO meeting. She said, 'they are just my thoughts with no attempt to criticise.'

Related to this are the rules for turn-taking. In a comparative study of turn-taking in Australian and Indonesian university seminars, Rusdi (1999) found that the Australian seminars were characterized by what appeared to be interruption and turn-stealing. In addition, hierarchy, gender or relative seniority appeared to play minor roles in determining whose turn it was to speak. In stark contrast, the Indonesian seminars were characterized by uninterrupted turns. Turn-taking was clearly determined by seniority and gender. In effect, the eldest male in the group always received the first invitation to speak. Other speakers would be identified by the moderator, whose choice would be influenced by their seniority and gender. Importantly for an insight into potential problems of cross-cultural communication, Rusdi also found that the Australians and Indonesians transferred their turn-taking rules and strategies into Indonesian and English respectively. That is to say, Indonesian students maintained their cultural rules for turn-taking when in English language environments, and this caused them great problems when attending seminars at Australian universities. They reported that they found these stressful and were unsure when they could make a contribution to the discussion. By the same token, Australian students who were studying Indonesian, transferred their turn-taking strategies to seminars conducted in Indonesian and some were thus considered rude and disrespectful.

This final section of the chapter has relied more on data from Asian languages and cultures than from the ASEAN data. However, the adoption of Asian pragmatic norms into Asian varieties of English and their use in lingua franca communication require a great deal of research, as the implications are possibly more significant for successful cross-cultural communication than an analysis of phonological and syntactic features alone. In part, this is because the transfer of pragmatic norms may be unremarked, and thus be interpreted by listeners as if the speaker were using the pragmatic norms of a different variety (their own) of English. This could have serious consequences in lingua franca communication. In Chapter 1, possible problems arising from different negotiating styles in ASEAN meetings were raised (Thambipillai 1992). The uniformity and mutual acceptance of the so-called ASEAN way, based on the two Malay concepts of *musyawarah* (dialogue) and *muafakat* (consensus) (Curley and Thomas 2007: 9), is likely to be challenged, given the recent signing of the formal ASEAN Charter. Research into the preferred pragmatic norms and negotiating styles of the ASEAN member states and their possible transfer into English as a lingua franca is thus of great importance.

The pedagogic implications of the linguistic features exemplified in this chapter will be considered in Chapter 7. In the next chapter, the communicative strategies adopted by the ASEAN speakers when engaged in lingua franca communication will be described and illustrated.

6
The communicative strategies of ASEAN ELF users[1]

The data upon which the findings in this chapter are primarily based come from the audio-recordings of six group discussions in which all ten ASEAN nations are represented. These are the same groups which were described in Chapter 4, but are repeated here for ease of reference and, because the individual speakers are referred to in slightly different ways, it is easier to refer to the speakers using these labels in the discussion of their communicative strategies. Naturally, some of the examples will be remembered from Chapters 4 and 5, but are here illustrating communicative strategies rather than linguistic features. Where lengthy, these are cross-referenced. For example, Extract 5 in this chapter is cross-referenced to [4: 47], meaning that Extract 5 below also occurred as Extract 47 in Chapter 4.

Each group comprised three or four people (see Table 6.1). The subjects were all English language teachers who had been selected to attend professional development courses in English language teaching conducted by staff at the Regional Language Centre (RELC) in Singapore. They were recorded in the RELC recording studio. Three groups were recorded in January 2004 and three in January 2005. The groups were asked to start their discussions by talking about the English language teaching situation in their country and were told they would be recorded for about half an hour. No group appeared to experience any hesitation or awkwardness, even though they had only known each other for two or three days. The letter and number in the brackets provided after each participant represents their reference in the data. Thus B1 refers to the Bruneian female in Group 1, while B4 refers to the Bruneian female in Group 4. Where relevant, the speaker's ethnicity and first language are also reported. Thus the Bruneian female in Group 1 (B1) is an ethnic Chinese who has a dialect of Chinese (Fuzhou in her case) as a mother tongue. Please also note that Burma is represented as 'Mn' and Malaysia as 'My'. The notation conventions are in Appendix 1.

Table 6.1 Composition of groups

Group	Composition
Group 1	Bruneian Female (Chinese) (B1); Filipina (F1); Thai Male (T1); Vietnamese Female (V1)
Group 2	Singaporean Female (Punjabi) (S2); Burmese Female (Mn2); Laotian Female (L2)
Group 3	Cambodian Male (C3); Indonesian Male (I3); Singaporean Female (Malay) (S3)
Group 4	Bruneian Female (B4); Malaysian Female (My4); Thai Female (T4); Vietnamese Female (V4)
Group 5	Indonesian Female (I5); Burmese Female (Mn5); Cambodian Male (C5)
Group 6	Malaysian Male (Chinese) (My6); Laotian Male (L6); Filipina (F6)

As detailed in the preceding two chapters of Part II, while speakers of ASEAN ELF share a range of non-standard forms, they also speak different varieties of English and, on occasion, their individual levels of proficiency in English may be lower than that of their peers. Given the different cultural, educational and linguistic backgrounds of these speakers, we would anticipate occasions where communication might become problematic, or even break down, and on such occasions for the speakers to adopt specific communicative strategies to try and repair the situation.

This chapter describes the communicative strategies adopted by these speakers and illustrates these from the data. These strategies are all deduced from the ASEAN ELF data. A major reason for this is that the SEAMEO meeting was more formal and it was conducted very much along the lines as described by Rusdi in his analysis of the Indonesian seminars (Rusdi 1999; see also Chapter 5). In the context of academic seminars in Indonesia Rusdi remarks,

> Each seminar session is opened by a moderator. In his/her opening remarks, the moderator greets the participants ... introduces the topic of the seminar, introduces members of the presentation team, sets the house rules for the activity and invites the presenter to give a presentation. After the presentation, the moderator summarises the main points of the presentation and calls for additional information from other presentation team members. The moderator then summarises the additional information and calls for questions from the audience. (Rusdi 1999: 71)

This represents an accurate description of the SEAMEO meeting. That is to say, turn-taking was directed by the chair and every person was told explicitly when it was their turn to speak. Turns were seldom interrupted. The chair of the meeting would also often summarize the main points of presentations. The overall layout of the room and seating arrangements were suited for this type of interaction. Thirty-seven representatives from the ASEAN centres were seated around an 'oblong' horseshoe and were grouped according to their respective centres. Observers and rapporteurs sat around an outer horseshoe. The director general (DG) sat at the head table with a deputy director general (DDG) to each side. The DG chaired the opening session and most of the others, although one of the two DDGs would occasionally take this role. In the opening session, he started by greeting the delegates in English, Malay (his own L1) and Thai (the language of the host country). This was the only time during the two days that a language other than English was used during the official proceedings. After the introduction, the DG invited each of the centre directors present to introduce themselves to the group. After the introductions, the DG introduced the house rules and urged delegates to keep to time saying 'keeping to your words is very crucial'. This was when he used the golfing metaphor referred to in Chapter 4, when pointing out how irritating it was for other members of a fourball if one of them turned up late for their tee time. He then introduced me and explained that I wished to record the meeting and asked them whether this would be acceptable. His request was greeted with complete silence (which I took to represent a certain lack of enthusiasm) but which he took as the silence of consent. Indeed, he explicitly announced to the participants that he would take their silence to mean consent.

This turn-taking model which comprised the DG, or one of his two deputies, taking the floor and then inviting reports or comments from specifically named delegates or centres was followed throughout the meeting. This meant that turns were never interrupted or stolen and that communicative strategies for turn-taking were not observable.

Generally speaking, the meeting passed without incident. There was one agenda item that did cause some discomfort, however, and this centred around the DG's wish that all the centres would use a new template when submitting their annual reports. This met with opposition for two reasons, namely the complexity of the form and because all centres, despite their diversity, were to use the same form. Centre delegates addressed the issue in turn, following the model described above (see Appendix 2 for a complete list of SEAMEO centres).

While it was apparent that the DG's proposal was extremely unpopular with the great majority of the delegates, no one expressed explicit criticism of it. Rather, they related how different the centres were from each other, but without adding something like 'and therefore for us all to have to complete the same form would be inappropriate'. Instead, delegates would conclude with a remark stressing that they were *not* criticizing the DG's proposals. Typical examples come from the final utterances of a Singaporean and an Indonesian speaker. These were from the Singaporean:

> They are just my thoughts, with no attempt to criticize.
>
> I just want to comment on some of the question with due respect to the Secretariat.

As such, the SEAMEO meeting was not a fruitful source for the study of communicative and spontaneous interactional strategies. Fortunately, the ASEAN ELF data provide a much richer source. However, in the same way that the speakers in the SEAMEO meeting were conscious not to cause criticism and ensure a smooth meeting, it is worth noting that the communicative strategies adopted by the ASEAN ELF speakers all seem to be aimed at ensuring collaborative communication among peers who see themselves as multilinguals and who have learned English as a 'second' language. In short, the strategies are aimed at ensuring communication and preserving the face of the participants. It is important to stress, therefore, that the communicative strategies illustrated here were adopted by people operating in a supportive atmosphere and with little crucial at stake. More data, especially of high-stakes interactions, is therefore needed.

In the analysis which follows, examples from the data are presented which show specific communicative strategies in action. These are italicized in the main text and presented in Table 6.2 (see p. 141), which forms the summary of the chapter. Where relevant, examples of the speakers' use of non-standard forms is also highlighted, especially when they illustrate issues raised in Chapter 5.

Having said that, the first example simply illustrates the successful communication that is characteristic of the data. In Extract 1, the participants share an understanding of the distinction between English as a second and English as a foreign language. The Laotian speaker's (L6) use of pronoun copying is highlighted (in bold). Also noteworthy is her non-use of the indefinite article as in 'English as foreign language' and 'only people from the city have opportunity to study'.

> (1)
>
> My6: I'm interested in the ... usage of English in your country how widely is English used?
> L6: oh ... in my country as you know we use and learn English as foreign language yeah
> My6: does this begin at the secondary school level?
> L6: no you know ehm only people from the city have opportunity to study English ... I mean the people who live far away from the city **they** don't have any opportunity to study English
> F6: do you do you mean English is not used as a second language it's a foreign language?
> L6: yeah it's a foreign language (F6: oh) some students **they** start learning English just only at the university (F6: ehm)

My6: I find that strange because in Malaysia well English is taught beginning at the primary school level (L6: ooh) it's taught as a second language (L6: I see) and ...

Lexical anticipation is one form of evidence that shows that the participants in a conversation are communicating successfully and are on the same wave length. This strategy of lexical anticipation is exemplified in Extract 2. First, B1 correctly anticipates the word 'income' and later, F1 returns the compliment, as it were, by correctly anticipating B1's use of 'better'. These are in bold. B1's pronunciation of 'these' as 'this' in line 14 is an example of a lack of distinction between short and long vowel sounds.

(2)

F1: and the parents are well educated whereas {T1:eh hm} those coming from the public er {B1: school} really come from lower er
B1: **income**
F1: **income families** {F+T1: ehm yeah} that's why er during our national exams [θɪs] children coming from the private schools they get higher scores than the ones who are {F+T ehm} in the government in the elementary {F+T1 ehm} school except for some science high schools {B1:ehm} and the University of the Philippines {B1: yes} system students [they get high grades
B1: for our high school] we get good results because we {F:ehm} we after standard six or primary six they primary school they go to a secondary {T1:correct} school so our school is a government school and we get students from private school {T: yes} and students from the government school F:eh hm so and ehm er these people who've who are who are from the government er the private school usually do better {T1:ehm} and they will continue doing
F1: **better**
B1: **better** until {T1: right} er ['O' levels {V1: yeah yeah or or high school {Fx2 +T: yeah} at the end of the high school year

In this example, there is also an instance of a speaker actually supplying the appropriate lexical item. In the opening line, BI provides 'school' and FI carries on with her turn. These strategies all indicate a high level of mutual understanding and co-operation. A related strategy that a participant can use to help out other participants is *lexical suggestion*. In Extract 3, B1 provides the word 'continuous' after the T1 speaker has said 'continuation continual'.

(3)

T1: right but actually {F:ehm} we can share some some experiences right {F: ehm} because teaching grammar is a continuation con[tinual process
B1: continuous process]
T1: right

It is hard to know whether the Thai speaker felt he was being corrected here or whether he was happy to accept the more appropriate word, although his use of 'right' suggests he was happy enough. A further instance of this strategy being used occurs in Extract 4, where S3 offers the more appropriate or sophisticated word 'benefits' for C3's more prosaic 'good things'. That he immediately adopts this suggestion is evidence that he welcomes it. Certainly, there is no clue in the intonation or tone of his voice to suggest that he is irritated by S3's interruption. I would suggest that, as all participants are multilingual English users, they are comfortable with helping strategies of this type and their use represents the 'solidarity of non-native ELF speakers' (House 2006: 94). If a native speaker were one of the participants and were to offer suggestions in this way, these might be viewed as corrections of errors, and thus make the other participants feel less comfortable.

(4)

C3: so Cambodian people rely and I will I will tell Cambodians I will tell them about the advantage advantages of English and ehm (...) er motivate them to learn English because I know the the **the good things** of English

S3: **the benefits**

C3: yeah the **benefit** you want to travel the world?

Extract 5 provides an example of the strategy of *lexical correction* rather than anticipation or suggestion. Here S3 actually provides the correct word 'stay', but her primary motive is to ensure successful communication rather than to correct the speaker, as she realizes that C3 has not understood I3's question and that the cause of the misunderstanding is I1's incorrect use of the word 'sit'. In this she is successful, as S3's provision of 'stay' leads C3 to understand I3's question. Again, there is no evidence of irritation and unease on the part of I3 here.

(5) [cf. 4: 47]

I3: so how long do do they have to **sit** in the junior high school and senior high school?

C3: ehm I've been teaching there for two years after my graduation er from er

I1: no I mean er er how many years do students have to **sit {S3: stay} to stay** in the junior high school {C3: ehm} and the senior high school?

C3: er in in in Cambodia er junior high school starts from grade seven

Extract 6 shows the lengths that participants will go to in order to work together to ensure they understand what is being said and represents a sort of *'don't give up' strategy*. This excerpt ends with shouts of delight when they realize they have 'solved' the problem and understood that the type of food being described by V4 is familiar to all of them, but by another name. Please note that it is sometimes difficult to distinguish between the Bruneian and Malay speakers in this extract, and this explains why both have occasionally been listed as speakers. The capital letters signal that the speaker is spelling the word out.

(6)

V4:	uhm uhm I think that the Western people when they come to the come to Vietnam they like nam pho [fɜ]
T4:	nam pho yeah
V4:	pho it is very very traditional you know
B4/My4:	V [viː]
V4:	P H O
B4/My4:	P H O
V4:	but you pronounce [it
B4:	what] is it actually?
V4:	[fɜ] [fɜ]
My4:	No no no she is she is just saying what is the dish actually is it fish is it what what is it rice?
V4:	ehn nam you know nam?
B4/My4:	nam nam
V4:	yes there are many kinds of [nam
My4:	what] is nam?
V4:	it is some kind of
My4:	made of pork?
V4:	yes it's made of pork and some green bean (yeah) no not green bean just some kind of
T4:	bean sprout
V4:	yes may be bean sprout and er some noodle (er I mean) you mix eggs you er mix them (ehm) and you use er some kind of it is also made from rice round a little and you pack it (yeah) and then you put in the oil (eh huh) and fry them
My4:	oh it must be very nice (yes) but minus the pork [of course (laughter)
B4:	put it in the packet and then you fry it
V4:	no no no no not the package
My4:	not the noodle
V4:	You use them I mean the package here it is made of rice sorry made of rice it is er ehm always circle or square you
My4:	is it something like
V4:	only use only only little and then you pack it so it is usu usually very small just (ehm) yeah round
My4:	may be our version of popiah
B4:	yeah popiah
V4:	yeah popiah
All:	popiah yeah popiah popiah [*loud laughter/shouting*]
B4/My4:	at least we find something that we know

In the event that a participant does not understand, he or she can *signal a request for repetition*. T1's 'ehm?' in Extract 7 provides an example of this strategy. It is also possible that the Thai speaker's 'ehm' with a rising intonation signals that he is not sure whether he is being addressed. Note that the Vietnamese speaker (V1) does not use the definite article or a personal pronoun in 'it's first time' and that she uses the bare infinitive form 'find'.

(7)

V1: well to me it's first time so I find everything very new and {T1 ehm} because I'm very excited to discover {T1 ehm}new things
B1: so how do you find the course so far?
T1: **ehm?**
B1: how do you find this course this course that we did so far?
T1: actually it's an it's an very intensive course {F: yeah} but for short period of time {F: yeah} (…) only two weeks {F: yeah}

A participant can also *signal a request for clarification*, as in Extract 8.

(8)

B1: when do] they start grade five as well?
V1: ehm you mean me?
B1: er no
V1: no grade six {B: grade six} the students now {B: no} {T: eh} you mean the children ehm now grade one?
B1: grade one ok
V1: not from not from kin[dergarten

The use of pardon in Extract 9 is another instance of this strategy of request for clarification.

(9)

S2: But how did you manage to cope when you were taught English at the very later stage? (1.4 second pause)
Mn2: Pardon?
S2: How how are you all able to cope you know when in your during your time, you were taught English only at secondary level?

On occasion, the participants use what Firth (1996: 243) has called the *'let it pass' strategy*. In Extract 10, for example, it is not clear if T1 or B1 really understand, particularly with the pronunciation of [tɔːtʃ] for 'taught', but they provide encouraging backchannels anyway to encourage V1 to continue in the hope that all will become clear.

(10)

V1: On the first year, um ... those students um will be taught [tɔːtʃ] all the basic er rules
T1: mm
V1: Like ... I I mean this, for the er for the sub- for the grammar subject itself, it's not for interpreter skills.
B1: mmm
V1: so, er ...

The pronunciation of 'taught' as /tɔtʃ/ occurs elsewhere in the data, but without causing misunderstanding. It is used by I3 in Extract 11, although, interestingly, he also uses the standard pronunciation the second time he mentions the word. Note also his non-use in the first instance and use in later instances of the indefinite article with 'a second language', as in 'English is becoming second language', 'launched as a second language' and 'officially launched as second language'.

(11)

I3: interesting thing in my er province it's a proper province ehm er now English is becoming second language is is has been launched as a second language ehm it's officially launched as a second language er so now we are working on the er what's it the curriculum {F: training} yeah and on er they way how English er
S3: is to be taught
I3: is to be [tɔtʃ] and then er and how English er is go is trying to be what to be taught in in in schools or in ehm ehm er in informal ...

To return to the *'let it pass' strategy*, in Extract 12, the pronunciation of 'us' sounds more like 'uts' which may confuse the others. But after a longish pause (1.2 sec), S2 provides a backchannel to encourage Mn2 to go on, in the hope it will get sorted out in time.

(12)

Mn2: They can catch, they can acquire more English than us [ʌts]/(1.2)
S2: hmm-mmm
Mn2: but mm er in our time we have to memorize some er most of the vocabulary in our mind and
S2: mmm
Mn2: we have to erm er r- repeat er before the teachers.

Linked to this, is the strategy of *listening to the message*. In other words, the listener attends to what the speaker says, even though it may be characterized by non-standard forms, as long as the message is clear. In Extract 13, L2's use of English suggests that her proficiency is lower than the others. Her English also carries a tonal quality, no doubt influenced by Lao phonology. However, S2, the most fluent of the group, makes no comment on this, but responds to her remarks in a way that encourages a smooth conversational flow. The non-standard forms used by the Laotian do not hinder the flow of the communication, even though these look like examples of learner English rather than of non-standard forms usually associated with the vernacular varieties of English.

(13)

L2: ehm last night [nai] we went there by walking.
S2: eh huh
L2: I enjoy walking [yeah
S2: you] mean all the way from [here
Mn2: yes yes
L2: yeah]
S2: oh ok
L2: some of my friend hurt his feet
S2: oh ok
L2: (laugh) he can't {Mn1: yes} walk and he is just stand and sit (quiet laugh)
S2: oh ok I would have taken the bus were you aware that there is a bus that goes …

When a listener realizes that a word is too important to let pass, however, she signals the need to clarify it immediately. In Extract 14, neither My6 nor F6 can make any sense out of L6's use of the word 'horns', so they seek to clarify it immediately. It is only when L6 adopts the strategy of *spelling out the word* (see also Extract 5 above) that My6 and F6 finally understand that he means 'holes'.

(14) [cf. 4:46]

L6: you know at the time that ehm tsunami occurs there were some problem in my country
My6: what problem
L6: yeah we've got some problem we have big holes [hoʊnz] in in some areas
My6: horns? Sorry
L6: hole [hoʊn] you know hole [hoʊnt]
F6: what houn
L6: yeah big hole [hoʊn]
My6: (laugh) what
F6: what's a horn
My6: sorry
L6: H-O-L-E something like this
My6: holes?

L6: yeah
My6: holes oh you mean a hole in the ground.
L6: yeah

Similarly in Extract 15, although Mn2 initially provides a positive backchannel, she then decides that 'drums' is an important part of the discourse, so she indicates she does not understand it.

(15)

S2: she wanted to get the erm ... Chinese drums for her son.
Mn2: yeah.
S2: um, an [er
Mn2 : [Chinese d
S2: the drums, the drums.
Mn2: drum, drum.
S2: yes [yes.
Mn2: [drum, oh oh.
S2: OK, and er

And again in Extract 16, neither F6 nor L6 initially understand My6's use of 'IT'. Although L6 initially provides an encouraging backchannel, F6 decides she needs to seek clarification by repeating the unknown term with a questioning intonation. Her signal for the need for clarification is promptly followed by L6's signal. F6 also uses the definite article in 'the information technology'.

(16)

My6: there has been a concerted effort by the government in my country to improve the standard of spoken written English because currently there are many unemployed graduates people who have degrees from Malaysian universities who can't find jobs basically because of their poor English and their lack of IT skills and the government has had to spend a lot of money retraining these people in a special training program to give them the basic proficiency the proficiency in the English language and IT skills (L6: I see) maybe you have read about this in your newspaper no
F6: IT?
L6: IT?
F6: did are you referring to the the information technology?
M6: yeah they lack IT skills and they lack a certain level of proficiency in the English language

As the final example of this strategy, in Extract 17 I5 realizes she cannot answer Mn5's question, as she does not recognize Mn5's pronunciation of 'pearl', so immediately asks for clarification. This makes Mn5 realize that her pronunciation of 'pearl' may be causing problems so she self-corrects.

(17) [cf.4:45]

Mn5: by the way er have you seen any er pearl [baː] beads at this shopping centre?
I5: ba bead what's that?
Mn5: er er pearl necklace
I5: yeah a lot but too expensive
Mn5: are they er very er high quality?

If the speaker feels that a phrase has not been understood, she can adopt the strategy of *repeating the phrase*. This is illustrated in Extract 18, where L1 pronounces only three teachers as [onwi tiː tiːtsə]. As this is followed by a second's pause, she realizes that the others may not have understood and so repeats herself. As reported in Chapter 4, her insertion of the 'r' sound in [triː] helps make her message clear.

(18) [cf. 4:48]

L2: especially in my nn school there are especially in my nn schoon here are only [onwi] three [tiː] teacher [tiːtsə] (1.0) [triː tiːtsə]
S2: three teachers
L2: [yes, three teachers

In Extract 19, I5 realizes that Mn5 has not realized he has tried to change the topic from 'food' to 'rooms' as she continues to talk about food. He therefore repeats his question, but only after he has politely listened to her comment about food. He also paraphrases his question and adopts the strategy of *making explicit* that what he wants to talk about is 'room'. The plural form 'fruits' used by the Indonesian speaker (I5) is common among many varieties of Asian English. The Burmese speaker (Mn5) also does not use 'BE' when she says 'I think the rice a little bit sticky', but does use it later when she says 'the price for them is also expensive'.

(19) [cf. 4:43]

I5: I think that er most of er fruits here are imported from other countries OK that's why er fruits and vegetables here are expensive (ehm) different our country (Mn5: maybe) we produce fruits a lot OK mango starfruit jambol OK oranges OK I think we can er find the fruit with er very cheap price (laugh)
Mn5: sure (laugh) sure (laugh)
I5: what about your rooms
Mn5: er
I5: you feel OK any [problems
Mn5: I] find the taste er quite ok (ehm) but er like yours is I think er ... er ... the rice a little bit sticky (C5: ehm) in our country we don't er eat er rice as sticky as that rice here er ehm and then ehm how shall

I say er ... and then vegetables er maybe er the same vegetables we eat (C5: ehm) in our country (I5: ehm) but er the price for them is also expensive (laughter) I think because I prefer eating vegetables (I5: OK) I prefer vegetables er than (I5: OK) to meat er

I2: OK what I'm asking is about **room** OK er do you feel cold like to our? to our neighbours (C5: ehm yes) cannot stay for air-conditioned room that's why

C5: for me it's OK for me (yeah) I get used to it air-conditioned (yeah)

The need to *signal topic change explicitly* is also illustrated elsewhere in the data and Extracts 20 and 21 are examples of this. The use of this strategy demonstrates participants' understanding that being explicit is a useful communicative strategy in ELF discourse. In this exchange, F6 also uses the preposition 'from' when the standard might expect either no preposition at all ('I would like to ask you ...') or possibly 'of' as in 'I would like to ask of you ...'.

(20)

L6: **now we can change our topic** to talk about I think about
F6: **I want to talk er something private** (laughter) (L2: yeah yeah) er Steven could it be
My6: er [sorry
L6: something] private
F6: I would like to ask from you something private
My6: like what
F6: like personal
My6: personal
F6: are you are you married or
My6: no I'm not married

(21)

S2: eh huh ok ... so that means the lessons were conducted in [English
Mn2: yes] yes
S2: OK it wasn't in your own dialect
Mn2: no {S2: eh hm} so er after my education and self-study is the most important to get {S1: eh hm} or to study ehm other languages {S2: eh hm} I think so {L2: laugh} do you think so (...) yeah {S2: eh hm} **shall we go shall we move on to another topic**?
S2: yeah OK

A fellow participant can also help the addressee if she realizes that the addressee has not understood the question. This strategy of *participant paraphrase* is illustrated in Extract 22, where Mn2 paraphrases S2's question for L2, as she realizes, possibly from L2's expression, that she has not fully understood.

(22)

S2: do they] do they write essays do they write essays do the pupils do the pupils write compositions?

Mn2: can your students write an essay or paragraph writing {S2: eh hm} a composition?

L2: yes I think they can because er as I ask them to write er the story they can write and some mistake I think that's ok for them because they have never learned English before.

Extract 23 provides an excellent illustration of the sincerity and depth of the desire to ensure that communication takes place while, at the same time, preserving the face of the participants. Extract 23 represents the most serious breakdown in understanding in the entire data. L2 clearly has great difficulty understanding S2's question and S2 resorts to paraphrase. She actually adopts the strategy of *speaker paraphrase* an extraordinary five times to help repair the breakdown. These are indicated by the numbers in brackets after each paraphrase. It is important to note that no underlying tone of irritation or impatience is evident. It is after S2's fourth attempt at paraphrase that the other participant, Mn2, tries to help by providing a possible answer for L2. This combination of *speaker paraphrase* and *participant prompting* is further evidence of the collaborative and supportive atmosphere, which has also been noted in other lingua franca contexts (see Firth 1996; House 2006). Note that *participant prompting* is different from the earlier strategy of *participant paraphrase*, as here Mn2 provides a possible answer to S2's question rather than a paraphrase of it.

(23)

S2: eh huh ehm do the do the children you know in er in your country those who come from a very poor families {L2: yes} are they given financial assistance?

L2: ehm

S2: are they in in terms of money? (1)

L2: ehm

S2: I mean does the government support them? (2)

S2: OK is there is there like you know those children who are very poor and their parents cannot afford to send them to school? (3) does the government actually given them assistance? (4)

Mn2: yeah the government will assist I think so{S2: eh hm}your government will assist

(two-second silence)

S2: example you know like buying uniform for them or textbooks and paying for their school fees (5)

L2: I th I think they don't do like that yes {S2: oh is it?} only the family or parents

S2: can afford

L2: yes afford them er for example {F ehm} in the (…) er countryside some students cannot learn because er it's hardly for them to er go to school/n/ {S2: eh hm}

Another important strategy designed to ensure mutual communication is to *avoid using local or idiomatic terms* which may not be understood by the other participants. This is particularly striking in the discussions that include any combination of Bruneians, Indonesians, Malays and Singaporeans, as they all share a knowledge of Malay. The conversation of such people, were they not joined by people from other linguistic backgrounds, would normally be characterized by code-switching between the shared languages (McLellan and David 2007). Yet, there is only one example in the entire data that could be classified as code-switching or the use of a local term and this occurs in Extract 24 where S3 and I3 use the Malay/Indonesian term, *rojak*. Even this can be explained by the topic, which is Singaporean English and 'Singlish', a term that the other participant, C3, would be expected to know given his presence on an ELT professional development course in Singapore. Note also that S3 does not use an indefinite article when she says 'we have to show good example', but uses it elsewhere.

(24) [cf.4:51]

S3: in school in class I will try to speak good English in fact we are supposed to speak good English {I3: ehm} so I will switch you know ehm {ehm} in the class I'm I am a teacher I see myself as a teacher we have to {C3: yes} show good example {I3: eh hm} so ehm there's no way that I will speak Singlish to my kids {I3: eh hm} not in class yeah er not in class not in school {I3: eh hm eh hm} but ehm like what you said just now when we go back to our friends {I3: (laugh) ok} and all that (I3: laugh) all the English (I3: laugh) and Singlish are all (I3: laugh) mixed together {I3: all right} like **rojak**
I3: oh like **rojak** right like that
S3: yes you know **rojak** right
I3: yes it's fruits mi[xed
S3: all] mixed up together
I3: all right all right {S3: yeah} ok oh all right

That this use of *rojak* is the only use of a local language, term or idiom in the data strongly suggests that these ELF speakers are consciously aware of the need to edit out any terms or idioms that might cause misunderstanding in ELF communication. This is evidence of a linguistic sophistication and sensitivity that is not always evident in native-speaker — non-native speaker communication, where there are frequent misunderstandings (House 2006).

To conclude these examples, it is important to mention the role and presence of laughter. Laughter is frequent in the data and appears to play a variety of roles. It signals relief and delight (see Extract 5 above). It is often used to hide nervousness, and may sometimes be used to hide lack of understanding or to signal that you did not understand, but now do. Extract 25 is a continuation of Extract 4 above. Here, when C3 asks, 'you want to travel the world', he is asking a rhetorical question but I3 does not realize this and tries to answer the question. C3's strategy is to override I3 by asking another rhetorical question to which he can give the same answer, 'you have to speak English'. S3 quickly understands the verbal game he is playing and joins in and then I3 also gets it and starts to laugh. The turn ends in general mirth.

(25)

C3: so Cambodian people rely and I will I will tell Cambodians I will tell them about the advantage advantages of English and ehm (...) er motivate them to learn English because I know the the the good things of English
S3: the benefits
C3: yeah the benefit you want to travel the world?
I3: well you [can you
C3: you you] have to speak English
I3: you [can
C3: you] want to do business with er {I: ehm ehm} other country you have [to
S3: you have] to speak English
I3: yeah
C3: use] English
I3: yeah yeah ok
C3: you want to do research? (I3: laugh)
S3: you have to do it in English
C3: you have to (S3+I3: laugh) to do in English (general laughter)

Conclusion

Extract 25 is an appropriate example to end with as it illustrates the humour, goodwill and collaborative atmosphere that characterizes this ELF data. The communicative strategies adopted by the participants are designed to ensure smooth communication between them. Smooth and collaborative communication is the main goal of the participants.

Although some of the strategies to negotiate meaning illustrated here are general-purpose strategies that would be found elsewhere in the world, it is also possible that some of them, particularly those that require patient paraphrase and negotiation and those that are designed to help participants and to preserve face, are part of the conversational behaviour that constitutes an emergent ASEAN ELF or ELF in general. However, as cautioned earlier, more data, especially from high-stakes interactions, is needed. Nevertheless, these ELF communicative strategies may have important implications for English language teaching in the ASEAN region and I consider these in more depth in Part III. Here, however, it is worth stressing that multilingual people are likely to be good at cross-cultural communication. Therefore, multilingual English speakers who are used to ELF communication represent valuable linguistic and communicative classroom models. A second point worth highlighting at this stage is that the variation and use of non-standard forms of the type found in the data does not seem to hinder communication. What does appear to hinder communication most is idiosyncratic pronunciation and a lack of explicitness. Third, it is also apparent that speakers in this ELF communication are conscious not to use lexis or idioms that might not be understood by people from their own speech community. As we also saw in Chapters 4 and 5, uses from local varieties of English are rare. One possible explanation of this is that ELF users are, by definition, seeking to communicate across linguistic and cultural boundaries. They are therefore operating at the communication end of the identity-communication continuum (I-CC) (cf. Kirkpatrick 2007a: 173).

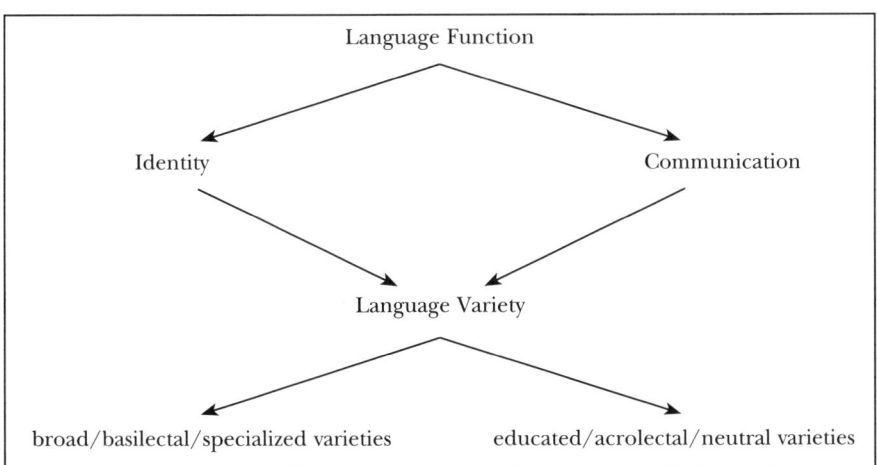

Figure 6.1 The Identity–Communication Continuum

The I-CC illustrates two major functions of language: language for communication; and language to establish identity. It shows that when speakers wish to highlight their identity and membership of a speech community, they will choose to use a highly localized, informal variety of English. Or, if they wish to identify themselves as members of a specialist profession, they may use a highly specialized variety or register for this purpose. These varieties are likely to be unintelligible to people outside the particular speech community. As Smith has pointed out, '[o]ur speech and writing in English needs to be intelligible only to those with whom we wish to communicate in English' (1992: 75). This helps explain the comparatively wide range of variation in local dialects of British English, as people want to be identified as members of a particular speech community.

The principles behind the I-CC are also at work when English is used as a lingua franca. The more *localized* the use of English as a lingua franca, the *more variation* it is likely to display. Conversely the *more international* its use, the *less variation* it is likely to display. When used in a local setting, ELF speakers will display identity markers. Thus code-switching and the explicit use of nativized norms can be expected. A conversation between Malays, Singaporeans and Bruneians, therefore, would be likely to be peppered with code-switching and nativized lexis and norms, as all participants would have at least some familiarity with the relevant local cultures and languages. When used for international communication, on the other hand, ELF speakers will consciously avoid the use of local and nativized norms and expressions. Thus, in the ASEAN ELF data, the only use of code-mixing occurred in the conversation that included a Singaporean and an Indonesian, when they referred to Singaporean English as '*rojak* English'. As explained in Chapter 4, *rojak* is an Indonesian-Malay word that usually refers to a kind of Indonesian mixed salad and the term '*rojak* English' would have been familiar to both of them, but not to the third member of the conversation, a Cambodian. With this single exception, avoiding the use of terms that might not be familiar to other participants was a strategy adopted by all the participants in their use of English for wider regional communication. This strategy displays sensitivity, as Seidlhofer reports that 'unilateral idiomicity' is a major cause of communication problems in her ELF corpus (2004: 220). Meierkord's study (2004), summarized in Chapter 5, in which she showed that the syntax of her outer circle subjects displayed little variation may also stem from the fact that they were using English for international communication with people who would not have been familiar with the cultures, say, of Africa or India. Thus they would consciously have excised nativized norms and cultural references from their speech in order to ensure all participants would understand them.

The English language classroom could profitably become a place where a major focus is on 'collaborative cross-cultural communication' and where a lingua franca approach to language teaching could be adopted. This will be explored in more depth in Part III. In the meantime, by way of summarizing this chapter, a list of the communicative strategies illustrated above, cross-referenced to the examples in which they occur is provided in Table 6.2. These are sub-divided into listener and speaker strategies.

Table 6.2 Communicative strategies of ASEAN ELF speakers

Strategy Type (Listener)	Illustration
Listener	
Lexical anticipation	[2]
Lexical suggestion	[3], [4]
Lexical correction	[5]
Don't give up	[6]
Request repetition	[7]
Request clarification	[8], [9], [14], [15], [16], [17]
Let it pass	[10], [12]
Listen to the message	[13]
Participant paraphrase	[22]
Participant prompt	[23]
Strategy Type (Speaker)	**Illustration**
Spell out the word	[5], [14]
Repeat the phrase	[18]
Be explicit	[19], [20], [21]
Paraphrase	[23]
Avoid local/idiomatic referents	[24]

Part III
Implications for Policy and Pedagogy

Introduction to Part III

In Part I, a review of the development and role(s) of English in each of the ten member states of ASEAN was provided. Despite the significant differences which exist, English is playing an increasingly important role in each, a role heightened by ASEAN's decision to make English the group's sole official and working language. The increasing importance attached to English in each of the member states — even Burma is now moving to promote the use of English — has seen its introduction as a compulsory part of the school curriculum of each country. In almost all the member states, it is taught as a subject from the early primary level. In Brunei, Malaysia and the Philippines, it is taught as a medium of instruction — typically, but not exclusively — for maths and science subjects. In Malaysia and the Philippines this use of English as a medium of instruction starts at Primary 1, although Malaysia has decided to rescind this policy from 2012 and revert to teaching English only as a subject. The Philippines has also signalled a radical shift in policy with the recently announced 'Mother Tongue-Based Multilingual Education', but it is too soon to be able to evaluate this new policy. In Brunei, the use of English as a medium of instruction currently starts at Primary 3, but, in sharp distinction from the new Malaysian and Philippines policies, it will be introduced from Primary 1 in 2011. In Singapore, it is *the* medium of instruction.

In Chapter 2, a number of concerns were listed connected with when to introduce English into the school curriculum, including whether to introduce it as a subject or as a medium of instruction and how to balance English with the other languages. These concerns can be summarized in these three questions:
(i) When should English be introduced into the school curriculum?
(ii) Should English be introduced as a subject or as a medium of instruction?
(iii) How can a mix of languages be equitably balanced in education?

Chapter 7 will consider the policy implications behind the three questions above and conclude with a possible language policy model in which English can complement local languages in the school curriculum rather than replace them. Chapter 8 will consider the pedagogical implications and conclude with a number of recommendations for language education policy and practice in ASEAN.

7
Implications for language education policy

As indicated earlier, Chapter 7 will first consider the implications for language education policy behind the following three questions:
  (i) When should English be introduced into the school curriculum?
  (ii) Should English be introduced as a subject or as a medium of instruction?
  (iii) How can a mix of languages be equitably balanced in education?

I now consider the first question, 'When should English be introduced into the school curriculum?', and begin by discussing the issue of resources.

As we have seen, almost all the member states of ASEAN have made English a compulsory part of the primary school curriculum, many countries teaching it from Primary 1. This has led to serious problems throughout the region, deriving from a lack of adequate resources. The situation in the Philippines and the problems associated with the lack of general resources in its government schools have been starkly recorded by Martin (2005: 274). Using figures based on Philippine Senate Committee, she reports:

> To this day, only 66.07% of elementary and secondary schools throughout the country have electricity. 13.3% have landline telephones. Only 2.9% have fax machines and 2% have internet access. In addition, 181,257 (out of roughly 450,000) public teachers reported that they had to bring their own tables to school; roughly the same number brought their own chairs. A smaller number (about 9,292) reported that they brought desks and chairs for their students.

These problems are common in rural areas of the Philippines, but are not restricted to them. The very numbers indicate how widespread the problems are. It should be recalled that, under the Philippines Bilingual Education Policy (BEP), Filipino primary children learn in Filipino and English from Primary 1. I shall return to the linguistic challenges this places on Filipino children below, but Martin's stark description underlines how desperately short government schools are of even the most basic resources. Schools simply do not have teaching materials and parents cannot afford them. Insisting on the teaching of (and in) English from Primary 1 adds tremendously to the cognitive burden on children and the financial and resources burden on schools and parents. As I shall argue below, a change of mindset about when and how to introduce English can help greatly alleviate these burdens.

Similar problems with resources and funding are reported in Indonesia, where teachers' low salaries force many to moonlight and take other jobs and where class sizes can make language teaching difficult even for the most experienced and dedicated teachers (Dardjowidjojo 2000). Results of many years learning English in primary and secondary schools are not good. In a comment which recalls Bautista's depressing summary of the situation in the Philippines where it pays to be middle class and have Tagalog as a first language, Dardjowidjojo writes: 'With few exceptions, generally a high school graduate is not able to communicate intelligibly in English. Those who can are suspected of having taken private courses or come from a certain family background' (2000: 27).

The question of teachers

The early introduction of English into the school curricula in so many countries has also led to serious problems connected with the shortage of adequately trained and linguistically proficient teachers of English. This led to the desperate measures taken by the Thai government reported in Chapter 3, when they advertised for 10,000 native speakers of English. As was also mentioned earlier, it was fortunate that this recruitment campaign failed, otherwise Thai schools could have been flooded with literally thousands of untrained and unvetted English teachers, appointed solely on the basis of being native speakers. Despite the failure of this particular campaign, however, it is common for governments in ASEAN and the region to try to overcome the shortage of local English teachers by recruiting native speakers, solely on the grounds that they are native speakers. This is a short-sighted and potentially dangerous policy and will be dealt with in detail in Chapter 8. Here it simply needs to be pointed out that any decision to introduce English into the primary curriculum as a compulsory subject will require a large number of suitably qualified and linguistically proficient teachers. No country in ASEAN has anything like an adequate number of such teachers. This alone should be reason enough to delay the teaching of English.

Linguistic demands on the child

The early introduction of English can also place heavy linguistic demands upon a child. One reason for this is that English is not of the same language family as any Southeast Asian language. In this respect, ASEAN provides a very different situation from the European Union, where most of the languages are members of the same Indo-European language family. Thus, children learning a selection of the major European languages of English, French, German, Italian or Spanish, are learning languages which belong to the same family. There are many points of familiarity between the languages, including a large number of vocabulary items. In addition, and very importantly, the scripts are the same, so that literacy in one leads to literacy in the others.

This is not the case in ASEAN. English is not cognate with any of the languages of ASEAN. This makes it more difficult to learn. And while many of the scripts of Asian languages share the Roman alphabet with English, many do not. Thus a Thai child who learns English has to learn two different scripts. While this is by no means impossible, it does mean that it takes more time. It also means that English will appear foreign with no points of reference or comparison. When we recall that the foreign language other than English which is most commonly found in the school curricula is Chinese (Putonghua), with its ideographic script, the linguistic demands being placed on children look overwhelming. As another example, a child from one of Vietnam's ethnic minority groups will face particular challenges, especially if the child's ethnic language has no script. Even though about half of Vietnam's ethnic minority languages now have scripts, the use of them in schools has not been successful in retaining ethnic minority children in the school system, as they have been used not to teach literacy in the mother tongue, but as a way of teaching literacy in the Vietnamese script, Quoc Ngu. This has been one cause of less than 10% of Hmong and Yao children attending school (Thaveeporn 2003: 231). But an ethnic minority child who does remain in school will have to learn Vietnamese (and the script), then English and then possibly Putonghua Chinese (and yet another script). In other words, in addition to the child's mother tongue, the child will have to learn three further languages — none of which are linguistically related to the mother tongue — and two different scripts.

The privileging of English

The privileging of English in ASEAN and its consequent early introduction into the school curriculum has, as its counter, the relative lack of attention paid to local languages. Once English is introduced, there is little or no room for other languages, with the exception of the respective national language. This has serious consequences. First, it means that children have no opportunity to learn local languages, other than their national language. As will be shown below, this also means that it is rare for children who come from ethnic minority backgrounds to receive education in their mother tongue. In this sense, English is privileged at the expense of local languages. Second, English is regarded as the language of knowledge creation and dissemination, and as the language of modernization. In this sense, English is privileged at the expense of the respective national language, and is a reason why English is sometimes adopted as the medium of instruction for maths and science, although, as will be argued below, there is no theoretical justification for this, especially at the level of primary school. As a consequence, scarce resources are channeled into the teaching of English when they might be better channeled to developing the lexicon of the national language. A common theme of Part 1 was how various national language institutes have been made responsible for making the national language a language of modernization. For example, Indonesia, Malaysia, the Philippines and Vietnam have all established national language institutes to work on this issue. It is interesting to note that two outer circle countries in which English has a colonial history and an institutional role, Malaysia and the Philippines, have been less successful in this enterprise (cf. Gill 2007, Garcia 1996) than either Indonesia or Vietnam, where the attempts to modernize national language have been more successful. There are certainly no theoretical or linguistic reasons why well-established languages with scripts should not perform perfectly adequately as languages of modernization. There is no doubt, however, that resources are needed in order to develop the vocabulary and produce dictionaries and text books. Governments should ensure they strike a sensible and practical balance between providing resources for the teaching of English and the development of the national language.

Before suggesting a final answer to the question of when English should be introduced into the school curriculum, I shall first consider the second of the two questions listed above.

Should English be introduced as a subject or as a medium of instruction?

The importance of time in second language learning

Although several of ASEAN's member states have introduced English as a medium of instruction, sometimes as early as in Primary 1, there are a number of reasons why this policy should be seriously questioned. The first reason for opposing the policy is that children need to attain a certain proficiency in the second language before they can use it as a medium of instruction through which to learn content. This is a point agreed upon by many scholars. For example, Benson (2008) argues that it is best for children to learn through the home language until at least Grades 5 or 6, as children require at least five years of L2 learning before they can learn content or academic subjects through the L2. 'Being taught academic content through the L2 represents a multiple burden for the learner' (Benson 2008: 2). Ideally, therefore, children should learn the second language for at least five years before the second language can become a medium of instruction. This is supported by the research findings of Cummins who shows that children are able to transfer L1 skills to learning the L2, but that this takes time (see also Gibson 2006). In a study of immigrant children in Canada, Cummins (1981) showed that, after the age, of six, children took between five and seven years to attain academic proficiency in English, although they were able to develop oral proficiency more quickly.

In the case where more than two languages are involved, however, even more time is needed. To take yet another example from ASEAN, a Filipino child from the area around Cebu will speak a local language as the mother tongue and will speak Cebuano as the regional lingua franca. It will be remembered from Chapter 2 that speakers of Cebuano and its related dialects number more than six million, compared with the four million native speakers of Tagalog. This bilingual child will enter Primary 1 and be expected to learn in two new languages, namely Filipino and English, one of which bears no relation to the child's mother tongue at all. The child will also be required to use both of these two new languages as media of instruction. English is used for maths, science and English communication arts. Filipino is used for the other subjects. In other words, the child will be required to learn mathematical and scientific concepts through English, a new and 'foreign' language. Along with all other Filipino children for whom Tagalog is not a first language, the child will have to learn the other subjects through another 'foreign' language. The child will therefore have to learn through two foreign languages from Primary 1 (Benton 1996: 309). It is not surprising then, that such children can end up as 'semi-linguals', as was the case in a study of Balara Primary 3 children (Maminto 2005: 339–340).

While it is clear that introducing English early into the primary curriculum even as a subject, let alone as a medium of instruction, can cause problems in terms of resources, teachers and learning, governments are increasingly adopting this policy. Why, then, are governments adopting this policy?

Three myths of language education

Benson (2008: 2*ff*) has identified the following three tenets (which she terms 'myths') as being, at least in part, the cause of current government policy in language education:

(i) the best way to learn a second language is to use it as a medium of instruction;
(ii) to learn a second language you must start as early as possible; and
(iii) the home language gets in the way of learning a second language.

With regard the first tenet above, a number of arguments suggesting that this needs to be carefully questioned have already been proposed. In short, the counter-claim is that a child needs between five and seven years' instruction in the second language before it can be used as a medium of instruction. This is particularly the case when the content matter to be learned includes maths and science, subjects which contain complex concepts. It places an unrealistically heavy cognitive load upon children to ask them to learn maths and science through English from Primary 1, especially when English is a different language family from the child's first language and/or the national language. The major reason for the Malaysian government's recent decision to rescind their policy of teaching maths and science through English from Primary 1, according to the Malaysian deputy prime minister, Tan Sri Muhyiddin Yassin, is that it has resulted in too many children failing the subject and has widened the gap between rural and urban children. The on-line edition of the *Star* newspaper of July 7 also quoted the minister pointing to a lack of suitably proficient teachers as being a further reason for the government's decision to scrap the system: 'Only 19.2% of secondary teachers and 9.96% of primary teachers were sufficiently proficient in English.'

Questioning the first myth

Maths and science as 'neutral' and modernizing

Two reasons why maths and science are commonly chosen as subjects to be taught through English are that they are seen to be culturally 'neutral' on the one hand and that, as they are crucial to development and modernization, they should be taught through the language of modernization on the other. However, it has been forcefully argued by the Filipino scholar, Bernardo (2000: 313), that, 'there seems to be no theoretical or empirical basis ... to obligate the use of English in teaching mathematics' and that,

> There are clear and consistent advantages to using the student's first language ... at the stage of learning where the student is acquiring the basic understanding of the various mathematical concepts and procedures.

As Bernardo stresses, the stage where the student is acquiring basic understanding is particularly important. In other words, maths and science, especially at the early stages, should be taught in the child's first language.

The other argument promulgated in favour of the teaching of 'culturally neutral' subjects such as maths and science is that they can be happily taught through a culture-free language such as 'scientific' English. Putting aside the idea that maths and science somehow live in a cultural vacuum, I shall argue later that, far from being used to teach supposedly culture-free subjects, English should be used to teach culture-rich subjects such as cross-cultural communication.

The first tenet above could therefore be rephrased to read:

> A child needs *at least* five years' instruction in a second language before it can be used as a medium of instruction to teach complex concepts.

Questioning the second myth

To turn now to the second of Benson's 'myths', namely:

> 'To learn a second language you must start as early as possible.'

All things being equal, this may be true. However, in order for successful language learning to take place at an early stage, a number of conditions need to be met. These include access to resources, the availability of competent, qualified and linguistically proficient teachers, a supportive language learning environment and a motivated learner who has already developed proficiency and literacy in the first language. As has been illustrated above, these conditions are seldom met in ASEAN contexts. The only children fortunate enough to find that these conditions are met will be members of the elite, who speak the national language as their first language and who live in urban centres. The *overwhelming majority* of ASEAN learners of English do not fall into this category. Instead, they come from the poorer socio-economic classes, have access to limited resources and overworked teachers, whose own levels of proficiency may be low. These children may also be learning two or more local languages as they acquire a regional lingua franca as well as a national language alongside their mother tongue. To force children from these backgrounds to learn English, even as a subject, from Primary 1 is to condemn them to cognitive overload and failure.

Start early or start late?

While there is research evidence to show that starting young is particularly valuable if you want to master the phonology of the language in the sense that you want to *sound like a native speaker*, this is the only area of language acquisition where starting early offers a clear advantage. However, with a pluricentric language such as English and its myriad varieties, both traditional and new, all with native speakers with significantly and noticeably different pronunciations, and with the countless billions of multilingual speakers using English as a lingua franca worldwide, the need to sound like a native speaker in today's post-Anglophone world needs to be seriously questioned. To put this another way, why would anyone of the speakers described in Part II necessarily need to sound like a native speaker of standard American or standard British English? If no reason can be found, even the phonological reason for an early start is removed. This is significant because, along with the research evidence showing the advantage of an early start for the acquisition of a native speaker accent, there is abundant research evidence to show that late learners can learn languages extremely successfully. A recent study that appears to be aimed at proving the importance of an early start in the acquisition of 'nativelikeness', can be interpreted to show the opposite. As this study is important to the argument here, I shall review it in some detail.

Abrahamsson and Hyltenstam (2009) identified second language learners of Swedish who passed as being native speakers. That is to say, they were perceived to be native speakers of Swedish by native speakers of Swedish. Then, in order to determine whether these 'interloper' Swedes really had complete native speaker competence in Swedish, the researchers subjected them to a battery of ten tests to measure their phonological and grammatical knowledge and competence. The ten tests were deliberately chosen to examine grammatical features renowned for their complexity. For example, the grammaticality judgement tests, which were both oral and written, included tests of: subject-verb inversion; reflexive possessive pronouns; placement of sentence adverbs in relative clauses; and gender and number agreement. They also used a 300-word cloze-test where every seventh word was deleted. Their results were then compared with the results achieved from testing 'real' native speakers.

The authors summarized the results of their experiment by saying that 'only a few of the early learners and none of the late learners exhibited actual, linguistic nativelikeness across the board when their performance was examined in detail' (2009: 293) and concluded that estimates and rates of 'nativelikeness' needed to be treated 'with caution, even suspicion' (2009: 294).

It should be noted, however, that none of the real native speakers scored 100% on all the tests and this raises the question as to what these tests were really testing. They were designed to test 'nativelikeness', but if native speakers themselves failed to score 100%, can these tests really have been measuring nativelikeness?

The results of this research can be interpreted in such a way as to be of value to applied linguistics and those engaged in 'real-world' language teaching and learning. Three points are of particular note in this context:
(i) starting early did not guarantee nativelikeness (as defined by the researchers and measured by them in their tests);
(ii) native speakers failed to score 100% on all these nativelikeness tests (does this mean they were therefore non-nativelike?); and
(iii) all the non-native speakers — including all those who started learning Swedish later in life — were considered to be native speakers of Swedish by 'real' native speakers of Swedish.

This would suggest that there is (a) no real advantage in starting to learn a language early, and (b) no real disadvantage in starting to learn a language late, as both sets of learners were assumed to be native speakers of the language by 'real' native speakers of it. This raises the important related question of the language learning target against which language learners are measured.

Second language acquisition (SLA) and language learning goals: Cognitivist SLA or social SLA?

In the study described above, the goal of second language learning is seen to achieve native speaker competence. This is the traditional position of second language acquisition (SLA) researchers. As second language learners' goals are assumed to be native speaker proficiency, their language is routinely measured against native speaker norms. When their language does not match native speaker norms, it is classified as deficient in some way. In this way, a dichotomy is created between the native speaker and the non-native speaker. The non-native speaker's task is to achieve native speaker norms. However, this cognitive view of language acquisition has recently been challenged by a number of scholars. In a well-known article published in 1997, Firth and Wagner argued that the concepts of native and non-native speaker had led to an idealized native speaker providing the norms against which non-native speakers were measured. The non-native speaker was then judged to be 'a defective communicator, limited by an undeveloped communicative competence' (1997: 285). In a more recent article, they argued that dominant SLA concepts 'were myopic vis-à-vis learning as social practice and language as social phenomenon' (2007: 801), and that SLA theory was not able to account for the use of English as a lingua franca. However, they concluded that, while the native speaker remained the baseline target for language learners, studies exploring second language acquisition from a socio-cultural and socio-interactional perspective had become more numerous. This is a point also made by Swain and Deters (2007) who give examples of second language acquisition research which prioritize socio-cultural and contextual factors and recommend that we need to 'pay balanced attention to social, cognitive and affective aspects' in second language learning (831).

The call for socio-cultural and contextual factors to be considered in SLA research has been made by a number of other scholars including Jenkins (2006). She makes a useful distinction between the goals and attitudes of traditional SLA, which, in the context of English, she labels English as a foreign language (EFL) and those of English as a lingua franca (ELF). Table 7.1 below contrasts these positions (slightly adapted from Jenkins 2006: 140, and see Kirkpatrick 2007d).

Table 7.1 EFL vs ELF

EFL	ELF
part of modern foreign languages	part of world Englishes
deficit perspective	difference perspective
metaphors of transfer/interference/ fossilization	metaphors of contact/evolution
code-mixing and switching are seen as interference errors	code-mixing and switching are seen as bilingual resources

The major difference between the two positions is that the ELF paradigm allows for diversity and sees this in a positive light, while the traditional ELF paradigm characterizes variation as deviation from a fixed and established standard norm. In multilingual societies such as those throughout ASEAN, insisting on a single target norm is inappropriate, impractical and unnecessary.

Larsen-Freeman (2007: 780) provides a useful overview of the different perspectives of cognitivist or mainstream SLA and the more recent sociocultural SLA. Basic differences are that, in the cognitivist view, language is a mental state, while in the social SLA view, language is a social construct. In the cognitivist view, therefore, the context in which learning takes place makes no difference to the acquisition process, while in the social SLA view, context is crucial. The primary research focus of cognitivist SLA is on how people learn a language. The primary research focus of social SLA is how people use language. In cognitivist SLA, learners are thought to have successfully acquired the language when their language matches that of the target. In social SLA, there is no real 'end' to language learning. I would add that the goal of language learning in cognitivist SLA is native speaker proficiency, and this is the linguistic benchmark against which the learner is constantly measured. In social SLA, on the other hand, the goal is functional proficiency. In other words, the learner learns a language in order to be able to use it successfully, and this is therefore the benchmark against which the learner should be measured.

As Larsen-Freeman and Firth and Wagner point out, cognitivist SLA remains the mainstream perspective and this is the approach adopted by ministries of education throughout the member states of ASEAN. This perspective translates as the following beliefs:

(i) The goal of the language learner is to achieve native-like proficiency in the language.
(ii) Progress towards the achievement of the goal needs to be measured against linguistic benchmarks derived from an idealized native speaker model. (In some countries this is a British model, in others it is an American model.)
(iii) As an early start is crucial for achieving native speaker proficiency, children should start learning English as soon as possible.
(iv) As learning content is an excellent way of second language learning, English should be used as a medium of instruction.

This helps explain, therefore, why so many governments accept the first two of Benson's 'myths' and introduce English into the curriculum so early, and why English is often used as a medium of instruction. In this book, I am urging a shift of perspective towards social SLA in the context of learning English, especially as the major role of English within ASEAN is as a lingua franca. Speakers and users of English within ASEAN need to be measured against their ability to use English as a lingua franca in ASEAN and international settings. They do not need to be measured linguistically against idealized native speaker norms. Not only is the language learning goal not the acquisition of native speaker proficiency, the idealized norms of the native speaker of English are less relevant in today's post-Anglophone world. In the multilingual world of ASEAN, we must adopt a new position. As Beacco and Byram have argued in the context of encouraging the learning of languages in the European Union, 'the teaching of English should be conceived so as to stimulate speakers' plurilingualism and not block its development in the name of a monolingual ideology' (2003: 28). It is important to note how plurilingualsim is defined here. It is not the acquisition of native speaker competence in a range of languages. Rather, it is the 'ability to use several languages to varying degrees of proficiency and for different purposes' (Beacco and Byram 2003: 8). One immediate consequence of this is the rejection of using native speaker norms to measure a learner's success in language learning. In Garcia's words, we must understand that a bilingual education 'doesn't accommodate to monolingual standards' and we therefore must 'avoid the inequities in comparing bilingual children to a monolingual child in one of the languages' (Garcia 2009: 386).

All this means that the second tenet or myth can be reformulated in the following way:

> To learn a second language, you do not have to start as early as possible.

Questioning the third myth

> 'The home language gets in the way of learning a second language.'

It is hard to know the origins of this belief, as all research shows that the opposite is true. In other words, far from getting in the way, the first language acts as a bridge to second and third language learning. What is important, however, is to ensure the child develops fluency and literacy in the first language. As Benson points out (2008: 4), building a strong foundation in the L1 helps the learning of a second language more than early exposure to the second language. Children are able to transfer the first language skills they have developed to learning later languages (Cummins 2008). For this reason, support for the first language is a key principle in the Canadian immersion programme (Swain and Johnson 1997). In order to facilitate second and later language learning therefore, governments would do well to invest in children's first language learning. The initial focus should be on developing fluency and literacy in the child's first language. Once this has been achieved, the child's readiness and ability to learn second and later languages will be greatly enhanced. This also argues for a later introduction of English in the ASEAN school curriculum.

Reformulating the tenets/myths

To sum up this part of Chapter 7, Benson's three tenets/myths can be reformulated in the following way:
(i) only use a second language as a medium of instruction after at least five year's instruction in it;
(ii) to learn a second language, you do not have to start early;
(iii) developing fluency and literacy in the first language will help the learning of second and later languages.

Answering the three questions

Three questions were posed at the beginning of this chapter. They were:
(i) When should English be introduced into the school curriculum?
(ii) Should English be introduced as a subject or as a medium of instruction?
(iii) How can a mix of languages be equitably balanced in education?

The answers to them should now be predictable.

(i) *When should English be introduced into the school curriculum?*

English should be introduced as a subject once the child has a solid grounding and literacy in the first language. In the context of ASEAN, curriculum time should also be given to other local languages, before the introduction of English. In other words, where the national language is different from the child's mother tongue, the child should be taught first in the mother tongue — *at least* for the first three years of school — and then move to the national language. In certain circumstances, where many local languages are spoken and it is impractical to offer the first three years of schooling in all of them, then it may be practical to teach first in a regional lingua franca and then the national language.

English need not be introduced until late primary or indeed secondary school, as it is quite possible to attain functional proficiency in English as a later learner in five or six years. The focus in primary schools should be on local languages.

(ii) *Should English be introduced as a subject or as a medium of instruction?*

English should first be introduced as a subject. Of course, content of some sort is *always* needed to teach language, but subjects with complex concepts such as science and maths should not be taught through a second language (English in this case) unless the child has *at least* five years' prior instruction in it. Generally speaking, the use of English as a medium of instruction should be delayed until secondary school, where it can be used to teach subjects such as cross-cultural communication rather than science or maths. This is further discussed in Chapter 8.

(iii) *How can a mix of languages be equitably balanced in education?*

In general terms, a very useful contribution to this topic is provided by Cenoz (2009) in the form of her concept of 'the continua of multilingual education' (2009: 31). In the ASEAN context, a general rule should be that primary schools should be concerned with the teaching of local languages.

These should be the child's mother tongue and the national language. Where this is impractical, the child's mother tongue can be replaced by a regional lingua franca. English can be delayed until secondary school. At the same time, resources should be provided to promote local languages, especially in the areas of script development and teaching materials. Resources should also be provided to develop the national language so that it can serve as a language of modernization. In the school context, subjects of 'modernization' and technology should be taught in the national language rather than English.

The need to focus on local languages in multilingual contexts is well recognized by experts. Table 7.2 is adapted from the UNESCO report, *Education for All by 2015* (UNESCO 2007). It identifies main challenges facing a selection of countries in ASEAN and suggests measures to help meet these challenges. The measures are all connected with the provision of bilingual and mother-tongue education designed to improve retention rates up to Primary (Grade) 5.

Table 7.2 Education for all: Challenges and measures

Country	Main challenges	Measures to help
Cambodia	reduce low levels of retention to Grade 5	develop bilingual education
Indonesia	reduce low levels of retention to Grade 5	add mother tongue education for early grades
Laos	reduce low levels of retention to Grade 5	develop multilingual materials
Philippines	reduce low levels of retention to Grade 5	make curriculum flexible to allow for cultural diversity
Vietnam	decrease number of children out of school	develop bilingual education for ethnic minorities

In the second part of this chapter, I propose a model based on the above principles. This has been designed for Hong Kong rather than an ASEAN member country as such, but the proposal is, I hope, transferable to comparable contexts. The next part of this chapter provides a brief review of the linguistic situation and language education policy in Hong Kong, before moving on to the description of a proposed new policy.

A language education policy model for Hong Kong

A brief review of Hong Kong's language policy

A full review of the language education policy in Hong Kong is beyond the scope of this chapter and here only a brief summary can be provided. A thorough discussion is provided in Bolton (2000, 2003).

Hong Kong was a British colony for some 150 years before being handed back to the People's Republic of China in 1997. Before the 1997 handover, the relative roles in the school curriculum of Cantonese — the first language of an overwhelming majority of the population — and English, were subjects of constant and heated debate, a debate dominated by whether Cantonese or English should be the medium of instruction in Hong Kong schools. Parental demand was for English. This was for the usual reasons: English was seen as a necessary tool for socio-economic advancement in the colony and its role as an international language and language of education was increasing. The University of Hong Kong, which had been established in 1911, had English as the medium of instruction. Hong Kong's second university, the Chinese University of Hong Kong, was set up in 1963 and offered Chinese as a medium of instruction. However, as students needed to pass an entrance exam in English, students from English-medium schools had an advantage even in applying for the Chinese-medium university (Boyle 1997). Today, English medium is the norm in university education in Hong Kong. Of Hong Kong's eight government-sponsored university-level tertiary institutions, only the Chinese University and the Hong Kong Institute of Education use Chinese as a medium of instruction. And even at the Chinese University, more and more courses are now being offered in English as the university seeks to attract international students.

In the 1980s and 1990s the colonial government commissioned a number of reports on education and the medium of instruction, and these reports all recommend the use of Cantonese as the medium of instruction. For example, the Llewellyn report of 1983 recommended the use of Cantonese in the early years of schooling 'accompanied by formal teaching of English as a first foreign language' (Bolton 2003: 91).

The recommendations of experts cut little ice with the parents, however. In 1990, although over 90% of primary students were in Cantonese-medium schools, the same percentage of students was enrolled in English medium secondary schools (Johnson 1994). One explanation for the high percentage of English-medium secondary schools was that the government allowed schools to choose the medium of instruction for themselves. Not surprisingly, given the overwhelming parental demand for English medium, secondary schools elected to teach through English.

This laissez-faire policy was altered shortly before Hong Kong's handover back to China in 1997. In place of allowing schools to choose the medium of instruction, the government decided to limit the number of English-medium schools to about 25% (114 schools out of a total of 460). Bolton offers two possible reasons for the sudden shift in policy. First, it was aimed at preserving Cantonese against Putonghua, a language that would inevitably increase in importance once Hong Kong became part of China again. Second, it was aimed at helping the government promote the language policy promoted in 1995, which was 'to develop a civil service which is biliterate in English and Chinese and trilingual in English, Cantonese and Putonghua' (2000: 270).

This remains the current policy, although it has been expanded beyond the civil service to include all educated Hong Kong citizens. The goal of Hong Kong's language education policy is thus to produce biliterate and trilingual citizens. Parental demand for English remains strong, and the government is keen to maintain proficiency in English as it promotes Hong Kong as 'Asia's world city'. Recent years have seen the predicted increase in demand for Putonghua, if not from parents, then from the students themselves. It is worth remembering that, while many of the older generations of Hong Kong have a negative attitude towards Mainland China — many chose to leave China and live in Hong Kong — this is not necessarily the case among the younger generation. Younger people have much fresher memories of the 2008 Beijing Olympics than they do of 1989 Tiananmen, when many current university students were not yet born. They naturally identify more closely with the Mainland than do their parents and grandparents, especially as Hong Kong is now formally an integral part of the Mainland (Kirkpatrick and Moody 2009).

In 2005, the Education Commission released a review of the medium of instruction issue in secondary schools (Education Commission 2005). This basically reiterated the policy described above. Primary schools would continue to teach through the mother tongue (Cantonese). Only those secondary schools which met strict criteria based on resources, student ability and the availability of suitable teachers would be allowed to use English as a medium of instruction.

'Fine-tuning' the policy

The post-handover policy has led to two major complaints: the first is that the division of schools into English medium of instruction (EMI) schools and Chinese medium of Instruction (CMI) schools has resulted in the CMI schools being perceived as inferior to the EMI schools. The second is that the reduction in the number of EMI secondary schools has led to declining overall standards of proficiency in English. These complaints, along with persistent parental demands for an increase in the number of EMI schools, have persuaded the government to agree to 'fine-tune' the policy (South China Morning Post 2009). From 2010, secondary schools will be allowed more flexibility to choose which *classes* to teach through English, although schools will still need to satisfy the students-teachers-resources criteria. Critics of the 'fine-tuning' policy have pointed out potential and unwanted outcomes. For example, one inevitable result of the new policy will be for secondary schools to try and increase the number of EMI classes they offer (parents will demand this). This in turn may lead to the unfortunate situation whereby maths, which has been so successfully taught through Chinese that Hong Kong students are routinely classified as being among the top students internationally, will now be taught in English in order to satisfy the demand for EMI classes. Second, the negative labelling effect may shift from between EMI and CMI *schools* to within schools and between EMI and CMI *classes*. What does it say of Hong Kong if people perceive those being educated through Chinese as being academically inferior to those being educated through English? Third, the work pressures and linguistic demands on teachers will grow, as teachers will have to be prepared to teach the same subject in two languages, for example, teaching maths in English to one class and then in Chinese to another.

Whatever the final outcome, I argue that any distinction between EMI and CMI schools or classes necessarily leads to the privileging of English over Chinese. The proposed policy outlined below therefore seeks to remove this distinction, while at the same time allowing children to become biliterate in English and Chinese and trilingual in Cantonese, Putonghua and English. In this way schools become multilingual sites, modelling speech communities of multilingual education (cf. Garcia and Bartlett 2007). At the same time, the proposal also anticipates and accommodates an increasing demand for the adoption of Putonghua as a medium of instruction, as Hong Kong moves even closer to China.

A proposed language education policy for Hong Kong

As the proposal draws heavily on the famous Canadian model of immersion and bilingual education (Lambert and Tucker 1972), I first briefly review it. Swain and Johnson (1997) describe the eight core features of the Canadian immersion model. They are:
1. The L2 is the medium of instruction (in the Canadian context the L2 is French).
2. The immersion curriculum parallels the local L1 curriculum (in the Canadian context the L1 is English).

3. Overt support exists for the L1 (in the Canadian context this is English).
4. The program aims for additive bilingualism.
5. Exposure to L2 is largely confined to the classroom.
6. Students enter with similar (and limited) levels of L2 proficiency.
7. The teachers are bilingual.
8. The classroom is that of the local L1 community.

There are obvious differences between the Canadian context and the Hong Kong context. First, the Canadian model concerns only two languages, French and English. These languages belong to the same language family and share the same script. In contrast, the Hong Kong context concerns three languages. Only two of these are cognates (Cantonese and Putonghua). The third, English, belongs to a different language family. A second major difference is that English and Chinese have different scripts. The difficulty associated with the learning of the Chinese script represents a further reservation in the wholesale adoption of the Canadian model, where the L2 (in Hong Kong's case this would be seen as English) is the medium of instruction. As pointed out in Chapter 1, it has been estimated that learning to become literate in Chinese takes two years longer than learning to become literate in an alphabetic language (Chen 1999: 143). Making English the medium of instruction would not allow enough time for children to develop literacy in Chinese. This is another powerful reason to be set alongside those outlined above for avoiding the use of English as a medium of instruction in similar contexts where the script of the first language is not alphabetic. This is precisely the case, for example, in Singapore, where, as reported in Chapter 2, the adoption of English as the medium of instruction has led to Chinese students graduating from secondary schools with poor literacy levels in Chinese (Goh 2009).

However, if instead of making English the medium of instruction, Putonghua were to take on this role, then the literacy problem would be overcome, as, with some exceptions, Cantonese and Putonghua share the same script, although the exceptions include some high frequency words (Snow 2004). Putonghua becomes the immersion language, but only in late primary, with Cantonese remaining the medium of instruction for the first five years. This will reassure parents that Cantonese will remain the language of Hong Kong identity, and that it is under no threat from Putonghua. During this time, Putonghua can be taught as a subject, in preparation for it becoming the medium of instruction and immersion language in Primary 6. This gives children five years of instruction in Putonghua before it becomes a medium of instruction. Continued support for Cantonese as the L1 is provided in late primary and secondary school.

The teaching of English as a subject can be delayed until the later years of primary school. In secondary school, English should become a medium of instruction in an in-depth course combining cross-cultural communication and international relations. I consider issues such as the English curriculum, the language learning targets, and teaching materials in more detail in Chapter 8.

If Swain and Johnson's immersion model were adapted for the Hong Kong context so that Putonghua became the immersion language, the Hong Kong model might look like this. An extra point (Point 4) has been added to include the third language, English.

1. Cantonese is the medium of instruction for the first five years of primary school. Putonghua is taught as a subject.
2. Putonghua becomes the immersion language from Primary 6 (a Chinese language as the L2 immersion language ensures that children will become literate in Chinese).
3. The immersion curriculum parallels the local (Cantonese) curriculum.
4. Overt support is given to the L1 (Cantonese).
5. English is taught as a subject in primary and in secondary as a medium of instruction for subjects such as cross-cultural understanding and international relations.
6. The programme aims for additive bi-(tri-)lingualism.
7. Exposure to the L2 immersion language is *not* confined to the classroom, as Putonghua is now commonly used in various domains in Hong Kong.
8. Students enter with similar (limited) levels of L2 proficiency (although an increasing number will have higher levels of proficiency in Putonghua).
9. The teachers are trilingual.
10. The classroom is that of the local L1 community.

Point 9 requires further elaboration. In the *original* Canadian model, the two languages, French and English, were taught monolingually. Lambert (1984: 13), one of the originators of the model, was quite clear about this:

> No bilingual skills are required of the teacher, who plays the role of a monolingual in the target language ... and who never switches languages ... In immersion programmes, therefore, bilingualism is developed through two separate monolingual instructional routes.

Belief in the efficacy of the monolingual model of language teaching remains commonly held in Hong Kong. I shall challenge this in Chapter 8, where a multilingual pedagogy will be proposed. Here, however, it needs to be stressed that the need for teachers to be trilingual does not mean that all teachers will be required to teach all subjects in all three languages. It simply means that, if the current language policy is successful in making all educated citizens trilingual — as defined in the sense of having functional proficiency in the three languages, but with one of the three operating as the main language — then all local teachers will be trilingual.

The implementation in Hong Kong of the model proposed above would, I believe, lead to the following outcomes:

> Children would develop literacy in Chinese and fluency in Cantonese, the language of Hong Kong identity.
>
> Children would develop high levels of proficiency in Putonghua, the national language.
>
> Children would develop high levels of proficiency in English which would allow them to use it as a lingua franca for intercultural communication.
>
> Children would graduate from Hong Kong schools, biliterate in Chinese and English and trilingual (in the sense defined above) in Cantonese, Putonghua and English.
>
> Schools become multilingual sites from where the invidious distinction between EMI and CMI schools and classes have been removed, thus allowing for a more equitable and effective education.

With regard to the final outcome listed above, it is also essential that special help be provided for Hong Kong children who are not ethnically Chinese or who are not literate in Chinese. While this may be a relatively small number of children, the numbers are increasing, as is the diversity across this group. The first language of these children needs to be explicitly valued and supported and special classes — especially those in the teaching of Chinese as a second language — need to be provided systematically and as a matter of course.

To conclude this discussion of language education policy in Hong Kong, it needs to be stressed that the language policies of the government-funded universities provide a major obstacle for the successful implementation of the government's trilingual and biliterate policy. Six of the eight government-funded tertiary institutions are officially English-medium only. The Chinese University of Hong Kong is bilingual — although students there have recently been protesting against the university for introducing more English-medium programmes, as the university attempts to meet key 'internationalization' criteria in order to climb the various international university ranking ladders, such as the Times Higher Education and the Shanghai Jiaotong scales. I have placed 'internationalization' in inverted commas, as this often means, in actual practice 'anglicization' (cf. Harder 2009). The Hong Kong Institute of Education is the sole government-funded tertiary institution to have a trilingual policy and where Cantonese, English and Putonghua all act as media of instruction. It is not surprising, therefore, that parents in Hong Kong are very keen to ensure that their children are educated though English as far as possible, in order to maximize their chances for university entry. This, of course, serves to undermine the trilingual-biliterate policy. It will only be when the universities of Hong Kong adopt policies to promote bilingual education that the government's language policy will have any real chance of success.

Summary

In this chapter I have considered ways in which ASEAN member states have implemented their respective language education policies with a particular focus on the teaching and learning of English. I have questioned the tenets upon which many of the policy decisions are based and argued that 'social SLA' offers a more relevant paradigm for language learning in the region than the traditional cognitivist SLA paradigms. I have therefore suggested radical reformulations of the tenets, which, I believe, would, if adopted, lead to much better and more equitable outcomes. I have also proposed a model of multilingual education for Hong Kong in the view that many of the issues there are relevant to other countries in ASEAN and East Asia. In doing this I have suggested answers for the three questions posed at the beginning of the chapter:

(i) When should English be introduced into the school curriculum?
(ii) Should English be introduced as a subject or as a medium of instruction?
(iii) How can a mix of languages be equitably balanced in education?

In Chapter 8, I move to consider pedagogical implications.

8
Pedagogical implications: The multilingual model and the lingua franca approach

In this chapter, the pedagogical implications of the role(s) of English within ASEAN will be considered. In particular, the following three questions will be addressed:

If English is to be taught in schools, what variety of English should be taught and how?
Who should teach it?
What should be taught through English and with what materials?

First, however, a brief summary of the current situation with regard ELT in the region is presented. This will be followed by a critical analysis of the current situation and proposals for radical changes.

The current situation: A summary

As illustrated in earlier chapters, all the member states of ASEAN are paying increasing importance to English and this is reflected in the introduction of English as a compulsory subject into the primary school curricula in all countries except Indonesia, often as a subject from Primary 1 and sometimes as a medium of instruction from Primary 1.

Major reasons for this increasing attention to English are that English is seen as the international language on the one hand, and as the major language of knowledge creation and dissemination and modernization on the other. In other words, these motivations are entirely instrumental and represent a demand for linguistic capital (Rappa and Wee 2006). It is assumed that countries need English in order to modernize and to participate in and to benefit from globalization. The motivation is driven by an 'if you can't beat 'em, join 'em' mentality and this motivation is not restricted to the member states of ASEAN. In South Korea, for example, learning English is linked to national survival, as exemplified in the Korean proverb, 'in order to win, know your enemy' (Tollefson and Tsui 2007: 264). This is also the motivation for the increase in spending on learning Arabic and languages spoken by 'troublesome others' in the United States. These reasons for language learning seem far distant from the integrative motivations for language learning which were traditionally proffered, such as learning to see the world through another's eyes, developing cross-cultural understanding, and enhancing cognitive ability. In ASEAN, the reasons for learning English are predominately instrumental.

Thus, despite the existence of established varieties of English in several of ASEAN's member states, the preferred model remains either a standard British or standard American model, as these are the models most closely associated with modernization. This privileging of British and American English gives advantage to native speakers of English and disadvantages others. Multilingual speakers of the local varieties of English are considered to provide inferior, if not deficient, models of English. Resources are spent on hiring so-called native English teachers (NETs) instead of on the training of local multilingual English teachers (METs). NETs are funded at the expense of METs.

The privileging of English — and a standard American or British English at that — and its consequent introduction into the primary curriculum also means that local languages are displaced from the curriculum. Instead of children being allowed to learn their mother tongue, in many cases the mother tongue and other local languages — with the exception of the national language — are not taught at all. Children most commonly learn English as the first foreign language. Sometimes they are asked to learn *through* English.

It is not only the local languages which are neglected as a consequence of the privileging of English. The region's national languages are also under-resourced. Instead of putting resources into developing the national languages as languages of modernization, resources are poured into the teaching and learning of English.

However, if the current language education policies continue to be implemented, the likely outcomes include the following.

Increasing failure and drop-out rates

Children will continue to fail to learn English *and* other subjects and drop out of school. Far from being a ladder to the path of success, English, if introduced too early in the curriculum provides a *barrier* to learning (Pennycook 2010). Children from rural and lower socio-economic backgrounds — and these represent the vast majority — are at particular risk. Far from providing the road map out of the village (Fishman 1973, and see Chapter 2), English, if introduced too early, means the child will be sentenced to lifelong service in the village. If the mother tongue is a language which is not used as a language of education or is not taught as a subject in schools — and this includes almost all of these languages — then the child is even further at risk. For example, less than 10% of Hmong and Yao children are in school in Vietnam (Thaveeporn 2003). Table 7.2 shows that many children are dropping out of school before Primary 5, and that the lack of bilingual education is a major cause of this. The figures for Cambodia reported in Chapter 3 indicate that only 10% of the Primary 1 cohort graduates from secondary schools.

Increasing inequality

If this is allowed to continue, the gap between the haves and the have-nots will increase. The current policies, while probably designed with the intention of allowing all children access to English, actually breeds inequality, as only children of the elite will be presented with the conditions in which they can learn English successfully. But it should be noted that their success in English often comes at a significant cost. It is becoming more and more common for middle-class parents to choose to send their children to schools where English is the medium of instruction, or even overseas (Wang 2007). In doing this, they often sacrifice proficiency and literacy in the local language on the altar of English. These elite can only be considered linguistic 'haves' in a very restricted sense of the term.

Increasing dominance of English

If English is allowed to increase its dominant position, local languages, especially those with relatively few speakers, will continue to die out at an alarming rate. It has been estimated (Dalby 2002: ix) that 2,500 languages will be lost this century. The Endangered Languages Project at the University of London estimates the number of endangered languages to be even higher, suggesting that half of the world's 6,500 languages are under the threat of extinction. The major reason for this is that children and young people are learning national and international languages at the expense of local and minority languages (Hans Rausing Endangered Languages Project Annual Report 2008: 3). Linguistic repertoires will increasingly comprise an instrumental form of bilingualism, the national language and English (and possibly Putonghua).

These outcomes are dire. They point to a region where children will continue to drop out of school, where inequality will increase, and where linguistic and cultural diversity will wither. In this chapter, I shall argue that it does not have to be this way. That by adopting the policies suggested in the previous chapter and the pedagogical principles outlined below, a radically revised language education policy can increase primary school retention rates, increase equality of opportunity, help maintain linguistic diversity and make English complementary to local languages.

This will require, among other things, changing the model of English and the learning targets. As shown throughout the book, the major role of English within ASEAN is as a lingua franca. That is to say, English is used as a medium of communication by multilinguals for whom English is a second or later language. It performs this role in formal settings as the sole working and official language of ASEAN. It also performs this role in a host of less formal communicative settings. Learners of English therefore need to be able to use English successfully in such settings. The great majority of people learning English in ASEAN require, above all, a functional proficiency in English to be able to use it as a lingua franca. In such circumstances, the insistence on a British or American model from which to derive linguistic benchmarks and targets for learners needs to be questioned. ASEAN provides an ideal opportunity for shifting away from the traditional cognitivist approach to second language acquisition (SLA) to a more socially and contextually sensitive approach to SLA. Multilinguals whose primary goal in learning English is as a lingua franca do not need to acquire native-like proficiency in the language, as measured against monolingual standards (Garcia 2009). Their English should not be measured against phonological and syntactic norms derived from monolingual speakers of English. Rather, their proficiency needs to be measured against their success in using English as a lingua franca (Firth and Wagner 1997, 2007).

The description in Part II of the English as used as a lingua franca by multilingual speakers from throughout ASEAN shows that, despite the presence of non-standard linguistic forms, communication is characterized by co-operation and mutual understanding. On the occasions where communication does breakdown, the breakdowns are repaired by a range of strategies which have been illustrated in Chapter 6. The key point to be made is that the frequent use of non-standard features does not interfere with intelligibility and understanding, especially when these non-standard features are shared by several participants. The non-standard phonological features shared by ASEAN speakers has been summarized in Table 4.5. The table is repeated here as Table 8.1 for ease of reference.

Pedagogical implications 173

Table 8.1 Summary of pronunciation features shared by ASEAN ELF users

Feature	Example(s)
reduction of consonant clusters	first – firs
dental fricative /θ/ as [t]	many thing [tɪŋ]
merging of long and short vowel sounds	[iː] and [i] to [i]
monophthongization of FACE and GOAT	diphthongs
reduced initial aspiration	they will teach [diːtʃ]
bisyllabic triphthongs	in our [aʊwə] time
lack of reduced vowels	officially [ɒfɪʃəlɪ]; to [tuː] visit
stressed pronouns	and HE has been in Singapore
heavy end-stress	the incidental WAY

An insistence on a British or American model within a traditional cognitivist SLA framework means all these features are classified as errors. They need, therefore, to be corrected, and curriculum time needs to be spent on ironing out these 'errors'. In fact, however, there is no need to spend curriculum time in 'correcting' most of these features. As we saw in Part II, few of these features cause problems in intelligibility in lingua franca communication. In fact, the only feature in the list above which may lead to misunderstanding is the merging of long and short vowels and these are included in Jenkins' lingua franca core (LFC) (2000). The LFC comprises phonological features which have been empirically shown to be important for intelligibility when English is being used as a lingua franca among non-native speakers. The suggestion is that these core features make up the core of the language syllabus. What the LFC does is 'reduce the number of pronunciation features to be learnt to those who opt for an ELF pronunciation syllabus, and thus reduce the *size* of the task while increasing teachability' (Jenkins 2007: 27). Other less problematic phonological features (in terms of ELF intelligibility) are classified as non-core. These non-core items will vary, being largely dependent upon the L1 of the speakers. The classroom model therefore 'is not the LFC but the local teacher whose accent incorporates both the core features and the local version of the non-core items' (2007: 25). ELF proficiency levels are thus not determined by their degree of closeness to native speaker norms, but are derived from ELF speakers themselves. This means that many linguistic features which are seen to be integral to all traditional teaching of English as a foreign language may not be relevant for ELF users. Table 8.2 is adapted from Jenkins' comparison between certain phonological features which are traditionally seen as crucial features of pronunciation for learners of English as a foreign language (EFL) but not important for ELF speakers (Jenkins 2007: 23).

Table 8.2 Targets for EFL and ELF compared

Feature	EFL Target traditional syllabus	ELF Target (non-core)
vowel quality	close to RP or GA	L2 (consistent) regional qualities
weak forms	essential	unhelpful to intelligibility
features of connected speech	all	inconsequential and may be unhelpful
stress-timed rhythm	important	unnecessary
word stress	critical	can reduce flexibility unteachable
pitch movement	essential for indicating attitudes and grammar	unnecessary/unteachable

In other words, Jenkins is proposing that the six phonological features listed here are either unnecessary, or even unhelpful, in a syllabus designed to teach English as a lingua franca, even though they would be considered essential features of any syllabus purporting to teach the standard British variety, Received Pronunciation (RP), and General American (GA).

While certain features of standard English may be unnecessary for an ELF syllabus, some *non-standard* features can be useful for lingua franca communication. In particular the lack of reduced vowels, noted in Table 8.1, leads to a tendency towards syllable-timed speech as opposed to stress-timed speech. This is helpful for intelligibility because each syllable receives more or less the same amount of prominence in the speech of ELF users. This is one explanation why the speech of Hong Kong and Singaporean speakers of English was found to be highly intelligible by native speakers of English in the study reported in Chapter 4 (Kirkpatrick, Deterding and Wong 2008). This syllable-timing can be contrasted to the 'swallowing' of vowel sounds, reflected in the omnipresent schwa sound in the stress-timed speech of native speakers. Thus, instead of coaching lingua franca speakers to move to a stress-timed pattern, they should be encouraged to retain their tendency towards syllable-timing.

Similar arguments can be made over the inclusion or exclusion of syntactic features for the ELF syllabus. For example, although the standard uses of verb forms remain an essential part of any syllabus aiming to teaching a standard British or American variety of English, the analysis of ELF speech shows that the non-marking of verb forms in certain contexts does not hinder intelligibility and communication. This suggests that, while it may be important to make sure learners know how English verb forms change and in what contexts, teachers do not have to worry over much if these are not always marked in speech. Similarly, an insistence on inversion in indirect questions of the type 'we don't know what it is for' seems unnecessary when the form, 'we don't know what is it for', is common in so many varieties of English and in ELF. Intelligibility overrides form, especially when curriculum time is necessarily limited. Other syntactic features which need little curriculum time include many of the others which have been identified and illustrated in Chapter 5. For example, the standard distinction between count and uncount nouns can be dispensed with. The treatment of nouns such as 'luggage', 'advice' and 'information' as countable is now so widespread among new varieties of English that the plural versions of these nouns is probably more common than the singular versions required in standard British and American English. In the same way, insisting on the use of a specific preposition in a specific context because this represents standard use is an unnecessary waste of curriculum time, especially as so much variation exists among vernacular dialects of English. Non-standard usage — in particular the extended range of 'about' exemplified in Chapter 5 as in 'mention about', 'discuss about', 'organize about' and 'explore about' — also needs no curriculum time. Again, the overarching principle is intelligibility. The ELF syllabus needs to prioritize linguistic features which may cause unintelligibility in lingua franca communication. It does not need to attempt to teach specific linguistic forms solely on the grounds that they are the forms used by an idealized native speaker of British or American English.

Adopting the perspective of a 'social' SLA in preference to a strictly 'cognitivist' SLA offers a way forward for syllabus design throughout ASEAN. Viewing language as something which is used for specific purposes in specific contexts rather than as a bonded system to be learned as a whole offers a radical alternative to the imposition of a British or American standard. This can be replaced by a 'multilingual model'. In the context of ASEAN, this means that the linguistic benchmarks against which learners will be measured will be derived from the speech of ASEAN multilinguals who successfully use English as a lingua franca.

The multilingual model

The 'multilingual model' is represented by multilinguals from ASEAN countries. Many of the subjects whose use of English as a lingua franca was illustrated in Part II are thus potential multilingual models. No doubt readers will be quick to point out that this is not a single model and that there may be as many 'models' as there are multilinguals. But this is to miss the crucial point. If a more social perspective of second language acquisition is to be adopted, then language learning 'success' is not measured solely against the acquisition of linguistic features derived from an idealized (i.e., unreal) speaker of a variety of standard English. Instead, success in language learning is measured against the ability to use language in real contexts. In short, learners need to be able to use the language in lingua franca contexts more than they need to be able to replicate the linguistic features of some imported exonormative standard of English.

It is nevertheless possible to identify classroom models in a number of ways. In addition to measuring success and proficiency against the ability to engage in lingua franca communication, countries in which a variety of English has been codified — and these include Brunei, Malaysia, Singapore and the Philippines — can use the educated formal variety of the variety as the standard. These varieties are, by definition, multilingual. However (and possibly because of their multilingual nature), these local varieties of English are often considered only suitable or acceptable as vernacular varieties by many key stakeholders in these countries. That is to say, these varieties are not considered as a possible source of classroom norms, hence their remaining dependence on the exonormative standards of British and American English. Again, we see the tyranny of using the norms of the monolingual native speaker being used to benchmark the multilingual. As an alternative to using a codified local variety of English, linguistic targets can be derived from speakers who are recognized as having successfully attained the goal of multilingual proficiency. This is similar to the 'multilingual model' outlined above, except that it narrows the model down to speakers of specific languages. Hong Kong can provide a good example of this, as the government policy is to produce citizens who are trilingual in Cantonese, Putonghua and English. Hong Kong has many first language speakers of Cantonese who have successfully achieved this goal and who are now functional trilinguals. They are therefore able to operate successfully both in Mainland China (in Putonghua) and internationally (through English). The English of these functional trilinguals should then provide the linguistic benchmarks for Hong Kong children. The trilingual speaker's variety of English thus provides the norms for the Hong Kong classroom. Much of the descriptive work of this variety has already been done (cf. Hung 2000; Bolton 2002; Deterding, Wong and Kirkpatrick 2008).

Coupled with the adoption of a multilingual model is the adoption of a lingua franca *approach* to language teaching. Seeing language as social practice requires accepting that it is more than just a finite system of rules. As Canagarajah has pointed out, English as a lingua franca 'does not exist as a system out there. It is constantly brought into being in each context of communication' (2007: 91). This is true, of course, of all language use, not just lingua franca communication. In the context of multilingual speakers, however, we need to understand the rich linguistic backgrounds such speakers bring to lingua franca communication and to see these as resources to be valued, and not as the cause of interference and mistakes. Pennycook (2007) refers to this as a translingual model of language.

Adopting a multilingual model has a number of significant implications for pedagogy. First, the inherent authority of the native speaker of English is removed, as to replicate standard norms is no longer the goal of language learning. This also removes the authority traditionally attributed to monolingual speakers, as standard norms are always derived from the idealized speech of the monolingual native speaker. In today's multilingual and post-Anglophone world, norms, as defined as the linguistic forms produced by idealized monolingual native speakers, no longer have much meaning. Instead, the ways multilinguals make meaning and ensure meaning is successfully communicated become more important. This also means that multilingual teachers now become not only the role models for their learners, but, crucially, they also become their *linguistic* models. And by linguistic models, we mean not only of the language they produce but, crucially, also of the way they *use* language. Such teachers will include, of course, the highly proficient English language teachers whose speech was described in Part II.

The linguistic aims of studying English need to be aligned to the role of English as a lingua franca. Linguistic benchmarks derived from monolingual speakers of standard American or British English against which the linguistic proficiency of the students need to be abandoned. 'Reliance on a native speaker model as the pedagogical target must be set aside' (McKay 2009: 238). Instead, benchmarks need to be adopted which are derived from multilingual speakers using English as a lingua franca. Garcia's plea (2009: 386) that we avoid the 'inequities' in measuring multilingual children against monolingual children was mentioned in Chapter 7. Instead, the second language speaker should be measured against the bilingual or multilingual speaker (House 2003).

The first question posed at the beginning of the chapter was, 'If English is to be taught in schools, what variety of English should be taught and how?' Rather than focusing on a specific variety of English, the ASEAN school curriculum needs to make a radical move to teach English as it is used in social contexts within the region. This I have called the 'multilingual model', combined with the adoption of a lingua franca approach to the teaching of English.

In response to the second question concerning who should teach English, the answer is that English should be taught by suitably trained multilingual speakers with high levels of English proficiency.

There is a long-standing debate over the relative advantages and disadvantages of native speaker and non-native speaker teachers of English (cf. Medgyes 1994, Braine 1999, Llurda 2005, 2009). Traditionally, the advantages associated with non-native speakers include their ability to empathize with their students, having themselves experienced learning the language as a second or foreign language. They are able to draw linguistic comparisons between the first and the target language, a linguistic ability unavailable to monolingual native speakers. They can therefore teach bilingually, although this is often considered a disadvantage by many, a point to which I return below. They are also often thought to have a more detailed and conscious knowledge of the grammatical system of the target language than many native speakers, for whom the grammatical system is intuitively, but not necessarily consciously, known. The major disadvantage associated with non-native speakers is the converse of the great advantage associated with native speakers, namely that they are non-native and native speakers of the language respectively. In other words, the major advantage attached to native speakers is through an accident of linguistic birthright. Whether one accepts a distinction between the native speaker or not (cf. Davies 1991), favouring one over the other on the grounds of linguistic birthright is discriminatory. In the same way that those who discriminate on the grounds of race or gender are rightly classified as racist or sexist, those who discriminate on the grounds of mother tongue can be classified as being guilty of 'linguicism', a term coined by Skutnabb-Kangas to describe 'ideologies, structures, and practices which are used to legitimate, effectuate, regulate and reproduce an unequal division of power and resources (both material and immaterial) between groups which are defined on the basis of language' (2000: 30).

While non-native speakers may often be looked down upon by native speakers (Llurda 2009: 123), equally unjust is for non-native speakers to be considered inferior by their fellow non-native speakers, especially by influential stakeholders and professionals. This prejudice leads to many ministries, deans of university language departments and school principals discriminating against highly qualified and linguistically proficient local multilingual teachers of English in favour of native speakers. This is particularly invidious, as native speakers are often not required to have any professional training. Thus an untrained and unqualified native speaker will be preferred to a qualified and highly proficient local non-native teacher. That many of these unqualified native teachers can also obtain employment in kindergartens and primary schools without any vetting makes this policy highly irresponsible. The following excerpts were taken from an advertisement in an international English-language newspaper. It was placed by an EFL recruitment company which was seeking teachers for schools in Japan. The teachers needed to be native speakers of English and to be 'enthusiastic, energetic graduates' who 'must like children'. 'No teaching or TEFL experience is required.'

The prejudice which favours the native speaker over the non-native speaker is, like all prejudices of this type, uninformed. As a result, the advantages offered by trained and proficient multilingual teachers remain unrecognized. One advantage — the ability to teach bilingually and to use both the first and target languages for language teaching — is commonly cited as a *disadvantage*. In Chapter 7, I mentioned that many people in Hong Kong still adhere to the belief that language is best taught monolingually. That is to say, the only language used in the language classroom should be the target language. This belief is shared by many through the ASEAN region, where one advantage of monolingual native speakers is seen to be their *inability* to use the children's first language. This belief extends to principals *not* employing bilinguals as teachers because they think these bilingual teachers will use the children's first language in the language classroom and, in this way, hinder learning. Cummins (2005: 9) points that this 'dominant monolingual instructional orientation' is based on three sets of assumptions, 'none of which is empirically supported'. They are:

> Instruction should be carried out exclusively in the target language without recourse to the students' L1. Bilingual dictionary use is discouraged (= *direct method* assumption).
>
> Translation between L1 and L2 has no place in the teaching of language or literacy. Encouragement of translation in L2 teaching is viewed as a regression to the discredited grammar/translation method; or in bilingual/immersion programs, use of translation is equated with the discredited concurrent translation methods in which teachers switch constantly between languages translating all relevant instructional content;
>
> Within immersion and bilingual programs, the two languages should be kept rigidly separate (= *two solitudes* assumption)

Cummins urges, however, the adoption of 'bilingual instructional strategies'. The children's first language can be used in systematic ways to enhance second language learning. For example, the use of the first language can explain concepts and phenomena in the most time-effective way. This can range from simple translations to explanations of grammatical structures and cultural values. This can be especially informative when ways of naming, patterning and doing in the first and target languages are compared.

More sophisticated uses of the first language include allowing children to use the first language while working on tasks which will need to be reported — either orally or in written form — in the target language. A strategy which promotes 'literacy engagement in both L1 and L2' (Cummins 2005: 9–10) is the creation of 'dual language books'. An example of the 'dual language books' strategy is the authoring of a bilingual Urdu-English book, *The New Country*, by three recent migrants to Canada. The three girls discussed the draft in Urdu but wrote the initial draft in English. The final product was a dual language book, and is an example of what Cummins refers to as an 'identity text'. More examples of these dual books and identity texts can be seen at http://thornwood.peelschools.org/DUAL/.

A second strategy involves schools establishing partnerships with other schools in different countries (Cummins 2005: 9). Groups of students from partner schools work together on projects in which they need to use English as a lingua franca. Establishing school and class partnerships of this type would be easy to establish in many ASEAN settings.

This use of more than one language in the language classroom has been called 'translanguaging', which is the receiving of information in one language and using it or applying it another language. The advantages of 'translanguaging' are described by Baker (2000: 104–5):

> Translanguaging has two potential advantages. It may promote a deeper and fuller understanding of the subject matter. It is possible in a monolingual context for students to answer questions or write an essay without fully understanding the subject. Whole sentences or paragraphs can be copied or adapted from a textbook without rarely understanding them. This is less easy in a bilingual situation. To read and discuss a topic in one language, and then to write about it in another, means that the subject has to be properly 'digested' and reconstructed.

A great advantage of multilingual language teachers is that they can adopt these bilingual strategies in the language class. This is yet another reason why English teachers in the ASEAN region need to be multilinguals who are able to use the language of the children in systematic ways in order to enhance the learning of English. Being monolingual represents a disadvantage here, not an advantage.

Having now suggested that the 'variety' of English should be a multilingual model and that it should be taught by multilinguals, I now turn to consider the third question raised at the beginning of this chapter, which was:

What should be taught through English and with what materials?

As has been shown, ASEAN member states see English as the language of knowledge creation and dissemination, and as the language of modernization. The desire to participate in modernization, the so-called knowledge economy and globalization is the major reason why ASEAN governments want their citizens to learn English. But as was also shown in Part I, while English is important for modernization and development, countries where only a relatively limited number of people speak and use English can be extremely successful. Indonesia and Vietnam are illustrations of this. Not everyone needs to know English for a country to modernize successfully. The proposition that, as English is the language of modernization, then the more people who speak it the better, does not stand up to serious scrutiny. First, as Graddol (2006) has pointed out, if everyone spoke English, then no particular advantage would accrue from being able to speak it, although monolingual English speakers would be disadvantaged. Second, the proposition that English is a guaranteed passport to economic success and social advancement and that therefore everyone must learn it, is equally problematic. Graddol's point still holds. If everyone knows English, how can knowing it give anyone an advantage? But this is the justification behind introducing English as early as possible into the primary curriculum. In fact, however, introducing English too early into the primary curriculum, especially when it is at the expense of local languages of education, does great disservice to most children (Bruthiaux 2002).

The truth is that the major role of English in ASEAN is as a lingua franca. This means that ASEAN speakers will be interacting with people from the region. It follows that a topic area which could be taught through English is cross-cultural communication and international relations, but with a focus on the cultures of ASEAN member states. Thus the English curriculum needs to be radically redesigned to become one in which local cultures are studied and where a 'critical cultural consciousness' is enhanced (Lie 2002/3: 72).

To give an example of such a course, I report on a project with which I was involved in Indonesia. This was funded by the Australia Indonesia Institute and came to be known as the 'Asian culture-based project' (see Kirkpatrick 2007e for a detailed report). The original aim was to develop materials aimed at interpreting aspects of different cultures within ASEAN for an English textbook for Indonesia university students. The textbook was published as *Culture Based English for College Students* (Aziz, Sudana and Noorman 2003). Although the final product was a culture-based textbook, the original aims for the project were inexorably altered and reshaped by the Indonesian members of the team. In this I received a salutary lesson in allowing stakeholders to include what they felt to be important, rather than what I had assumed would be considered important.

As reported earlier, English language teaching in Indonesia has not been successful (Dardjowidjojo 2000). The common problems have been described as including 'unskilled teachers, abject facilities, and unfavourable learning environments' (Alwasilah 2001: 20).

At tertiary level, non-English majors are commonly required to take two to three hours per week of an ESP-based English course. This is usually taught as a grammar-translation class. These courses are not successful in developing students' proficiency in English, not least because the students enter these courses with such low levels of English proficiency. This was the background to the project to develop culture-based materials for these students. A planning seminar under the title 'Specific English

for Indonesians' was held at a university in Bandung in 2001. The four interrelated themes and questions discussed at the seminar were:
1. English is now an Asian language; it is commonly used as a lingua franca throughout Asia by so-called non-native speakers in order to communicate with other non-native speakers.
2. When these speakers use English, they need to be able to talk about each other's cultures in English.
3. There are many different varieties of English. Why can't Indonesians choose a culturally appropriate local variety, Malaysian, for example, instead of a native speaker variety?
4. If the English taught in Indonesia is to be based on a local model and if the materials are to be based on local and regional cultures, does that not imply that local and regional English teachers who speak the model to be taught, and have knowledge of the cultures to be taught are the most appropriate teachers?

These themes promoted some heated discussion. In answer to the third question, for example, about Indonesians adopting the Malaysian variety of English as a model, it was quite clear that this would be the last variety that Indonesians would want to adopt, although they clearly saw the linguistic and cultural advantages of doing so.

However, there was enough agreement to decide to form a team to develop an English textbook based on a range of ASEAN cultures. The team was set up by Professor Chaedar Alwasilah of the University of Education (IUE) and headed by Dr Aziz, also of IUE. The plan was that the team would first write six trial units and then send them to me in Australia for my comments.

When the six units duly arrived, I was surprised to find that they dealt exclusively with the cultures of Indonesia rather than with those of ASEAN. There was nothing about Vietnam, Thailand or the Philippines, for example. Instead, the units all dealt with different aspects of Indonesian cultures. As illustrated in Chapter 3, Indonesia is an extraordinarily diverse nation in which more than 200 ethnic groups speak more than 400 languages, and it was clear that it was these cultures that were of most interest to the textbook writers. This presented me with a problem, as the original idea had been to develop a textbook based on ASEAN cultures, but the team was writing a textbook based on the cultures of Indonesia itself. I was also unclear why these topics would not be more appropriately discussed through Bahasa Indonesia, the national lingua franca, rather than through English. I thus had my concerns, but when the results of the student evaluations of the trial units arrived, I had to put my concerns aside, as they were overwhelmingly positive, with, for example, *all* the students classifying the materials as suitable.

Table 8.3 Student evaluation of the trial materials (Kirkpatrick 2007e: 25)

Evaluative statements	Percentage% of students who agreed with the statements
Appropriate for MKDU course	83.35%
Appropriate for achieving course objectives	75%
Support their study	95.8%
Materials are suitable	100%
Need to incorporate global culture	79.2%
Activities are useful	95.8%
Materials improve reading ability	91.7%
Materials improve listening and speaking	75%
Materials improve writing ability	54.2%
Time allocated is sufficient	45.8%
The design is not attractive	66.7%

Thus the final textbook focused entirely on Indonesian cultures, as evidenced by the titles of the fifteen units. These are listed in Table 8.4.

Table 8.4 Unit titles

Unit 1	Our capital city
Unit 2	Becak
Unit 3	We love dangdut
Unit 4	Harmonious life
Unit 5	Students and brawls
Unit 6	Preserving the traditions: Textiles
Unit 7	Rendra
Unit 8	The world of mysticism
Unit 9	Business matters
Unit 10	Traditional wedding ceremony
Unit 11	Traditional arts: Wayang
Unit 12	Wanted urgently: Are you the right person?
Unit 13	The top five!
Unit 14	Caring for fauna
Unit 15	Indonesian cuisine: Ayam Taliwang

Even those units which do not make an explicit reference to Indonesia or Indonesian culture actually describe these. For example, Unit 9 lists the characteristics of Indonesian business people. The 'top five' of Unit 13 is a reference to Transparency International's list of the world's most corrupt countries which placed Indonesia in the 'top five', coming 88th out of the 91 countries surveyed. This also illustrates that the textbook writers were prepared to deal with tricky subjects. While some of the units deal with uncontroversial topics, this was not a textbook which uncritically celebrated the joys of Indonesian diversity, but one which tackled subjects that were discomfiting to Indonesians. These subjects were included as Indonesians themselves felt they were important and needed to be discussed. This may also explain their selection for inclusion in an English textbook, as it may well have been easier for the Indonesians to discuss 'tricky' subjects in English than in Bahasa Indonesia.

In any event, the textbook was successful and was reprinted. It turned out that the textbook writers were right in including local cultures. This gave students the opportunity to discuss issues of importance to them, while allowing them to develop the language to be able to talk about and explain their own cultural heritage and values to non-Indonesians through English. Any English language curriculum for ASEAN must have as a major goal the ability of people to talk about and explain *their own* cultural values to outsiders.

In addition to preparing students to be able to talk about their own cultures, the cross-cultural curriculum, could, however, also include information about other cultures of the region. This is of particular importance when the major languages of the region are not taught in these schools, as is currently the case. Ideally, students in ASEAN should learn about the cultures of each other's countries while taking a relevant language course. For example, Thai students should learn about Indonesia while taking a course in Bahasa Indonesia. As, however, the national languages of ASEAN are not taught as foreign languages in government schools — Putonghua is by far the most common Asian language taught as a 'foreign' language — then the cultures of ASEAN can be taught through English. Thus Vietnamese students can learn about the cultures of Malaysia in a cross-cultural course which uses English as the medium of instruction. Such courses provide excellent opportunities for schools within the region to establish school partnerships and 'sister-class' arrangements of the type described earlier (Cummins 2005: 9). In this way, Vietnamese schools can, for example, work in partnership with Malaysian schools on projects in which students compare and contrast Vietnamese and Malaysian cultural values. This would help students in ASEAN become familiar with the cultures of ASEAN and to understand the extraordinarily rich level of cultural diversity which exists across the member states.

A course in cross-cultural communication and international relations could include a history of ASEAN itself and an introduction to the various workings of ASEAN. A critical reading of the ASEAN Charter could be part of such a course, which could include a discussion on the reasons for and the advantages and disadvantages of privileging of English as the sole working and official language.

Topics of shared concern should also be part of the course. These might include environmental concerns — logging and deforestation, for example; political concerns — ways of negotiating with Burma, for example; and social concerns — the position of ethnic minorities, for example.

The pragmatic norms discussed in Chapter 5 could also be course components. The transfer of pragmatic norms is of particular importance in lingua franca communication, as participants may not realize that such a transfer is being made. Thus, for example, if a request pattern which is appropriate in Filipino is inappropriate in Vietnamese, then the transfer of this pattern from Filipino into English in lingua franca communication with Vietnamese may be interpreted as inappropriate by the Vietnamese interactants, as they will respond to the request pattern from the point of view of Vietnamese norms. Questions such as 'Do all Asian cultures give and receive compliments in the same way?' and 'Are there significant differences in the appropriate ways of making request between Asian and Anglo cultures?' therefore become important topics for study in any course on cross-cultural communication. As McKay has argued, it is important that courses of this type address 'the hybridity of modern life and the manner in which English as an international language is often used to negotiate various identities' (2009: 239).

In addition, individual member states could offer courses in literatures in English which would allow students to read about their own and other cultures through the eyes of people with whom they can identify. One interesting example of such a course comes from the Philippines, where each year the children read texts in English that fit in with an annual theme (Thompson 2003: 51). In the first year, they read stories and texts written in English by Filipino authors about being a Filipino. In the second year, they move to read texts written in English by Asian authors about what it is like to be an Asian. In the third year, they read stories taken from 'Anglo' literatures, and in the fourth year, the theme is extended further to being a citizen of the world. This is summarized below:

Year	Theme
1	I am a Filipino
2	I am an Asian
3	I am an English speaker
4	I am a citizen of the world

A course in cross-cultural communication and international relations would therefore contain a wide variety of content aimed to provide an in-depth comparative study of ASEAN cultures, concerns and literatures. Such a course could extend throughout secondary school. It would also need to include a study of Asian varieties of English and, of course, the role of English as a lingua franca in ASEAN.

This would have important implications for teaching materials, for which multilingual speakers engaged in lingua franca communication should be used. That is to say, interactional ELF data of the type described in Part II should play a prominent role as teaching material in showing students how English is used as a lingua franca by ASEAN multilinguals such as themselves. While there must obviously be some focus on form, the overarching goals are to ensure intelligibility and to achieve communicative success in lingua franca communication. Thus the communicative strategies illustrated in Chapter 6 should also be taught, as these help ensure smooth and successful communication.

So, to answer the third question concerning what should be taught and with what materials, I propose that an in-depth course in cross-cultural communication and international relations made up of the components illustrated above should be the subject taught through the medium of English. Materials modelling ELF interactions should also help students recognize that the major role of English in ASEAN is as a lingua franca, and that it is used by multilinguals such as themselves with whom they can identify and upon whom they can model their own performance. They are learning English primarily to be able to use English as a regional lingua franca in this way.

Conclusion

At the beginning of this chapter, three questions were posed. These were:

> If English is to be taught in schools, what variety of English should be taught and how?
> Who should teach it?
> What should be taught through English and with what materials?

I hope that my suggested answers to these questions and the justifications for them are now clear. However, it is also clear that an ASEAN English curriculum which incorporates an English-medium secondary school course in cross-cultural communication and which is to be taught by trained local multilingual teachers of English using themselves as linguistic models along with other teaching materials of ASEAN ELF interactions represents a radical departure from current practice. I shall conclude then by reiterating the reasons for the proposals made here and in Chapter 7 and by suggesting a number of results that could be seen, if the proposals presented in this book were adopted.

1. It is much better to start learning English late than to start too early.

Currently almost all ASEAN countries introduce English as a compulsory subject at primary level. The reason for this is that it is believed that the earlier one starts to learn a language the better. I have presented counter-arguments and research results to show that it is not necessary to start early in order to gain a high degree of proficiency in a second language. The tenet: 'to learn a second language you *must* start as early as possible', should therefore be reformulated to read:

'To learn a second language *you don't have* to start as early as possible.'

Indeed, in the great majority of ASEAN contexts I have argued that it is actually harmful for too early a start to be made, as there are insufficient resources, a chronic and severe lack of suitably qualified and linguistically proficient teachers, and the learning environment is anything but supportive. As a result, large number of children fail or drop out of primary school.

2. English should not be used as a medium of instruction in primary schools.

Several ASEAN countries use English as a medium of instruction, usually for the teaching of science and maths. Some use English as a medium of instruction from Primary 1. This is based on the belief that the best way to learn a second language is to use it as a medium of instruction. I have offered counter-arguments and research results to show that a second language should only be used as a medium of instruction once the learner has gained at least five years' instruction in it. Using the L2 too early as a medium of instruction places far too heavy a cognitive burden on the child, who will end up learning neither the L2 nor the content subject. This has now been recognized by the Malaysian government in their decision to abandon their current policy of using English to teach maths and science, not only just from Primary 1, but as a medium of instruction altogether. The tenet that, 'the best way to learn a second language is to use it as a medium of instruction' should therefore be reformulated to read:

'Only use a second language as a medium of instruction after at least five years' instruction in it.'

3. The linguistic focus of primary schools in ASEAN should be on local languages, not English.

The use of local languages as languages of education is currently neglected in almost all government primary schools throughout ASEAN.

The common situation is that primary children learn the national language and English. This neglect of the child's first language is based on the belief that the home language gets in the way of learning a second language. I have offered counter-arguments and research results to show that the opposite is true. In other words, the first language acts as a bridge to literacy and fluency in the second and third languages. Ensuring children achieve literacy and fluency in their first language therefore represents an excellent investment in the child's linguistic future. Where possible, therefore, the first five years of primary school should be taught through the child's first language. If this is impractical, then a local regional lingua franca should be used instead. The tenet that, 'the home language gets in the way of learning a second language' should therefore be reformulated to read:

> 'Fluency and literacy in the home language acts as a bridge to learning a second and later languages.'

The proposal that English should be delayed as a subject until the later years of primary school, and as a medium of instruction until secondary school, is likely to meet with parental resistance. However, Baetens Beardsmore has argued in the context of Europe that the primary curriculum should focus on encouraging linguistic diversity and that English should therefore be delayed until secondary school (2009: 207). This is comparable to the proposal being presented here. It will be important to stress the value of linguistic diversity to parents while reassuring them that delaying English until secondary school still gives students plenty of time in which to gain high levels of proficiency in the language, especially if they have already developed fluency and literacy in other languages.

Adopting the principles expressed in the 'reformulated' tenets above, along with the multilingual model, would, I believe, lead to the following results:

> children who graduate from primary school will be functionally bilingual or multilingual in the relevant national language and local languages;

> children who graduate from secondary school will be: multilingual in the national language and at least one local language; have high levels of proficiency in English; and will have a solid understanding of the cultural diversity of the ASEAN region;

> a far higher retention rate in primary schools, as local languages replace English as languages of education;

> a far more equitable balance of local languages and English within the government education systems of the ASEAN member states;

an increase of resources for the maintenance and development of local languages, including development of the respective national languages as languages of modernization;

an understanding of the post-Anglophone use of English as a lingua franca in ASEAN and the de-privileging of native speaker varieties of English and the native speaker teacher;

the adoption of equitable linguistic benchmarks based on language use in multilingual contexts and the abandonment of highly inequitable monolingual benchmarks based on a monolingual native speaker standard;

the understanding that local multilingual teachers represent excellent role *and* linguistic models for the language classroom and the consequent validation of the multilingual language teacher.

Adopting these proposals would mean that at least some of the linguistic and cultural diversity which currently characterizes the member states of ASEAN would be preserved. It would go some way in helping ASEAN meet one of the aims identified in Article 1 of the new ASEAN Charter, namely 'to promote an ASEAN identity through the fostering of greater awareness of the diverse culture and heritage of the region'. At the same time, adopting the multilingual model and the lingua franca approach to the teaching of English would lead to an increase in the numbers of citizens of ASEAN becoming multilingual and literate in local languages, with those graduating from secondary schools also attaining high levels of functional proficiency in English. Otherwise, the predictable outcome will be a region marked by increasing inequality between the haves and the have-nots, and a region in which local languages become increasingly threatened and displaced by English. English may now be the sole working and official language of ASEAN. We need to ensure that this does not mean that it becomes the dominant language of ASEAN. It is hoped that the recommendations made in this book will provide ASEAN countries with ways and ideas for promoting and valuing multilingualism in Asian languages, while at the same time ensuring its citizens the opportunity to become proficient multilingual speakers of English.

Appendices

Appendix 1: Notation Conventions

(a) { }: The use of { } brackets indicates a 'please continue, I'm listening' signal from a fellow participant. Thus, {T1: eh hm} indicates that the Thai participant makes this signal at this point in the conversation. {F +T1: ehm yeah} indicates that the Thai and one of the female participants say this, but it is not clear which of the female participants it is. {Fx2+T1: yeah} indicates that both the two other females and the Thai speaker say 'yeah' at this stage.

(b) [ ]: The use of [ ] brackets indicates overlapping speech. Thus the excerpt below that reads,

> F1: ... Philippines {B: yes} system students [they get high grades
> B1: for our high school] we get good results

indicates that B1 starts to say 'for our high school' while F1 is saying 'they get high grades'. Please note that these markers are only indicative.

(c) ? : The use of ? indicates that the words of the speaker are not clear at this point.

(d) Phonetic symbols: These are only used in these transcriptions when relevant to the argument being made or to explain a particular transcription.

Appendix 2: SEAMEO Centres

Name	Name	Place
BIOTROP	Tropical Biology	Indonesia
CHAT	History and Tradition	Burma
INNOTECH	Educational Innovation and Technology	Philippines
RECSAM	Education in Science and Maths	Malaysia
RELC	Language Centre	Singapore
RETRAC	Training Centre	Vietnam
RIHED	Higher Education and Development	Thailand
SEAMOLEC	Open Learning Centre	Indonesia
SEARCA	Graduate Study and Research in Agriculture	Philippines
SPAFA	Archaeology and Fine Arts	Thailand
TROPMED	Tropical Medicine and Public Health	(5 Centres)
VOCTECH	Vocational Education and Training	Brunei

Notes

Preface

1. The origin of the term 'lingua franca' stems from when Germanic Franks moved into Gaul in the fifth century and adopted the local language, which became known as the language of the Franks, lingua franca (Phillipson 2008: 261). Ostler (2005: 407) says the term was first used in the Levant. It has a number of possible plural forms, including *lingue franche*, *linguae francae* and *linguas franca*, but 'lingua francas' is now the most common.
2. While the official name of the country is now Myanmar, I refer to it as Burma, as this remains the name most people are familiar with.

Chapter 1

1. As of May 2009 they were: Bulgarian, Czech, Danish, Dutch, English, Estonian, Finnish, French, German, Greek, Hungarian, Italian, Irish, Latvian, Lithuanian, Maltese, Polish, Portuguese, Romanian, Slovak, Slovenian, Spanish, and Swedish. As more nations join with national languages other than these, so will the number of official and working languages increase.

Introduction to Part II

1. A list of these is provided in Appendix 2.

Chapter 4

1. Wells' lexical sets are: KIT, DRESS, TRAP, LOT, STRUT, FOOT, BATH, CLOTH, NURSE, FLEECE, FACE, PALM, THOUGHT, GOAT, GOOSE, PRICE, CHOICE, MOUTH, NEAR, SQUARE, START, NORTH, FORCE, CURE (Wells 1982: xviii).
2. Unless otherwise indicated, the examples of ASEAN ELF all come from Deterding and Kirkpatrick (2006: 391–409).

Chapter 6

1. This chapter draws on Kirkpatrick (2007b), 'The communicative strategies of ASEAN speakers of English as a lingua franca', in D. Prescott (ed.), *English in Southeast Asia: Literacies, Literatures and Varieties* (Newcastle: Cambridge Scholars Publishing), pp. 121–139.

References

Abas, Husen (2000) The crystallization of the Malay language: The Indonesian experience. In *Parangalcang Brother Andrew: A Festschrift for Andrew Gonzalez on His sixtieth Birthday*. Edited by Ma. Lourdes Bautista, Teodoro A. Llamzon, and Bonifacio P. Sibayan. Manila: Linguistic Society of the Philippines, pp. 239–246.
Abrahamsson, Niklas, and Hyltenstam, Kenneth (2009) Age of onset and nativelikeness in a second language: Listener perception versus linguistic scrutiny. *Language Learning*, **59**(2), 249–306.
Aglionby, John (2005) Chinese whispers as a lingua franca. *The Guardian Weekly*, 23 February.
Ahmad Zakaria Haji (1992) The structure of decision making. In *The ASEAN Reader*. Edited by K. S. Sandhu. Singapore: Institute of East Asian Studies, pp. 96–100.
Alisjahbana, Takdir S. (1966) *Indonesia: Social and Cultural Revolution*. Kuala Lumpur: Oxford University Press.
Alisjahbana, Takdir S. (1976) *Language Planning and Modernisation: The Case of Indonesian and Malaysian*. The Hague: Mouton.
Alwasilah, Chaedar (2001) The emerging Indonesian English (Indoenglish): A pedagogical exploration. In *Proceedings of the Seminar on Specific English for Indonesians*. Edited by Daniel Wibowo. Bandung: Universitas Kristen Maranatha, pp. 18–22.
Anderson, Liz (1999) *Red Lights and Green Lizards: A Cambodian Adventure*. Maidenhead: Wayfarer Publishing.
Aziz, Aminudin, Sudana, Dadang, and Noorman, Safrina (2003) *Culture-Based English for College Students*. Jakarta: Grasindo.
Baetens Beardsmore, Hugo (2009) Language promotion by European supra-national institutions. In *Bilingual Education in the 21st Century: A Global Perspective*. Edited by Ofelia Garcia. Malden, MA: Wiley-Blackwell, pp. 197–217.
Bailey, Guy (1997) When did Southern American English begin? *Englishes Around the World, Vol. 1*. Edited by Edgar Schneider. Berlin: Mouton de Gruyter, pp. 255–276.
Baker, Colin (2000) *The Care and Education of Young Bilinguals*. Clevedon: Multilingual Matters.

Baker, Frederick J., and Giacchino-Baker, Rosalie (2003) Lower secondary school curriculum development in Vietnam. http:/www.csuponoma.edu/~jis/2003/ Baker_Baker pdf. Accessed on 22 February 2008.

Bamgbose, Ayo (1998) Torn between the norms and innovations in World Englishes. *World Englishes*, **17**(1), 1–14.

Baskaran, Loga (2004) Malaysian English: Phonology. In *A Handbook of Varieties of English. Volume 1: Phonology*. Edited by Edgar W. Schneider, Kate Burridge, Bernd Kortmann, Rajend Mesthrie, and Clive Upton. Berlin: Mouton de Gruyter, pp. 1034–1046.

Bautista, Ma. Lourdes (1996) Outline: The national language and the language of instruction. In *Readings in Philippine Sociolinguistics*. Edited by Ma. Lourdes Bautista. Manila: De la Salle University Press, pp. 223–227.

Bautista, Ma. Lourdes (1997) The lexicon of Philippine English. In *English Is an Asian Language: The Philippine Context*. Edited by Ma. Lourdes Bautista. Sydney: Macquarie Library, pp. 49–72.

Bautista, Ma. Lourdes (2000) The grammatical features of educated Philippine English. In *Parangalcang Brother Andrew: A Festschrift for Andrew Gonzalez on His Sixtieth Birthday*. Edited by Ma. Lourdes Bautista, Teodoro A. Llamzon, and Bonifacio P. Sibayan. Manila: Linguistic Society of the Philippines, pp. 146–160.

Bautista, Ma. Lourdes (ed.) (1996) *Readings in Philippine Sociolinguistics*. Manila: De la Salle University Press.

Bautista, Ma. Lourdes (ed.) (1997) *English is an Asian Language: The Philippine Context*. Sydney: The Macquarie Library.

Bautista, Ma. Lourdes, Llamzon, Teodoro A., and Sibayan, Bonifacio P. (eds.) (2000) *Parangalcang Brother Andrew: A Festschrift for Andrew Gonzalez on His Sixtieth Birthday*. Manila: Linguistic Society of the Philippines.

Beacco, Jean-Claude, and Byram, Michael (2003) *Guide for the Development of Language Education Policies in Europe (Draft 1 (rev)*. Strasbourg: Council of Europe, Language Policy Division.

Benson, Carol (2008) Summary overview. Mother tongue-based education in multilingual contexts. In *Improving the Quality of Mother Tongue-based Literacy and Learning: Case Studies from Asia, Africa and South America*. Edited by Caroline Haddad. Bangkok: UNESCO, pp. 2–11.

Benton, Richard A. (1996) The Philippine bilingual education program: Education for the masses or the preparation of a new elite? In *Readings in Philippine Sociolinguistics*. Edited by Ma. Lourdes Bautista. Manila: De la Salle University Press, pp. 308–326.

Bernard, Jacques (2003) Language policy and the promotion of national identity in Indonesia. In *Fighting Words: Language Policy and Ethnic Relations in Asia*. Edited by Michael Brown and Sumit Ganguly. Cambridge, MA: MIT Press, pp. 263–290.

Bernardo, Allan B.I. (2000) The multifarious effects of language on mathematical learning and performance among bilingual: A cognitive science perspective. In *Parangalcang Brother Andrew: A Festschrift for Andrew Gonzalez on His Sixtieth Birthday*. Edited by Ma. Lourdes Bautista, Teodoro A. Llamzon, and Bonifacio P. Sibayan. Manila: Linguistic Society of the Philippines, pp. 303–316.

Bernardo, Allan B.I. (2005) Bilingual code-switching as a resource for learning and teaching: Alternative reflections on the language and education in the Philippines. In *Linguistics and Language Education in the Philippines and Beyond: A Festschrift for Ma. Lourdes S. Bautista.* Edited by Danilo T. Dayag and J. Stephen Quakenbush. Manila: Linguistic Society of the Philippines, pp. 151–170.

Berns, Margie (2008) English as a lingua franca, and intelligibility. *World Englishes,* **27**(3–4), 327–334.

Bernstein, Cynthia (2003) Grammatical features of southern speech: *Yall, might could,* and *fixin' to.* In *English in the Southern United States.* Edited by S. J. Nagle and S. L. Saunders. Cambridge: Cambridge University Press, pp. 106–118.

Bhumirat, Chinnapat (2007) Enhancing education and forging national unity through the use of mother-tongue: The experience of Thailand. *SEAMEO Education Agenda,* **1**, 20–22.

Bickerton, Derek (1981) *Roots of Language.* Ann Arbor, MI: Karoma.

Blake, Norman Francis (1996) *A History of the English Language.* London: Macmillan.

Blum-Kulka, Shoshana, House, Juliane, and Kasper, Gabriele (eds.) (1989) *Cross-cultural Pragmatics: Requests and Apologies.* Norwood: Ablex.

Bolton, Kingsley (2000) The sociolinguistics of Hong Kong and the space for Hong Kong English. *World Englishes,* **19**(3), 265–286.

Bolton, Kingsley (ed.) (2002) *Hong Kong English: Autonomy and Creativity.* Hong Kong: Hong Kong University Press.

Bolton, Kingsley (2003) *Chinese Englishes: A Sociolinguistic History.* Cambridge: Cambridge University Press.

Bolton, Kingsley (2008) English in Asia, Asian Englishes, and the issue of proficiency. *English Today,* **24**(2): 3–12.

Bolton, Kingsley (2010) 'Thank you for calling': Asian Englishes and 'native-like' performance in Asian call centres. In *The Handbook of World Englishes.* Edited by Andy Kirkpatrick. London: Routkedge, pp. 556–564.

Bolton, Kingsley and Kwok, Helen (1990) The dynamics of the Hong Kong accent: Social identity and sociolinguistic description. *Journal of Asian Pacific Communication,* **1**(1), 147–172.

Boyle, Joseph (1997) Imperialism and the English language. *Journal of Multilingual and Multicultural Development,* **18**(3), 265–286.

Braine, George (ed.) (1999) *Non-native Educators in English Language Teaching.* Mahwah, NJ: Lawrence Erlbaum Associates.

Breiteneder, Angelika (2005) The naturalness of English as a European lingua franca: The case of the 'third person -s'. *Vienna English Working Papers,* **14**(2), 3–26.

Breiteneder, Angelika (2009) English as a lingua franca in Europe: An empirical perspective. *World Englishes,* **28**(2), 256–269.

Britain, David (2007) Grammatical variation in England. In *Language in the British Isles.* Edited by David Britain. Cambridge: Cambridge University Press, pp. 75–104.

Brown, Adam (1999). *Singapore English in a Nutshell: An Alphabetical Description of its Features.* Singapore: Federal Publications.

Brown, Michael (2003) Language policy and ethnic relations in Asia. In *Fighting Words: Language Policy and Ethnic Relations in Asia.* Edited by Michael Brown and Sumit Ganguly. Cambridge, MA: MIT Press, pp. 413–447.

Brown, Michael E., and Ganguly, Sumit (eds.) (2003) *Fighting Words: Language Policy and Ethnic Relations in Asia.* Cambridge, MA: MIT Press.

Brunei Ministry of Education (2009) *Sistem Pendidikan Negara Abad 21 (SPN–21).* Bandar Seri Begawan: Ministry of Education.

Bruthiaux, Paul (2002) Hold your courses: Language education, language choice, and economic development. *TESOL Quarterly,* **36**(3), 275–296.

Bruthiaux, Paul (2006) Restandardising local Englishes: Aspirations and limitations. *International Journal of the Sociology of Language,* **177**, 31–50.

Bruthiaux, Paul (2008) Language education, economic development, and participation in the Greater Mekong subregion. *International Journal of Bilingual Education and Bilingualism,* **11**, 134–148.

Budianta, Melani (2007) Diverse voices: Indonesian literature and nation building. In *Language Nation and Development.* Edited by Lee Hock Guan and Leo Suryadinata. Singapore: Institute of Southeast Asian Studies, pp. 51–73.

Burchfield, Robert (1985) *The English Language.* Oxford: Oxford University Press.

Butler, Susan (2002) Language, literature and culture – and their meeting place in the dictionary. In *Englishes in Asia: Communication, Identity, Power and Education.* Edited by Andy Kirkpatrick. Melbourne: Language Australia, pp. 143–168.

Butler, Susan (2007) Dictionary publishing in Asia. In *English in Southeast Asia: Varieties, Literacies and Literatures.* Edited by David Prescott. Newcastle: Cambridge Scholars Publishing, pp. 30–46.

Callahan, Mary P. (2003) Language policy in modern Burma. In *Fighting Words: Language Policy and Ethnic Relations in Asia.* Edited by Michael Brown and Sumit Ganguly. Cambridge, MA: MIT Press, pp. 143–175.

Canagarajah, Suresh (2007) The ecology of global English. *International Multilingual Research Journal,* **1**(2), 89–100.

Card, James (2008) Shock tactics split Korea. In *The Guardian Weekly, Learning English.* 8–14 February.

Carruthers, Ashley (2007) Vietnamese language and media policy. In *Language Nation and Development.* Edited by Lee Hock Guan and Leo Suryadinata. Singapore: Institute of Southeast Asian Studies, pp. 195–216.

Cenoz, Jasone (2009) *Towards Multilingual Education.* Bristol: Multilingual Matters.

Chambers, J. K. (2004) Dynamic typology and vernacular universals. In *Dialectology Meets Typology: Dialect Grammar from a Cross-linguistic Perspective.* Edited by Bernd Kortmann. Berlin: Mouton de Gruyter, pp. 124–145.

Chambers, J. K. (2009) Cognition and the linguistic continuum from vernacular to standard. In *Vernacular Universals and Language Contacts: Evidence from Varieties of English and Beyond.* Edited by Markku Filppula, Juhani Klemola, and Heli Paulasto. London: Routledge, pp. 19–32.

Chen, Ping (1999) *Modern Chinese: History and Sociolinguistics.* Cambridge: Cambridge University Press.

Cheshire, Jenny (2005) Syntactic variation and beyond: Gender and social class variation in the use of discourse-new markers. *Journal of Sociolinguistics,* **9**(4), 479–508.

Chua, Chee Lay (ed.) 2005. *Keeping My Mandarin Alive: Lee Kuan Yew's Language Learning Experience.* Singapore: World Scientific Publishing.

Clayton, Thomas (2006) *Language Choice in a Nation under Transition: English Language Spread in Cambodia.* Boston, MA: Springer.

Cogo, Alessia and Dewey, Martin (2006) Efficiency in ELF communication: From pragmatic motives to lexico-grammatical innovation. *Nordic Journal of English Studies,* **5**(2), 59–93.

Cruttenden, Alan (2001) *Gimson's Pronunciation of English.* Sixth edition. London: Arnold.

Crystal, David (2004) *The Stories of English.* London: Allen Lane.

Cukor-Avila, Patricia (2003) The complex grammatical history of African-American and white vernaculars in the South. In *English in the Southern United States.* Edited by S. J. Nagle and S. L. Sanders. Cambridge: Cambridge University Press, pp. 82–105.

Cummins, Jim (1981) Age on arrival and second language learning in Canada: A reassessment. *Applied Linguistics,* **1**, 132–149.

Cummins, Jim (2005) Teaching for cross-language transfer in dual language education: Possibilities and pitfalls. TESOL Symposium on Dual Language Education, Bogazici University, Turkey, 23 September. http://www.achievementseminars.com/seminar_series_2005_2006/readings/tesol.turkey.pdf

Cummins, Jim (2008) Teaching for transfer: Challenging the two solitudes assumption in bilingual education. *The Encyclopedia of Language and Education. Vol. 5. Bilingual Education.* New York: Springer, pp. 65–75.

Curley, Melissa G., and Thomas, Nicholas (2007) Advancing East Asian regionalism: An introduction. In *Advancing East Asian Regionalism.* Edited by Melissa G. Curley and Nicholas Thomas. London: Routledge, pp. 1–25.

Dalby, Andrew (2002) *Language in Danger: How Language Loss Threatens Our Future.* London: Allen Lane, The Penguin Press.

Dardjowidjojo, Soenjono (2000) English teaching in Indonesia. In *The English Australia Journal,* **18**(1), 2–30.

David, Maya, and McLellan, James (2007) Nativised varieties of English in news reports in Malaysia and Brunei. In *Varieties, Literacies and Literatures.* Edited by David Prescott. Newcastle: Cambridge Scholars Publishing, pp. 93–117.

Davies, Alan (1991) *The Native Speaker in Applied Linguistics.* Edinburgh: Edinburgh University Press.

Dayag, Danilo T., and Quakenbush, J. Stephen (eds.) (2005) *Linguistics and Language Education in the Philippines and Beyond: A Festschrift for Ma. Lourdes S. Bautista.* Manila: Linguistic Society of the Philippines.

Deterding, David (2007) *Dialects of English: Singapore English.* Edinburgh: Edinburgh University Press.

Deterding, David (2010) Variation across Englishes: Phonology. In *The Routledge Handbook of World Englishes.* Edited by Andy Kirkpatrick. London: Routledge.

Deterding, David, Low, Ee-Ling and Brown, Adam (eds.) (2003) *English in Singapore: Research on Grammar.* Singapore: McGraw-Hill.

Deterding, David, Brown, Adam, and Low, Ee-Ling (eds.) (2005) *English in Singapore: Phonetic Research on a Corpus.* Singapore: McGraw-Hill.

Deterding, David, and Kirkpatrick, Andy (2006) Emerging Asian Englishes and intelligibility. *World Englishes,* **25**(3–4), 391–410.

Deterding, David, Wong, Jennie, and Kirkpatrick, Andy (2008) The pronunciation of Hong Kong English. *English World-Wide,* **29**(2), 148–175.

Diffloth, Gérard (1994) The linguistic treasures of Vietnam. *Vietnamese Studies,* 42.

Diller, Tony (1991) What makes Central Thai a national language? In *National Identity and Its Defenders: Thailand 1939–1989*. Edited by Craig J. Reynolds. Melbourne: Centre of Southeast Asian Studies, Monash University, pp. 91–107.

Dussek, O.T. (1983) Education in British Malaya. In *Honourable Intentions: Talks on the British Empire in South-East Asia Delivered at the Royal Colonial Institute 1874–1928*. Edited by Paul H. Kratoska. Singapore: Oxford University Press, pp. 447–448.

Education Commission (2005) *Report on Review of Medium of Instruction for Secondary Schools and Secondary School Places Allocation*. Hong Kong.

Elder, Cathy, and Davies, Alan (2006) Assessing English as a lingua franca. *Annual Review of Applied Linguistics*, **26**, 282–301.

Fabricius, Anne (2002) Ongoing change in modern RP: Evidence for the disappearing stigma of t-glottalling. *English World-Wide*, **23**(1), 115–136.

Ferguson, Gibson (2006) *Language Planning and Education*. Edinburgh: Edinburgh University Press.

Filppula, Markku, Klemola, Juhani and Paulasto, Heli (eds.) (2009a) *Vernacular Universals and Language Contacts: Evidence from Varieties of English and Beyond*. London: Routledge.

Filppula, Markku, Klemola, Juhani and Paulasto, Heli (2009b) Vernacular universals and language contacts: An overview. In *Vernacular Universals and Language Contacts: Evidence from Varieties of English and Beyond*. Edited by Markku Filppula, Juhani Klemola, and Heli Paulasto. London: Routledge, pp. 1–16.

Firth, Alan (1996) The discursive accomplishment of normality: On 'lingua franca' English and conversation analysis. *Journal of Pragmatics*, **26**, 237–259.

Firth, Alan, and Wagner, Johannes (1997) On discourse, communication, and (some) fundamental concepts in SLA research. *Modern Language Journal*, **81**, 285–300.

Firth, Alan and Wagner, Johannes (2007) Second/foreign language learning as a social accomplishment: Elaborations on a reconceptualised SLA. *Modern Language Journal* **91**, **1** (Special Focus Issue), 800–819.

Fishman, Joshua A. (1973) Language modernization and planning in comparison with other types of national modernization and planning. *Language in Society*, **2**(1), 23–43.

Galang, Rosita G. (2000) Language planning in Philippine education in the 21st century: Toward language-as-resource orientation. In *Parangalcang Brother Andrew: A Festschrift for Andrew Gonzalez on His Sixtieth Birthday*. Edited by Ma. Lourdes Bautista, Teodoro A. Llamzon, and Bonifacio P. Sibayan. Manila: Linguistic Society of the Philippines, pp. 267–276.

Ganguly, Sumit (2003) The politics of language policies in Malaysia and Singapore. In *Fighting Words: Language Policy and Ethnic Relations in Asia*. Edited by Michael E. Brown and Sumit Ganguly. Cambridge, MA: MIT Press, pp. 239–261.

Garcia, Ester A. (1996) The language policy in education. In *English Is an Asian Language: The Philippine Context*. Edited by Ma. Lourdes Bautista. Sydney: The Macquarie Library, pp. 73–86.

Garcia, Ofelia (2009) *Bilingual Education in the 21st Century: A Global Perspective*. Malden, MA: Wiley-Blackwell.

Garcia, Ofelia, and Bartlett, Lesley (2007) A speech community model of bilingual education: Educating Latino newcomers in the USA. *The International Journal of Bilingual Education and Bilingualism*, **10**(1), 1–25.

Gibson, Ferguson (2006) *Language Planning and Education*. Edinburgh: Edinburgh University Press.

Gill, Saran Kaur (2005) Language policy and planning: Understanding UKM's past, present and future concerns and responses. *Akadamika*, **66** (Januari), 31–50.

Gill, Saran Kaur (2007) Shift in language policy in Malaysia. In *Linguistic Inequality in Scientific Communication Today, The AILA Review, Vol. 20*. Edited by Augusto Carli and Ulrich Ammon. Amsterdam: John Benjamins, pp. 106–122.

Goethals, Michael (1997) English in Flanders (Belgium). *World Englishes*, **16**(1), 105–114.

Goh, Yeng Seng (2009) Bilingual education policy in Singapore: Challenges and opportunities. In *Language Teaching in a Multilingual World*. Edited by Chris Ward. Singapore: SEAMEO Regional Language Centre (RELC) Anthology Series 50, pp. 171–190.

Gonzalez, Andrew B. (1996a) The history of English in the Philippines. In *English is an Asian Language: The Philippine Context*. Edited by Ma. Lourdes Bautista. Sydney: The Macquarie Library, pp. 25–40.

Gonzalez, Andrew B. (1996b) Evaluating bilingual education in the Philippines: Towards a multidimensional model of education in language planning. In *Readings in Philippine Sociolinguistics*. Edited by Ma. Lourdes Bautista. Manila: De la Salle University Press, pp. 327–340.

Gonzalez, Andrew B. (2007) Language, nation and development in the Philippines. In *Language Nation and Development*. Edited by Lee Hock Guan and Leo Suryadinata. Singapore: Institute of Southeast Asian Studies, pp. 7–16.

Gottlieb, Nancy, and Chen, Ping (eds.) *Language Planning and Language Policy: East Asian Perspectives*. Richmond: Curzon.

Graddol, David (2006) *English Next*. London: The British Council.

Greenbaum, Sydney (ed.) (1996) *Comparing English Worldwide*. Oxford: Oxford University Press.

Gupta, Anthea Fraser (1988) A standard for written Singapore English. In *New Englishes: The Case of Singapore*. Edited by James Foley. Singapore: National University of Singapore Press, pp. 27–50.

Haddad, Caroline (ed.) (2007) *Mother Tongue-Based Literacy Programmes: Case Studies of Good Practice from Asia*. Bangkok: UNESCO.

Haddad, Caroline (ed.) (2008) *Improving the Quality of Mother Tongue-Based Literacy and Learning: Case Studies from Asia, Africa and South America*. Bangkok: UNESCO.

Hagiwara, Yoshiyuki (1992) The formation of ASEAN. In *The ASEAN Reader*. Edited by Kernial Singh Sandhu. Singapore: Institute of East Asian Studies, pp. 35–37.

Hans Rausing Endangered Languages Project Annual Report (2008) http://www.hrelp.org/publications/reports/HRELP_annual_report_2008.pdf. Accessed on 10 August 2009.

Harder, Peter (ed.) (2009) *Angles on the English Speaking World*. Copenhagen: University of Copenhagen Press.

Hau, Caroline S., and Tinio, Victoria L. (2003) Language policy and ethnic relations in the Philippines. In *Fighting Words: Language Policy and Ethnic Relations in Asia*. Edited by Michael E. Brown and Sumit Ganguly. Cambridge, MA: MIT Press, pp. 319–350.

Heder, Steve (2007) Cambodia. In *Language and National Identity in Asia*. Edited by Andrew Simpson. Oxford: Oxford University Press, pp. 288–311.

Hickey, Ray (2004) *Legacies of Colonial English*. Cambridge: Cambridge University Press.
Hinds, John (1983) Contrastive rhetoric: Japanese and English. *Text*, **3**, 183–195.
Ho, Esther Sui-chu, and Man, Evelyn Yee-fun (2007) *Student Performance in Chinese Medium of Instruction (CMI) and English Medium of Instruction (EMI) Schools: What We Learned from the PISA Study*. Hong Kong: Hong Kong Institute of Educational Research, The Chinese University of Hong Kong.
Ho, Wah Kam, and Wong, Ruth (eds.) (2000a) *Language Policies and Language Education: The Impact in East Asian Countries in the Next Decade*. Singapore: Times Academic Press.
Ho, Wah Kam, and Wong, Ruth (2000b) Introduction. In *Language Policies and Language Education: The Impact in East Asian Countries in the Next Decade*. Edited by Ho Wah Kam and Ruth Wong. Singapore: Times Academic Press, pp. 1–39.
Ho, Wah Kam, and Wong, Ruth Y.L. (eds.) (2004) *English Language Teaching in East Asia Today*. Singapore: Eastern Universities Press.
Ho, Wah Kam, and Wong, Ruth Y.L. (2006) Applied linguistics in Southeast Asia. In *The Encyclopedia of Language and Linguistics*. Edited by Keith Brown. Oxford: Elsevier, pp. 385–393.
Honey, P. J. (1987) Vietnamese speakers. In *Learner English: A Teacher's Guide to Interference and Other Problems*. Edited by Michael Swan and Bernard Smith. Cambridge: Cambridge University Press, pp. 238–251.
Honna, Nobuyuki (n/d) English is an Asian language: Some thoughts for action proposals. http:www.jafae.org/Englishes/sample%20in%20Enlgish.doc. Accessed on 13 February 2008.
House, Juliane (2002) Developing pragmatic competence in English as a lingua franca. In *Lingua Franca Communication*. Edited by K. Knapp and C. Meierkord. Frankfurt: Peter Lang, pp. 73–89.
House, Juliane (2003) English as a lingua franca: A threat to multilingualism? *Journal of Sociolinguistics*, **7**(4), 556–578.
House, Juliane (2006) Unity in diversity: English as a lingua franca in Europe. In *Reconfiguring Europe*. Edited by Constant Leung and Jennifer Jenkins. London: Equinox, pp. 87–104.
Hülmbauer, Cornelia (2007) 'You moved, aren't?' — The relationship between lexicogrammatical correctness and communicative effectiveness in English as a lingua franca. *Vienna English Working Papers*, **16**(2), 3–35.
Hung, Tony T. N. (2000) Towards a phonology of Hong Kong English. *World Englishes*, **19**(3), 337–356.
Hung, Tony T.N. (2002) English as a global language: Implications for teaching. *The ACELT Journal*, **6**(2), 3–10.
Ihalainen, Ossi (1994) The dialects of England since 1776. In *Cambridge History of the English Language, Vol. 5, English in Britain and Overseas. Origins and Development*. Edited by Robert Burchfield. Cambridge: Cambridge University Press, pp. 197–274.
James, Alan (2000) English as a European lingua franca: Current realities and existing dichotomies. In *English in Europe: The Acquisition of a Third Language*. Edited by J. Cenoz and U. Cessner. Clevedon: Multilingual Matters, pp. 22–38.

James, Alan (2005) The challenges of the lingua franca: English in the world and types of variety. In *The Globalisation of English and the English Language Classroom*. Edited by C. Gnutzmann and F. Inteman. Tubingen: Narr, pp. 133–144.
Jenkins, George (1988) *Times Dictionary of Problem Words*. Singapore: Federal Publications.
Jenkins, Jennifer (2000) *The Phonology of English as an International Language*. Oxford: Oxford University Press.
Jenkins, Jennifer (2006) Points of view and blind spots: ELF and SLA. *International Journal of Applied Linguistics*, **16**(2), 136–162.
Jenkins, Jennifer (2007) *English as a Lingua Franca: Attitudes and Identity*. Oxford: Oxford University Press.
Jenkins, Jennifer, Modiano, Marko, and Seidlhofer, Barbara (2001) Euro-English. *English Today*, **68**(17), 4, 13–21.
Jeon, Mihyon, and Lee, Jiyoon (2006) Hiring native-speaking English teachers in East Asian countries. *English Today*, **22**(4), 53–58.
Johnson, R.K. (1994) Language policy and planning in Hong Kong. *Annual Review of Applied Linguistics*, **14**, 177–199.
Jones, Gary M. (2000) Some language planning questions facing Brunei Darussalam, Singapore, Malaysia and the Philippines. In *Parangalcang Brother Andrew: A Festschrift for Andrew Gonzalez on His Sixtieth Birthday*. Edited by Ma. Lourdes Bautista, Teodoro A. Llamzon, and Bonifacio P. Sibayan. Manila: Linguistic Society of the Philippines, pp. 226–238.
Jones, Gary M. (2002/3) Mono, bi or trilingual education? A question facing many education planners. *Southeast Asia: A Multidisciplinary Journal*, **4**(1–2), 63–72.
Jones, Gary M. (2007) Twenty years of bilingual education: Then and now. In *English in Southeast Asia: Varieties, Literacies and Literatures*. Edited by David Prescott. Newcastle: Cambridge Scholars Publishing, pp. 246–258.
Kachru, Braj B. (ed.) (1992a) *The Other Tongue: English across Cultures*. 2nd edn. Urbana and Chicago: University of Illinois Press.
Kachru, Braj B. (1992b) Models for non-native Englishes. In *The Other Tongue: English across Cultures*, 2nd edn. Urbana and Chicago: University of Illinois Press, pp. 48–74.
Kachru, Braj B. (1992c) Teaching World Englishes. In *The Other Tongue: English across Cultures*, 2nd edn. Urbana and Chicago: University of Illinois Press, pp. 355–365.
Kachru, Braj B., Kachru, Yamuna and Nelson, Cecil L. (2006) *The Handbook of World Englishes*. Malden, MA: Blackwell.
Kettle, Kelvin Charles (2007) In search of a Southeast Asian identity. *SEAMEO Education Agenda*, **2**, 22–25.
Keuk, Chan Narik (2007) An emergence of English language variety in Cambodia. Paper given at the XIIth English in South East Asia Conference, King Mongkut University of Technology, Bangkok, 12–14 December.
Kesavapany, K. (2005). Foreword. In *Framing the ASEAN Charter*. Edited by Rodolfo C. Severino. Singapore: Institute of Southeast Asian Studies, pp. vii-viii.
Keyes, Charles F. (2003) The politics of language in Thailand and Laos. In *Fighting Words: Language Policy and Ethnic Relations in Asia*. Edited by Michael Brown and Sumit Ganguly. Cambridge MA: MIT Press, pp. 177–210.

Kirkpatrick, Andy (1991) Information sequencing in Mandarin in letters of request. *Anthropological Linguistics,* **33**(2), 1–20.
Kirkpatrick, Andy (1993) Information sequencing in Modern Standard Chinese in genre of extended spoken discourse. *Text,* **13**(3), 422–452.
Kirkpatrick, Andy (1996) Topic-comment or modifier-modified? *Studies in Language,* **20**(1), 93–116.
Kirkpatrick, Andy (2007a) *World Englishes: Implications for International Communication and English Language Teaching.* Cambridge: Cambridge University Press.
Kirkpatrick, Andy (2007b) The communicative strategies of ASEAN speakers of English as a lingua franca. In *English in Southeast Asia: Varieties, Literacies and Literatures.* Edited by David Prescott. Newcastle: Cambridge Scholars Publishing, pp. 118–137.
Kirkpatrick, Andy (2007c) The arrangement of letters: Hierarchy or culture? From Cicero to China. *Journal of Asian Pacific Communication,* **17**(2), 245–258.
Kirkpatrick, Andy (2007d) Setting attainable and appropriate English language targets in multilingual settings: A case for Hong Kong. *International Journal of Applied Linguistics,* **17**(3), 353–368.
Kirkpatrick, Andy (2007e) Teaching English across cultures. *English Australia Journal,* **23**(2), 20–36.
Kirkpatrick, Andy (2008) English as the official working language of the Association of Southeast Asian Nations (ASEAN): Features and strategies. *English Today,* **94**(24–2), 37–44.
Kirkpatrick, Andy (2009) English as the working language of ASEAN: Pedagogical principles and implications. In *Language Teaching in a Multilingual World.* Edited by Chris Ward. Singapore: SEAMEO Regional Language Centre (RELC) Anthology Series 50, pp. 215–232.
Kirkpatrick, Andy, and Chau, Michael (2008) One Country, two systems, three languages: A proposal for combining Cantonese, Putonghua and English in Hong Kong's schools. *Asian Englishes,* **11**(2), 32–45.
Kirkpatrick, Andy, Deterding, David, and Wong, Jennie (2008) The international intelligibility of Hong Kong English. *World Englishes,* **29**(3–4), 359–377.
Kirkpatrick, Andy, and Moody, Andrew (2009) A tale of two songs: Singapore versus Hong Kong. *English Language Teaching Journal (ELTJ),* **63**(3), 265–271.
Kirkpatrick, Andy, and Saunders, Neville (2005) The intelligibility of Singaporean English: A case study in an Australian university. In *English in Singapore: Phonetic Research on a Corpus.* Edited by David Deterding, Adam Brown, and Low Ee-Ling. Singapore: McGraw-Hill, pp. 153–162.
Kirkpatrick, Andy, and Xu, Zhichang (2002) Chinese pragmatic norms and China English. *World Englishes,* **21**(2), 269–280.
Kortmann, Bernd, Burridge, Kate, Mesthrie, Rajend, Schneider, Edgar W. and Upton, Clive (eds.) (2004) *A Handbook of Varieties of English. Volume 2: Morphology and Syntax.* Berlin: Mouton de Gruyter.
Kosonen, Kimmo (2003) Community participation in minority language education in Thailand. *Journal of Southeast Asian Education,* **4**(1), 104–136.
Krasnick, Harry (1995) The role of linguaculture and intercultural communication in ASEAN in the year 2020: Prospects and predictions. In *Language and Culture in Multilingual Societies.* Edited by Makhan Tickoo. Singapore: SEAMEO Regional Language Centre, pp. 81–93.

Kratoska, Paul H. (ed.) (1983) *Honourable Intentions: Talks on the British Empire in South-East Asia Delivered at the Royal Colonial Institute 1874–1928*. Singapore: Oxford University Press.
Kumar, Sree, and Siddique, Sharon (2008) *Southeast Asia: The Diversity Dilemma*. Singapore: Select Books.
Kyaw, Yin Hlaing (2007) The politics of language policy in Myanmar. In *Language Nation and Development*. Edited by Lee Hock Guan and Leo Suryadinata. Singapore: Institute of Southeast Asian Studies, pp. 150–180.
Lambert, Wallace E. (1984) An overview of issues in immersion education. In *Studies on Immersion Education: A Collection for United States Educators*. Sacramento, CA: California State Department of Education.
Lambert, Wallace E., and Tucker, G. Richard (1972) *Bilingual Education of Children: The St Lambert Experiment*. Rowley, MA: Newbury House.
Larsen-Freeman, Diane (2007) Reflecting on the cognitive-social debate in second language acquisition. *Modern Language Journal*, **91**(1) (Special Focus Issue), 773–787.
Le, Minh-Hang, and O'Harrow, Stephen (2007) Vietnam. In *Language and National Identity in Asia*. Edited by Andrew Simpson. Oxford: Oxford University Press, pp. 415–441.
Lee, Hock Guan (2007) Ethnic politics, national development and language policy in Malaysia. In *Language Nation and Development*. Edited by Lee Hock Guan and Leo Suryadinata. Singapore: Institute of Southeast Asian Studies, pp. 118–149.
Lee, Hock Guan and Suryadinata, Leo (eds.) (2007) *Language Nation and Development*. Singapore: Institute of Southeast Asian Studies.
Lee, Su Kim (2007) Silent border crossings: The unspoken ESL dilemma. In *Border Crossings*. Edited by Lee Su Kim, Thang Siew Ming, and Lee King Siong. Kuala Lumpur: Pelanduk, pp. 1–22.
Leung, Constant, and Jenkins, Jennifer (2006) *Reconfiguring Europe: The Contribution of Applied Linguistics*. London: Equinox.
Levis, John (2005) Changing contexts and shifting paradigms in pronunciation teaching. *TESOL Quarterly* **39**, 369–377.
Li, David C.S. (2002) Pragmatic dissonance: The ecstasy and agony of speaking like a native speaker of English. In *Discourses in Search of Members: In Honor of Ron Scollon*. Edited by David C.S. Li. Lanham, MD: University Press of America, pp. 559–595.
Li, David C.S. (2006) China as a lingua franca in greater China. *Annual Review of Applied Linguistics* **26**, 149–176.
Li, David C.S. (2007) Researching and teaching China and Hong Kong English. *English Today*, **23**(3–4), 11–17.
Li, Charles, and Thompson, Sandra (1976) Subject and topic: A new typology of language. In *Subject and Topic*. Edited by Charles Li. London: Academic Press, pp. 457–489.
Lie, Anita (2002/3) English curriculum in multicultural societies. *Journal of Southeast Asian Education*, **3–4**, 59–74.
Lieberman, Erez, Michel, Jean-Baptiste, Jackson, Joe, Tang, Tina, and Nowak, Martin A. (2007) Quantifying the evolutionary dynamics of language. *Nature*, **449**(11), 713–716.

Lintner, Bertil (2009) The battle for Thailand. *Foreign Affairs*, July/August, 110–118.
Llurda, Enric (2005) *Non-native Language Teachers: Perceptions, Challenges and Contributions to the Profession*. New York: Springer.
Llurda, Enric (2009) Attitudes towards English as an international language: The pervasiveness of native models among L2 users and teachers. In *English as an International Language: Perspectives and Pedagogical Issues*. Edited by Farzad Sharifian. Bristol: Multilingual Matters, pp. 119–134.
Lo Bianco, Jo (2001) Vietnam: Quoc Ngu, colonialism and language policy. In *Language Planning and Language Policy: East Asian Perspectives*. Edited by Nanette Gottlieb and Ping Chen. Richmond: Curzon, pp. 159–206.
Luangthongkum, Theraphan (2007) The positions of non-Thai Languages in Thailand. In *Language Nation and Development*. Edited by Lee Hock Guan and Leo Suryadinata. Singapore: Institute of Southeast Asian Studies, pp. 181–194.
Mackinnon, Ian (2008) Immersion is a difficult lesson. In *The Guardian Weekly, Learning English*, January, 18–24.
Makarenko, Victor and Pogadaev, Victor (2000) Language situation and policy in Southeast Asia. In *Parangalcang Brother Andrew: A Festschrift for Andrew Gonzalez on His Sixtieth Birthday*. Edited by Ma. Lourdes Bautista, Teodoro A. Llamzon, and Bonifacio P. Sibayan. Manila: Linguistic Society of the Philippines, pp. 213–225.
Maminto, Rosario E. (2005) Program design and implementation of Philippine language education: Research and theoretical perspectives. In *Linguistics and Language Education in the Philippines and Beyond: A Festschrift for Ma. Lourdes S. Bautista*. Edited by Danilo T. Dayag and J. Stephen Quakenbush. Manila: Linguistic Society of the Philippines, pp. 335–348.
Martin, Isabel P. (2005) Conflicts and complications in Philippine education: Implications for ELT. In *Linguistics and Language Education in the Philippines and Beyond: A Festschrift for Ma. Lourdes S. Bautista*. Edited by Danilo T. Dayag and J. Stephen Quakenbush. Manila: Linguistic Society of the Philippines, pp. 267–279.
Martin, Peter, and Abdullah, Kamsiah (2002) English language teaching in Brunei Darussalam: Continuity and change. *Asia-Pacific Journal of Education*, **22**(2), 23–34.
Mauranen, Anna (2003) The corpus of English as a lingua franca in academic settings. *TESOL Quarterly*, **37**(3), 513–527.
Mauranen, Anna (2006) A rich domain of ELF: The ELFA corpus of academic discourse. *Nordic Journal of English Studies* **5**(2), 145–159.
Maxwell, George (1983) Some problems of education and public health in Malaya. In *Honourable Intentions: Talks on the British Empire in South-East Asia Delivered at the Royal Colonial Institute 1874–1928*. Edited by Paul H. Kratoska. Singapore: Oxford University Press, pp. 401–422.
McArthur, Tom (2002) *The Oxford Guide to World Englishes*. Oxford: Oxford University Press.
McArthur, Tom (2003) English as an Asian language. *English Today*, **19**(2), 19–23.
McCafferty, K. (2003) The Northern subject rule in Ulster: How Scots, how English? *Language Variation and Change*, **15**, 105–139.
McFarland, Curtis D. (1996) Subgrouping and number of the Philippine languages or how many Philippine languages are there? In *Readings in Philippine Sociolinguistics*. Edited by Ma. Lourdes Bautista. Manila: De la Salle University Press, pp. 13–22.

McKay, Sandra Lee (2009) Pragmatics and EIL pedagogy. In *English as an International Language*. Edited by Farzad Sharifian. Bristol: Multilingual Matters, pp. 227–253.
McLellan, James (2010) Mixed codes or varieties of English? In *The Routledge Handbook of World Englishes*. Edited by Andy Kirkpatrick. London: Routledge.
McLellan, James and David, Maya Khemlani (2007) A review of code-switching research in Malaysia and Brunei Darussalam. In *English in Southeast Asia*. Edited by David Prescott. Newcastle: Cambridge Scholars Publishing, pp. 69–92.
Medgyes, Peter (1994) *The Non-native Teacher*. London: Macmillan.
Meierkord, Christiane (2004) Syntactic variation in interactions across international Englishes. *English World-Wide*, 25(1), 109–132.
Mesthrie, Rajend (2004) Synopsis: Morphological and syntactic variation in Africa and South and Southeast Asia. In *A Handbook of Varieties of English Volume 2*. Edited by Bernd Kortmann, Kate Burridge, Rajend Mesthrie, Edgar W. Schneider, and Clive Upton. Berlin: Mouton de Gruyter, pp. 1132–1141.
Mesthrie, Rajend and Bhatt, Rakesh (2008) *World Englishes*. Cambridge: Cambridge University Press.
Ministry of Education, Youth and Sport (2004) *Policy for Curriculum Development 2005–2009*. Phnom Penh: Ministry of Education, Youth and Sport.
Mitaray, Sikhamtath (2000) Education in the Lao People's Democratic Republic: Challenges in the new millennium. *Journal of Southeast Asian Education*, 1(1), 103–112.
Modiano, Marko (2006) Euro Englishes. In *The Handbook of World Englishes*. Edited by Braj B. Kachru, Yamuna Kachru, and Cecil L. Nelson. Malden, MA: Blackwell, pp. 223–239.
Mollin, Sandra (2006) English as a lingua franca: A new variety in the new expanding circle? *Nordic Journal of English Studies*, 5(2), 41–57.
Montolalu, Lucy R., and Suryadinata, Leo (2007) National language and nation-building: The case of Bahasa Indonesia. In *Language Nation and Development*. Edited by Lee Hock Guan and Leo Suryadinata. Singapore: Institute of Southeast Asian Studies, pp. 39–50.
Moody, Andrew (2007) Features of the syntax of Asian Englishes: Using the Asian ICE corpora to investigate norms. In *English in Southeast Asia: Varieties, Literacies and Literatures*. Edited by David Prescott. Newcastle: Cambridge Scholars Publishing, pp. 47–68.
Mufwene, Salikoko (2001) *The Ecology of Language Evolution*. Cambridge: Cambridge University Press.
Mufwene, Salikoko (2009) Some offspring of colonial English are Creole. In *Vernacular Universals and Language Contacts: Evidence from Varieties of English and Beyond*. Edited by Markku Filppula, Juhani Klemola, and Heli Paulasto. London: Routledge, pp. 280–303.
Neau, Vira (2003) The teaching of foreign languages in Cambodia: A historical perspective. *Language, Culture and Curriculum*, 16(3), 253–268.
Nelson, Cecil (2008) Intelligibility since 1969. *World Englishes*, 29(3–4), 297–308.
Nelson, Gerald (1996) The design of the corpus. In *Comparing English Worldwide*. Edited by Sydney Greenbaum. Oxford: Oxford University Press, pp. 27–35.

Okudaira, Akiko (1999) A study on international communication in regional organizations: The use of English as the "official" language of the Association of South East Asian Nations (ASEAN). *Asian Englishes,* **2**(1), 91–107.

Ong Keng Yong (2009) At close quarters with the drafting of the ASEAN Charter. In *The Making of the ASEAN Charter.* Edited by Tommy Koh, Rosario Manolo and Walter Woon. Singapore: World Scientific Publishing, pp. 105–113.

Ostler, Nicholas (2005) *Empires of the Word: A Language History of the World.* London: HarperCollins.

Ostler, Nicholas (2009) Review of *Language and National Identity in Asia. Language Policy,* **8**(2), 193–195.

Pakir, Anne (2000) Singapore. In *Language Policies and Language Education: The Impact in East Asian Countries in the Next Decade.* Edited by Ho Wah Kam and Ruth Wong. Singapore: Times Academic Press, pp. 259–284.

Pennycook, Alastair (2007) *Global Englishes and Transcultural Flows.* London: Routledge.

Pennycook, Alastair (2010) The future of Englishes: One, many, or none? In *The Handbook of World Englishes.* Edited by Andy Kirkpatrick. London: Routledge.

Phillipson, Robert (2003) *English-only Europe: Challenging Language Policy.* London: Routledge.

Phillipson, Robert (2008) Lingua franca or lingua frankensteinia. *World Englishes,* **27**(2), 250–267.

Phommanimith, Khounmy (2008) *Country Report on Basic Education Curriculum in Lao PDR.* Vientiane: Department of General Education, Ministry of Education.

Pickering, Lucy (2006) Current research on intelligibility in English as a lingua franca. *Annual Review of Applied Linguistics,* **25**, 219–233.

Platt, John (1991) Social and linguistic constraints on variation in the use of two grammatical variables in Singapore English. In *English Around the World. Sociolinguistic Perspectives.* Edited by Jenny Cheshire. Cambridge: Cambridge University Press, pp. 376–387.

Platt, John, and Weber, Heidi (1980) *English in Singapore and Malaysia: Status, Features, Functions.* Kuala Lumpur: Oxford University Press.

Poon, Franky Kai Cheung (2006) Hong Kong English, China English and World English. *English Today,* **22**(2), 23–28.

Prodromou, Luke (2007a) Is ELF a variety of English? *English Today,* **23**(2), 47–53.

Prodromou, Luke (2007b) Kettles of fish: Or, does unilateral idiomaticity exist? *English Today,* **23**(3–4), 34–39.

Puteh, Alis (2006) *Language and Nation Building.* Petaling Jaya: Strategic Information and Research Development Centre.

Quirk, Randolph, Greenbaum, Sidney, Leech, Geoffrey, and Svartvik, Jan (1985) *A Comprehensive Grammar of the English Language.* London: Longman.

Ramsey, S. Robert (1989) *The Languages of China.* Princeton: Princeton University Press.

Ranta, Elena (2006) The 'attractive' progressive: Why using the *-ing* form in English as a lingua franca? *Nordic Journal of English Studies,* **5**(2), 95–116.

Rappa, Antonio, and Wee, Lionel (2006) *Language Policy and Modernity in Southeast Asia: Malaysia, Singapore, the Philippines and Thailand.* New York: Springer.

Rashid, Rehman (1993) *A Malaysian Journey.* Petaling Jaya: Rehman Rashid

Rusdi, Taib (1999) Schema of group seminar presentations and rhetorical structures of presentation introductions: A cross-cultural study of Indonesian and Australian students in university academic settings. *Asian Englishes,* **2**(1), 66–89.
Sand, Andrea (2004) Shared morpho-syntactic features in contact varieties of English: Article use. *World Englishes,* **23**(2), 281–298.
Sandhu, Kernial Singh (1992) *The ASEAN Reader.* Singapore: Institute of Southeast Asian Studies.
Schmied, Josef (1991) *English in Africa.* London: Longman.
Schneider, Edgar W. (2003) The dynamics of new Englishes: From identity construction to dialect rebirth. *Language,* **79**(2), 233–281.
Schneider, Edgar W. (2007) *Postcolonial Englishes: Varieties around the World.* Cambridge: Cambridge University Press.
Seidlhofer, Barbara (2001) Closing a conceptual gap: The case for a description of English as a lingua franca. *International Journal of Applied Linguistics,* **11**(2), 133–157.
Seidlhofer, Barbara (2004) Research perspectives in teaching English as a lingua franca. *Annual Review of Applied Linguistics,* **24**, 209–239.
Seidlhofer, Barbara (2005) English as a lingua franca. In *Oxford Advanced Learner's Dictionary of Current English.* Edited by A. S. Hornby. Oxford: Oxford University Press, R92.
Seidlhofer, Barbara (2007) Common property: English as a lingua franca in Europe. In *The International Handbook of English Language Teaching.* Edited by Jim Cummins and Chris Davison. New York: Springer, pp. 137–153.
Severino, Rodolfo C. (ed.) (2005) *Framing the ASEAN Charter.* Singapore: Institute of Southeast Asian Studies.
Severino, Rodolfo C. (2008) *ASEAN.* Singapore: Institute of Southeast Asian Studies.
Sharifian, Farzad (2010) Semantic and pragmatic conceptualisations within an emerging variety: Persian English. In *Handbook of World Englishes.* Edited by Andy Kirkpatrick. London: Routledge, pp. 442–458.
Shin, Yoon Hwan (2007) Malay/Indonesian for an official language of the East Asian community. http://www.arenaonline.org/content/view/305/151/.
Sibayan, Bonifacio P. (1996) The intellectualisation of Philippino. In *Readings in Philippine Sociolinguistics.* Edited by Ma. Lourdes Bautista. Manila: De la Salle University Press, pp. 240–253.
Siddique, Sharon (ed.) (2003) *The Second ASEAN Reader.* Singapore: Institute of Southeast Asian Studies.
Simpson, Andrew (ed.) (2007a) *Language and National Identity in Asia.* Oxford: Oxford University Press.
Simpson, Andrew (2007b) Indonesia. In *Language and National Identity in Asia.* Edited by Andrew Simpson. Oxford: Oxford University Press, pp. 312–336.
Simpson, Andrew, and Noi, Thammasathien (2007) Thailand and Laos. In *Language and National Identity in Asia.* Edited by Andrew Simpson. Oxford: Oxford University Press, pp. 391–414.
Siti, Jamilah (2008) English in Indonesian primary schools. *Pendidikan Network.* http://re-searchsengines.com/siti0908.html. Accessed on 10 August 2009.
Skutnabb-Kangas, Tove (2000) *Linguistic Genocide in Education: Or Worldwide Diversity and Human Rights?* Mahwah, NJ: Lawrence Erlbaum Associates.

Smith, Larry E. (1992) Spread of English and issues of intelligibility. In *The Other Tongue: English Across Cultures*. Edited by Braj B. Kachru. Chicago: University of Illinois Press, pp. 75–90.
Smith, Larry E., and Bisazza, J. A. (1982) The comprehensibility of three varieties of English for college students in seven countries. *Language Learning* **32**, 259–269.
Smith, Larry E., and Nelson, Cecil L. (2006) World Englishes and issues of intelligibility. In *The Handbook of World Englishes*. Edited by Braj B. Kachru, Yamuna Kachru, and Cecil L. Nelson. Malden, MA: Blackwell, pp. 428–445.
Smith, Larry E., and Rafiqzad, Khalilulla (1979) English for cross-cultural communication: The question of intelligibility. *TESOL Quarterly*, **13**, 371–380.
Smyth, David (1987) Thai speakers. In *Learner English: A Teacher's Guide to Interference and Other Problems*. Edited by Michael Swan and Bernard Smith. Cambridge: Cambridge University Press, pp. 252–263.
Snow, Don (2004) *Cantonese as Written Language*. Hong Kong: Hong Kong University Press.
Sonntag, Suzanne K. (2003) *The Local Politics of Global English: Case Studies in Linguistic Globalisation*. Lanham, MD: Lexington Books.
South China Morning Post (2009) Mother-tongue education going in right direction, says Minister. Education Supplement, 17 March, p. 3.
Su, Heng (2008) *The Linguistic Realization of Face in Chinese Political Discourse*. PhD thesis. Perth: Curtin University of Technology.
Survey of Overseas Filipinos (2008) http://www.census.gov.ph/pressrelease2009/of08tx.html. Accessed on 10 July 2009.
Swain, Merrill, and Deters, Ping (2007) "New" mainstream SLA theory: Expanded and extended. *Modern Language Journal*, **91**(1) (Special Focus Issue), 820–836.
Swain, Merrill, and Johnson, R. K. (1997) Immersion education: A category within bilingual education. In *Immersion Education: International Perspectives*. Edited by Merrill Swain and R. K. Johnson. Cambridge: Cambridge University Press, pp. 1–16.
Szmrecsanyi, Benedikt, and Kortmann, Bernd (2009) Vernacular universals and angloversals in a typological perspective. In *Vernacular Universals and Language Contacts: Evidence from Varieties of English and Beyond*. Edited by Markku Filppula, Juhani Klemola, and Heli Paulasto. London: Routledge, pp. 33–53.
Tagliabue, John (2006) English is the EU's lingua franca. http://www.taipeitimes.com/News/editorials/archives/2006/12/08/2003339612. Accessed on 22 February 2008.
Tai, James (1985) Temporal sequence and Chinese word order. In *Iconicity and Syntax*. Edited by John Haiman. Amsterdam: John Benjamins.
Tan, Eugene B. (2007) Language policy and discourse in Singapore. In *Language Nation and Development*. Edited by Lee Hock Guan and Leo Suryadinata. Singapore: Institute of Southeast Asian Studies, pp.74–117.
Taylor, Insup, and Taylor, Martin M. (1995) *Writing and Literacy in Chinese, Korean and Japanese*. Amsterdam: John Benjamins.
Temasek Review (2009) MM Lee admits 'mistake' made in his education policy. http://www.temasekreview.com/2009/11/18/mm-lee-admits-mistake-made-in-his-education-policy/. Accessed on 3 December 2009.
Thambipillai, Pushpa (1992) Negotiating styles. In *The ASEAN Reader*. Edited by Kernial Singh Sandhu. Singapore: Institute of East Asian Studies, pp. 72–75.

Thaveeporn, Vasavakul (2003) Language policy and ethnic relations in Vietnam. In *Fighting Words: Language Policy and Ethnic Relations in Asia*. Edited by Michael Brown and Sumit Ganguly. Cambridge, MA: MIT Press, pp. 211–238.

Thomas, Anne (2002) Bilingual community-based education in the Cambodian Highlands: A successful approach to enabling access to education by indigenous peoples. *Journal of Southeast Asian Education*, 3(1), 26–55.

Thomason, Sarah G. (2009) Why universals versus contact-induced change. In *Vernacular Universals and Language Contacts: Evidence from Varieties of English and Beyond*. Edited by Markku Filppula, Juhani Klemola, and Heli Paulasto. London: Routledge, pp. 349–364.

Thompson, Roger M. (2003) *Filipino English and Taglish: Language Switching from Multiple Perspectives*. Amsterdam: John Benjamins.

Tollefson, James W. (ed.) (2002a) *Language Policies in Education*. Mahwah, NJ: Lawrence Erlbaum Associates.

Tollefson, James W. (2002b) Introduction. In *Language Policies in Education*. Edited by James W. Tollfeson. Mahwah, NJ: Lawrence Erlbaum Associates, pp. 3–15.

Tollefson, James W., and Tsui, Amy B. (eds.) (2004a) *Medium of Instruction Policies: Which Agenda? Whose Agenda?* Mahwah, NJ: Lawrence Erlbaum Associates.

Tollefson, James W., and Tsui, Amy B. (2004b) Contexts of medium-of-instruction policy. In *Medium of Instruction Policies: Which Agenda? Whose Agenda?* Edited by James W. Tollefson and Amy B.M. Tsui. Mahwah, NJ: Lawrence Erlbaum Associates, pp. 283–294.

Tollefson, James W., and Tsui, Amy B. (2007) Issues in language policy, culture and identity. In *Language Policy, Culture and Identity in Asian Contexts*. Edited by Amy B. Tsui and James Tollefson. Mahwah, NJ: Lawrence Erlbaum Associates, pp. 259–270.

Tosi, Arturo (ed.) (2003) *Crossing Barriers and Bridging Cultures*. Clevedon: Multilingual Matters.

Trudgill, Peter (2002) Linguistic and social typology. In *Handbook of Linguistic Variation and Change*. Edited by Jack K. Chambers, Natalie Schilling-Estes and Peter Trudgill. Oxford: Blackwell, pp. 707–728.

Tsui, Amy B. M., and Tollefson, James W. (2004) The centrality of medium of instruction policy in sociopolitical processes. In *Medium of Instruction Policies: Which Agenda? Whose Agenda?* Edited by James W. Tollefson and Amy B. M. Tsui. Mahwah, NJ: Lawrence Erlbaum Associates, pp. 1–18.

Tsui, Amy B. M., and Tollefson, James W. (eds.) (2007) *Language Policy, Culture and Identity in Asian Contexts*. Mahwah, NJ: Lawrence Erlbaum Associates.

Tupas, Ruanni F. (2007) Go back to class: The medium of instruction debate in the Philippines. In *Language Nation and Development*. Edited by Lee Hock Guan and Leo Suryadinata. Singapore: Institute of Southeast Asian Studies, pp. 39–50.

UNESCO (2007) *Education for All by 2015: Will We Make It?* Oxford: Oxford University Press. http://unesdoc.unesco.org/images/0015/001547/15473e.pdf. Accessed on 27 March 2009.

Wang, Gungwu (2007) Keynote Address. In *Language Nation and Development*. Edited by Lee Hock Guan and Leo Suryadinata. Singapore: Institute of Southeast Asian Studies, pp. ix–xvii.

Watkins, Justin (2007) Burma/Myanmar. In *Language and National Identity in Asia* Edited by Andrew Simpson. Oxford: Oxford University Press, pp. 263–287.

Wee, Lionel (2004) Singapore English: Morphology and syntax. In *A Handbook of Varieties of English Volume 2*. Edited by Bernd Kortmann, Kate Burridge, Rajend Mesthrie, Edgar W. Schneider, and Clive Upton. Berlin: Mouton de Gruyter, pp. 1058–1072.

Wells, John (1982) *Accents of English*. Cambridge: Cambridge University Press.

Winford, Donald (2009) The interplay of 'universals' and contact-induced change in the emergence of new Englishes. In *Vernacular Universals and Language Contacts: Evidence from Varieties of English and Beyond*. Edited by Markku Filppula, Juhani Klemola, and Heli Paulasto. London: Routledge, pp. 206–230.

Wolf, Hans-Georg (2010) East and West African Englishes: Differences and commonalities. In *Handbook of World Englishes*. Edited by Andy Kirkpatrick. London: Routledge, pp. 197–211.

Wolfram, Walt, and Schilling, Estes Natalia (2003) Parallel development and alternative restructuring: The case of weren't intensification. In *Dialectology: In Honour of Peter Trudgill*. Edited by David Britain and Jenny Cheshire. Amsterdam: John Benjamins, pp. 131–154.

Wong, Ruth, and James, Joyce (2000) Malaysia. In *Language Policies and Language Education: The Impact in East Asian Countries in the Next Decade*. Edited by Ho Wah Kam and Ruth Wong. Singapore: Times Academic Press, pp. 209–240.

Wright, Sue (2002) Language education and foreign relations in Vietnam. In *Language Policies in Education*. Edited by James W. Tollfeson. Mahwah, NJ: Lawrence Erlbaum Associates, pp. 225–244.

Wright, Sue (2007a) The right to speak one's own language: Reflections on theory and practice. *Language Policy,* **6**, 203–224.

Wright, Sue (2007b) English in the European parliament: MEPs and their language repertoires. *Sociolinguistica,* **21**, 151–165.

Xu, Zhichang (2010) Chinese English: A future power? In *The Routledge Handbook of World Englishes*. Edited by Andy Kirkpatrick. London: Routledge, pp. 282–298.

Yin, Binyong and Rohsenow, John (1994) *Modern Chinese Characters*. Beijing: Sinolingua.

Index

User's Note: The subject entries are arranged in letter-by-letter order.

Abell, Sir Anthony, 22
'about', non-standard use of, 114, 175
Adulayev, King Bhumibol, 50
African-American vernacular English, 98
African Englishes (*see also* Black South African English, Indian South African English), 121
  shared features of, 103–4
Alexandre de Rhodes, 59
'alphabet', semantic scope of, 87, 88
alphabetization, of Chinese, 16
Alwasilah, Professor Chaedar, 182
American English, 73, 86, 170
'Anglo' rhetorical style, 119
Anna and the King of Siam (Landon), 48
Anvil-Macquarie Dictionary of Philippines English for High School, 88, 89
Arabic, 50, 170
articles (definite and indefinite), usage of, 102, 104–5
ASEAN (*see also* working language of ASEAN)
  aims and purposes of, 4–5, 6–7
  linguistic and cultural diversity in, xi–xii, 189
  ethnic diversity in, 4
  formation of, x, 3, 4, 46
  identity, 6, 7
  membership of, 3, 54
  member states, motivations for learning English, 169–70, 180–1
  negotiating styles of, 9
  structure, 5
  'way', the, 5, 121, 122
ASEAN Charter, x, 5–7, 184
ASEAN ELF (ASEAN English Lingua Franca)
  audio-recordings of, 69, 123
  composition of groups providing data on, 69, 124 (Table 6.1)
  corpus, 71
  data, 69, 71, 91, 100, 102, 113, 114
  distinctive nature of, 93
  non-standard features of, 104–11
  phonological features of, 74–80, 92, 172–3
ASEAN + 3 grouping, 15, 67
ASEAN Reader, The, 9
Asian languages, teaching of, in ASEAN countries, 18
Asia and Pacific Council (ASPAC), 3
Association of South Asia (ASA), 3
Association of Southeast Asian Nations, *see* ASEAN
audio-recordings, 69–70, 123
Aung San, 51
Aung San Su Kyi, 51, 52
AUPELF (Association des universités partiellement ou entièrement de langue française), 14, 56, 62
Australia Indonesia Institute, 181
Australian English, 86–7, 88
Aziz, Dr, 182

Index

backchannels, encouraging, 131, 133
Bahasa Indonesia (BI)
    first grammar of, 46
    as medium of instruction, 46
    as national language, 44
    as national lingua franca, 7, 10, 11, 12, 44–6, 47, 64
    unified orthography with Malay, 45
Baki-Chang Report (1959), 34
Balinese (language), 46
Bangkok Declaration (1967), x, 3, 4–5, 7, 8
Barnes Commission (1951), 23
Batak (language), 46
bilingual education, 31, 32, 34–5, 37–41
    Canadian model, 163–4, 165
Birch, J. W. W., 20
Black South African English, 100, 101
British colonies, 10, 19, 20, 29, 34, 43
British English, 77, 86, 170
    historical variation in, 95–7
    non-standard dialects of, 97–9, 140
Brunei, 12
    language education policy, 34–5, 62
    1959 Constitution, 34
Buginese (language), 46
bumiputra policy, 24
Burma, x, 19, 51–3, 63
    ethnic and linguistic diversity, 51
    language education policy, 52, 53
    1947 Constitution, 52
    use of English in, 10, 43, 51, 53
Burmese (language), as medium of instruction, 52
Burmese Socialist Programme Party (BSPP), 10, 52
Butler, Susan, 88

call centres, 40
Cambodia, 14, 55–8
    use of English in, 57
Cambodian Communist Party, *see* Khmer Rouge
Cambodian speaker, example of spoken English, 109
Cambridge Advanced Learners' Dictionary, 87
Canadian Model, immersion and bilingual education, 163–4, 165

Cantonese (language)
    as medium of instruction, 33, 161
    preservation of, 162, 164
Cebuano (language), 151
Chalermpalanupap, Termsak, 14
children
    cognitive load on, x, 152
    linguistic demands on, 149
    dropping out of school, 62, 149, 160, 170–1
Chinese (language) (*see also* Cantonese, Mandarin)
    banned in Indonesia, 46
    clause sequencing patterns in, 116–17
    dialects, 31, 33
    literacy in, 15–16, 31–2
    request pattern in, 117–19
    script, 15–16, 59, 149
Chinese (people), 21, 29
    compliments and, 120
    presence in ASEAN countries, 15
Chinese English (*see also* Hong Kong English, Singaporean English), 87
Chinese University of Hong Kong, 161, 166
Choeng Ek extermination camp, English sign at, 115
Chu Nho script, 59
Chu Nom script, 59
Cia-Cia tribe, preservation of language of, 47
clarification, 130, 133
classification of countries, based on history and status of English in, 10, 18
clause order, 116–7
'clipping', in Australian English, 87
Cobbold Commission (1962), 22
Cobbold, Lord, 23
code-mixing, 90, 91
code-switching, 90–1, 137, 140
cognitive load, on children, x, 152
communication (*see also* cross-cultural communication)
    English as medium of, 172
communication strategies, 82, 123–41, 186
communism, 4, 46
compliments, 120

comprehensibility, 80, 81
Confucius Institutes, 15, 50
consonants, pronunciation of, 74–6
Constitution Amendment Act, 1971 (Malaysia), 25
contact linguistics, 102
Council of Europe, 8
criticism, 121, 125
cross-cultural communication, 121–2
    proposed course in, 165, 181, 184–6
cultural diversity, in ASEAN, xi–xii, 189
cultural values
    new varieties of English shaped by, 119–22
    reflected in lexis, 87–8
Culture Based English for College Students, 181
cultures
    based textbook, 181–4
    languages and, ix, 28

declension, of nouns in standard English, 95–6
'deleter', as variety of English, 100
Dewan Bahasa dan Pustaka (Malaysia), 22
dialects, non-standard, of British English, 97, 98–9, 140
dictionaries, 86–9
Dien Bien Phu, 54, 59
discourse features, 116–19
    transfer of, 116
Do Bama Asiayone (Our Myanmar Association), 51
Doi Moi policy, in Vietnam, 61
double comparison, 98
'dual language books', 179
Dussek, O. T., 21
Dutch (language), 44, 45
Dutch (people), colony of, 10
dwibahasa policy, in Brunei, 34–5

early learners, 153–4
economic growth
    in ASEAN countries, 64
    perceived role of English in, 181
Education Act, 1960 (Malaysia), 24
Education Act, 1961 (Malaysia), 24
Education Act, 1966 (Burma), 52
Education Act, 1979 (Malaysia), 25

Education for All by 2015 (UNICEF), 160
Education Law, 1991 (Vietnam), 60
Education Ordinance, 1952 (Federation of Malaya), 23
Education Ordinance, 1957 (Federation of Malaya), 23–4
ekkalak, concept of, 49
Endangered Languages Project, 171
English (language) (*see also* ASEAN ELF, individual varieties of English)
    curriculum for ASEAN, 184
    demand for, 49, 61
    diaspora, 74
    failure to learn, 148, 170
    first foreign language, ix, 10–11, 14, 48, 54, 63 (Table 3.2)
    history and status of, as basis for classification, 10
    home language, 12, 31, 71
    increasing dominance of, 171
    institutional role of, 10, 43, 63
    introduction to school curriculum, x, 20, 145, 147, 159, 188
    local varieties of, 36
    medium of instruction, ix, 17, 27, 31, 34, 36–7, 145, 150–1, 159, 161, 186, 187, 188
    non-pro-drop language, 100
    not a *sine qua non* of modernization, 48
    not cognate with ASEAN languages, 149
    'post-Anglophone' role of, 57
    privileging of, 149–50, 163, 170, 184, 189
    reintroduction of, as medium of instruction, 25
    role of, in Malaysia, 28
    role of, in Singapore, 29, 31, 32–3, 34
    roles and status of, in ASEAN founder member countries, 10–11
    science and modernity, perceived as language of, 12, 14, 42, 49, 152, 169, 170, 180
    speakers of, 67
    teaching of, questions relating to, 169, 186
    Thailand, introduction to, 48
    threat to local languages, x, 20, 18, 50, 170, 171, 189

216 Index

working language of ASEAN, ix, 7, 8–10, 12, 15, 61, 145
Vietnam, introduction to, 60
English, as a foreign language (ELF)
   distinguished from English as lingua franca, 156
English, as a lingua franca (*see also* ASEAN ELF)
   corpus of, 68, 69, 71
   definition of, 67–8
   distinguished from English as a foreign language, 156
   phonological features of lingua franca core, 68, 173
   recordings of speakers of, 69–70, 123
   role as, in ASEAN, 181
   shared linguistic features, 68–9, 85
   teaching of, 174
   variation as factor in, 140
English, new varieties of, 74, 88
   cultural influences on, 119–22
   variation in, 99–104
'epenthetic' -s, 109–10
ethnic diversity, in ASEAN, 4
ethnic minorities, in Burma, 51, 53
ethnicity, 21
European Centre for Modern Languages, 8
European Commission, 8
European Cultural Convention, 8
European Union (EU), 149
   language policy in, 7–8, 14
'expanding circle countries', in ASEAN, 11

'face', preservation of, 126, 136, 138
Federated Malay States, 20
Federation of Malaya, 22
Fenn and Wu Report (1952), 23
Filipino (language), 40, 151
   'intellectualizing' of, 39
   national language, 36, 37–8
Fifth Language Congress (1988), 46
first language, 158, 179, 188
foreign direct investment (fdi), in ASEAN countries, 64
foreign languages, teaching of, 18, 184
French (language), 12, 14, 54, 56, 61, 62
French colonies of, 12, 54, 55, 59

Geneva Conference (1954–56), 60
Goh Keng Swee, 31
Goh Report (1979), 31
Gonzalez, Brother, 38
greetings, 120

Hangul script, 47
Hmong, 54
Ho Chi Min, 59, 60, 61
home language, English as, 12, 31, 71
Hong Kong
   Filipina domestic helpers in, 40
   language education policy, xi, 33, 161–7, 176
Hong Kong English
   intelligibility of, 81
   pronunciation of 'TH' in, 75–6
Hong Kong Institute of Education, 161, 167
human rights, 6, 7
Hunminjeongeum Research Institute, 47
Hun Sen, 56
Hussein, Hishamuddin, 27
hybridization, 89–90
hypotaxis, 117

identity
   ASEAN, 6, 7
   communication continuum and, 139 (Fig 6.1)
   English as marker of, 32–3, 34
   language and, ix, 28, 33, 47, 49, 139–40, 164
idioms, 89, 92
   avoiding use of, 137, 139
immersion education, Canadian model, 163–4
immersion languages, Putonghua proposed as, 164, 165
Indian English, 113
Indian South African English, 113
Indo-Chinese Union, 59
Indonesia, 10, 43–8, 63
   culture based textbook for, 181–4
   'failure' of English language teaching in, 17, 148
   inadequate school resources, 148
   language education policy, 46–7

language policy, 11
   linguistic diversity of, 43–4
   1945 Constitution, 44
Indonesian Language Committee (1942), 45
Indonesian speaker, example of spoken English, 110, 112
inequality, in access to English, 171
Institute of Language and Literature (Malaysia), 22
Institute of Linguistics (Vietnam), 60
intelligibility, 79, 80, 81, 85, 174
International Corpora of English (ICE), 69, 87, 88 (Table 4.6), 102
international relations, proposed course on, 165, 181, 184–6
interpretability, 80, 81
interpretation services, cost of, 14
inversion, 113, 174
irregular verbs, 96–7

Japan, 178
   effect of compliments in, 120
Japanese (language), words adopted from, 86
Javanese (language), 43, 44, 46
Jenkins, Jennifer, 68

Kachin (language), 51
Khmer (language), 56
   as medium of instruction, 56, 57
Khmer Rouge, 55, 56
Kw'enlun, as Malay lingua franca, 13, 44

Lahu (language), 51
'language alternation', 90–1
language education (*see also* multilingual education)
   aims of, 156–7, 177
   balance of languages in, 159–60, 188
   challenges, 160 (Table 7.2)
   early start to, 153–4, 187
   myths of, 152, 158
language education policies (*see also* individual countries)
   implications for, 147–60
   likely outcomes of current, 170–2
   shared concerns, 19–20

language policies (*see also* individual countries)
   in European Union, 7–8
   universities in Hong Kong, 166
Lao (language), as national lingua franca, 54
Laos, 14, 54–5, 63
   linguistic diversity, 54
Laotian speaker, examples of spoken English, 108–9
laughter, 137–8
Lee Hsien Loong, 31
Lee Kwan Yew, 11, 29, 31, 32, 33
left-branching, 117
left-dislocation, 116
Lembaga Bahasa Nasional (Indonesia), 45
Leonowens, Anna, 48
'let it pass' strategy, 130–1
letter writing, manuals, Medieval European, 119
lexical anticipation, 127
lexical correction, 128
lexical suggestion, 127–8
lexis, of varieties of English, 86–92, 93
Lie Kim Hok, 46
lingua franca (*see also* ASEAN ELF, English as a lingua franca)
   origin of term, 193n1
linguistic benchmarks, 176, 177, 189
linguistic diversity, in ASEAN, xi–xii, 189
linguistic elites, 50, 171
listening, 131
literacy, 149
   in Chinese, 15–16, 31–2, 164
Llewellyn Report (1983), 161
local languages (*see also* minority languages, mother tongue)
   declining interest in, 61
   English as threat to, x, 18, 20, 50, 170, 171, 189
   identity and, 47
   Indonesian, speakers of, 47 (Table 3.1)
   lack of attention to, 149–50, 187–8
   medium of instruction, 63
   recommended as medium of instruction, 38, 41, 46
   threats to survival of, 62
   within primary schools, 159, 160, 187
Lon Nol, 55

Mabini, Apolinario, 36
Macquarie Dictionary, 86, 88
Macquarie Junior Dictionary, 88, 89
Mahathir, Dr, 11, 13, 25, 27
Malay (language), 8, 13–14, 24–8, 29
  coining new words in, 45
  grammar of, 46
  medium of instruction, 23, 24–5, 34, 63
  national language, 12, 13, 30, 34, 36, 44
Malay Chinese Association (MCA), 23, 24
Malay English, 86
Malay Language Academy, 26, 28
Malays (people), 22
  discrimination in favour of, 24
Malaysia, 20–8
  language education policy, 13, 19, 20, 21, 23–8, 63, 152, 187
  language policy, 11
  negotiating style, 9
  population balance in, 22, 23
Malayanization, policies, 11
  monolingual Malays created by, 28
Malay speaker, example of spoken English, 112
Malay States, 20
Mandarin, 15, 18, 28, 29, 184
  demand for, 50, 61, 62, 162, 163
  immersion language in Hong Kong, 164, 165
  medium of instruction, 58
  'mother tongue' of ethnic Chinese in Singapore, 30, 31
MAPHILINDO, 3
markers and marking, 96–8, 100, 106
  non-marking, 110, 114–15
maths and science
  English as medium of instruction for, 25, 26, 27, 34, 62, 145, 152
  Malay as medium of instruction for, 26–7, 34, 63, 187
  teaching of, 152–3
Mauranen, Anna, 69
Maxwell, George, 20, 21, 44
measurement
  language learning, 175–6
  proficiency in English, non-native speakers, 155–6, 172, 173

medium of instruction
  Bahasa Indonesia, 46
  Burmese, 52
  Cantonese, 33, 161
  choice of, in Hong Kong, 162
  English as, ix, 17, 27, 31, 34, 36–7, 145, 150–1, 159, 161, 186, 187, 188
  in ASEAN, 63 (Table 3.2)
  in universities, 25
  Khmer, replaced French as, 56
  local languages recommended as, 38, 41–2
  Malay, 23, 24–5, 34, 63
  Mandarin, 30, 58
  reintroduction of English as, 25
  second language as, 151, 152
  Tamil, 24
  Thai, 49, 50
  Vietnamese, 59, 60
middle classes, educational advantages of, 148, 171
minorities, *see* ethnic minorities
minority languages (*see also* local languages)
  newspapers in, closed, 53
  promotion of, 60–1
  teaching of, 52, 60
missionaries, 22, 51, 59
misunderstanding, 82–5
modality, 112
modernization
  English as language of, 12, 14, 19, 40, 42, 152, 169, 170, 180
  English not a *sine qua non* of, 48, 63
Mongkut, King (Rama IV), 48
Mon-Khmer languages, 51, 54
monolingual model, of language teaching, 165, 176, 177, 179
monolinguals, 28
monophthongization, 77
mother tongue (*see also* local languages), 30
  education, 23, 41, 160, 162
  identity and, ix
  Mandarin as, 30, 31
  retention of, 62
multilingual education, 41–2
  model of, 175–80, 188, 189

multilingualism, 157
multilinguals, 'English knowing', 67
multiple negation, 98
Myanmar, *see* Burma

Nanyang Siang Pau, 30
Nanyang Technological University, 30
Nanyang University, 30
National Council for the Union of Myanmar, 53
National Language Act, 1967 (Malaysia), 11, 12, 24
National Language Institute (Cambodia), 57
National Language Institute (Indonesia), 45
National Language Institute (Philippines), 37, 39
National Language Law (Philippines), 37
national languages
  development of, 23–4, 37–8, 43, 44–6, 60, 150, 189
  in primary school curriculum, 160, 188
  teaching of, 184
  under-resourced, 170
National League of Democracy (NLD), 52
National Operations Council (NOC) (Malaysia), 24
National University of Malaysia, 25
National University of Singapore (NUS), 30
'nativelikeness', in acquisition of language, 154–5
native English speakers
  non-native speaker communication and, 137
  privileging of, 170, 189
  recruitment of, as teachers, 17, 49, 148
Ne Win, General U, 10, 43, 52, 63
negotiating styles, in ASEAN, 9
New Economic Policy (Malaysia), 24
New Oxford Dictionary, 87
New Straits Times, 26–7
non-native speakers, of English, 67
  measurement of proficiency in, 155–6, 172, 173, 175–6
Norodom Sihanouk, King, 55
northern subject rule, 97–8

notation conventions, for transcripts of audio-recordings, 123, 190
nouns, non-countable, 105–6, 175
Nuclear Weapon-Free Zone, 6, 7
Nu, U, 51, 52
number, marking of, 105–7

Old English, 95, 96
Ong Keng Yong, 9
Our Myanmar Association, 51
'outer circle countries', in ASEAN, 10, 19
Overseas Contract Workers (OCWs), 40

paraphrase, participant, 135–6
parataxis, Chinese preference for, 117
parental demands, for learning English, 19, 29, 161, 162
partnerships, 180, 184
Pathet Lao, 54
People's Action Party (PAP), 30
Persian English, cultural conceptualizations in, 120–1
Philippine Commission (1898), 36
Philippines, 35–42, 148
  language education policy, 36, 37–42, 63, 147
  linguistic diversity of, 35
  negotiating style, 9
  1987 Constitution, 37
  population, 35
  school resources, lack of, 147–8
phonetic symbols, in transcriptions of audio-recordings, 190
phonology, lingua franca core of international English, 68, 173
Pigafetta, Antonio, 46
pinyin, 16
plural, marking of, 96, 106–7
plurilingualism, *see* multilingualism
Pol Pot, 55
'post-Anglophone', stage of English, 57, 74
'pragmatic dissonance', 120
pragmatic norms, 119–22
  transfer of, 116, 185
prepositions, 113
  non-standard use of, 99, 114
'preserver', as variety of English, 100, 101, 112

primary schools
    curriculum, local languages in, 159, 160, 187–8
    English as subject in, ix, 17, 147, 169, 187
    mother tongue teaching in, 162
Principles of the Thai Language, 48–9
private schools, 18, 58
Private Higher Education Institutions Act, 1996 (Malaysia), 25
pro-drop languages, 100, 117
prompting, participant, 136
pronouns, 79
pronunciation (*see also* phonology), 73, 74–80, 127, 173
    idiosyncratic, 83–5, 139
Putonghua, *see* Mandarin

Quoc Ngu (script), 59, 60, 149

racial tensions, in Malaysia, 24
Radio Australia, 117–18
Rahman, Tunku Abdul, 24
Rajaratnam, S. (Sinnathamby), 3
Rama IV, King, 48
Rama VI, King, 48, 49
Ramkhamhaeng, King, stele of, 48
Razak Report (1956), 23
Razak, Tun Abdul, 24
Received Pronunciation (RP), *see* British English
Regional Language Centre (RELC), Singapore, 71, 123
regional lingua franca, ix, 13, 44, 160
religious schools, 50
repetition, 130, 134
request patterns, 117–19
resources, 170, 189
    lack of adequate school, 147
Rhodes, Alexandre de, 59
right-branching, 117
romanization
    of Chinese, 16
    of ethnic languages, 60
Royal University of Phnom Penh, 56
Russian (language), 54, 56

Sabah, 22, 23
Sarawak, 22, 23
Saw Maung, General, 52, 53
school curriculum
    English in, ix, 17, 181
    introduction of English to, x, 20, 145, 147, 159
    in Vietnam, 18
schools (*see also* primary schools, private schools, religious schools, secondary schools, vernacular schools)
    Chinese medium, 162, 163
    English medium, 18, 20, 22, 162–3
    enrolments, 22 (Table 2.1)
    partnerships, 180, 184
    racially segregated, 24
    retention of children in, 62, 149, 160, 170–1, 188
science, *see* maths and science
scripts, 15–16, 47, 59, 60, 62, 149, 164
SEAMEO
    Centre Directors meeting, recorded, 70, 124–5
    Centres, 192
    corpus of English, 102
    data, 92, 100, 105, 106, 116
    data, non-standard forms in, 111–15
Second ASEAN Reader, The, 9
Second Congress of Indonesian Youth, 44
second language
    early learning of, conditions for, 153
    medium of instruction, 151, 152
second language acquisition (SLA), 155–8, 167, 172, 175
Second Philippine Commission, 36
secondary schools, medium of instruction in, 159, 161, 162, 183
Seidlhofer, Barbara, 68
'semi-linguals', 151
seminars, academic, turn-taking in, 121–2, 124
sensitivity, linguistic, 137, 140
Shinawatra, Thaksin, 5, 50
Siam, *see* Thailand
Singapore, 29–34
    Constitution, 30

English as identity marker in, 32–3, 34
expulsion from Federation of Malaya, 23, 29
language education policy, 29, 30–4
language policy, 11, 29–30
negotiating style, 9
population of, 29
'Speak Mandarin' campaign, 31
Singapore English in a Nutshell (Brown), 88
Singaporean English, 100, 105, 140, 137
'alphabet' in, 87, 88
intelligibility of, 81
vowels in, 77 (Table 4.4)
Smith, Larry E, 80
socio-economic classes
disadvantaged learning of lower, 153, 170–1
educational advantages of middle, 148, 171
Songkhram, Phibun, 49
South Korea, 17, 47, 169–70
Southeast Asian Ministers of Education Organization, *see* SEAMEO
Spanish colonies, 35–6
Speak Good English Movement, 33
Special Assisted Plan (SAP) schools, 32
spelling out, 132
State Law and Order Restoration Council (SLORC), 53
State Peace and Development Council (SPDC), 53
Straits Settlements, 20, 29
stress-timed languages, 79–80, 174
Sultan Idris College, 21
Sundanese (language), 43–4, 46
Swedish, second language learners of, 154
syllable timing, 79, 81, 93, 174

Tagalog, *see* Filipino
tag-question, 99
Tai-Kadai languages, 51, 54
Talib Report (1957), 24
Tamil (language), 24, 29
Tamils (people), 21
teachers, English language
low proficiency of, 58, 153
multilingual, 177, 178–9, 180, 189

native speakers, 178–9
non-native speakers, 177–8
recruitment of native speakers as, 17, 49, 148
sent to Philippines, 36
shortage of qualified, 17, 26, 49, 53, 55, 148, 152
teacher training, institutions, 21
teaching English
as a lingua franca, 174, 176
implications of communicative strategies for, 139
questions relating to, 169, 186
teaching materials, 186
textbooks
culture-based, 181–4
local and minority language, 46, 52
Thai, 49
'TH', pronunciation of, 75–6
Thai (language)
development of, 48–9
medium of instruction, 49, 50
Thai (people), identity and unity, 49, 50
Thailand, 5, 10, 48–50
introduction of English to, 48
language education policy, 49
language policy, 11
population, 49
recruitment of native English speakers, 17, 49, 148
Thai speaker, examples of spoken English, 111–12
Thomasites, 36
Tibeto-Burman languages, 51, 54
Times Dictionary of Problem Words (Jenkins), 88
topicalization, 116
topic change, 135
'translanguaging', in classroom, 180
translation services, cost of, 14
Transparency International, 183
Treaty of Pangkor (1874), 20
Treaty of Paris (1898), 36
trilingualism, promotion of, in Hong Kong, 162, 163, 166, 167, 176
Tunku Abdul Rahman University, 25
Tupas, Ruanni F, 38
turn-taking, 121–2, 124–5

U Ne Win, *see* Ne Win, General U
U Nu, *see* Nu, U
UNESCO, 160
'unilateral idomaticity', absence of, 91
United Malay National Organisation (UMNO), 23
United Nations Transitional Authority in Cambodia (UNTAC), 56, 14
United States, 35, 36, 170
  colonies of, 10, 35
Universiti Kebangsaan Malaysia (UKM), 25
universities
  language policies of, in Hong Kong, 166
  medium of instruction in, 25, 30, 56, 57, 161
  private, 25–6
University of Hong Kong, 161

Vajiravudh, King (Rama VI), 48, 49
Vejjajiva, Prime Minister Abhisit, 50
verbs
  forms, regularization and simplification of, 96–7, 115
  non-marking of, 174
  non-standard forms, 107–12
vernacular languages, *see* local languages
vernacular schools, 21, 24, 29, 58
vernacular universals, 69, 101–2
Victorian Institute, Kuala Lumpur, 22
Vienna-Oxford Corpus of English (VOICE), 68, 104
Vietnam, 12, 14, 17, 58–62, 63
  language policy, 60–1
Vietnamese (language), 56
  medium of instruction, 59, 60
  lexicon, 60
  national language, 60
Vietnamese diaspora, 62
Vietnam War, 55, 60
VOICE, *see* Vienna-Oxford Corpus of English
vowels
  pronunciation of, 76–9
  reduced, 78–9, 174

word order, 117
words,
  adoption of, 86
  differences in meaning of, 86
  hybrid, 89–90
Working Committee on the Indonesian Language (1947), 45
working language of ASEAN
  advantages of using English as, 10, 14
  English as, ix, 7, 8–10, 12, 15, 145
  other languages proposed as, 12–16, 61